The Military Conquest
of the Southern Plains

The Author

WILLIAM H. LECKIE, who is newly appointed assistant dean for graduate stud-
ies in the University of Toledo, received
the Ph.D. from the University of Oklahoma. His long-time interest in Indians and in military history prepared
him well for writing this comprehensive book on Southern Plains Indian
warfare.

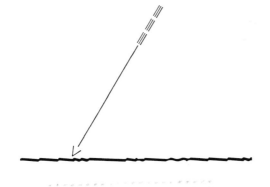

The Military Conquest
of the Southern Plains

WILLIAM H. LECKIE

UNIVERSITY OF OKLAHOMA PRESS · NORMAN

Library of Congress Catalog Card Number: 63–17160

Copyright 1963 by the University of Oklahoma Press,
Publishing Division of the University.
Composed and printed at Norman, Oklahoma, U.S.A.,
by the University of Oklahoma Press. First edition.

To Mon, Stewart, and Jo Marie

Preface

THE WARS BETWEEN RED MAN AND
white on the many frontiers of the United States form significant
and highly colorful episodes in the nation's history. Thus they
have engaged and held the interest of Americans in all walks of
life. This has led to an enormous literature on various aspects of
these struggles, ranging from the most scholarly history to the
most lurid dime novel.

The military conquest of the nomadic Southern Plains Indians—
the Comanches, Kiowas, Kiowa-Apaches, Southern Cheyennes,
and Arapahoes—is no exception. Precipitated by the advance of
white settlement into the Plains region, this struggle, inaugurated
in earnest at the close of the Civil War, raged intermittently for a
decade. A far-flung and dramatic contest, it has evoked a number
of formal histories, a still greater number of books for popular
consumption, literally hundreds of reminiscences by participants,
and many more articles in journals and magazines.

However, the sporadic nature of the war, the vastness of the arena in which it was fought, the many compelling personalities both Indian and white who engaged in it, and the tendency to note only a few outstanding incidents widely separated in both time and distance have all contributed to a literature dealing with isolated phases of the conflict. In the great mass of such material are many works of merit that contribute much to a knowledge and understanding of the war, but a book dealing with the struggle as an integrated whole is lacking. It is hoped that this book will fill that need.

In this effort I am deeply indebted to many persons who have given generously of their time and talents. This is especially true of Miss Sara Jackson, Mrs. Anne Henry, and Mr. Frank Heppner of the War Records Division of the National Archives, Washington, D.C. Without their assistance the research for this book could never have been completed. I owe much to the aid given me by Miss Opal Gladys Carr of the University of Oklahoma Library, Mr. Boone McClure, curator of the Panhandle-Plains Historical Society, and to the staff of the Library and of the Indian Archives Division of the Oklahoma Historical Society. Professors Donnell Owings, A. K. Christian, Donald J. Berthrong, Jim E. Reese, and Charles C. Bush of the University of Oklahoma have given me invaluable advice and encouragement. I shall be forever grateful to Dr. Ernest H. Poteet, President Emeritus, Texas College of Arts and Industries, Kingsville, Texas, for a research grant that cleared the last financial hurdle to the completion of my work.

In preparation of the manuscript, my wife, Glorieta Leckie, typed and retyped the manuscript with skill and unfailing good temper and was a constant source of encouragement. The errors and shortcomings of this book are, of course, entirely my own.

WILLIAM H. LECKIE

Kingsville, Texas
May 27, 1963

Contents

Illustrations

xi

Maps

The Military Conquest
of the Southern Plains

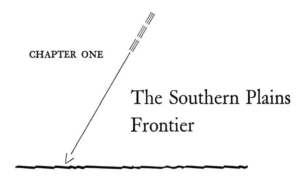

CHAPTER ONE

The Southern Plains Frontier

T HE DECADE IMMEDIATELY AFTER the Civil War was one of almost constant warfare between the armed forces of the United States and the nomadic Indians of the Southern Plains. Fundamentally the struggle stemmed from a determination of these Indians to hold fast to their homeland and maintain their way of life as opposed to an equal resolution of the white settler to possess the Plains and to civilize or exterminate the roving red man.

The Southern Plains, at once arena and prize in this far-flung contest, are vast in extent, stretching south from the Platte River to the Río Grande and eastward from the Rocky Mountains to about the ninety-eighth meridian. In general the region is level, semiarid or subhumid, almost treeless, and covered by a thick grassy sod, all of which makes it one of the finest natural grazing areas to be found anywhere in the world.

Topographically this area comprises two distinct divisions, the

3

High Plains and the Low or Rolling Plains. The latter, sloping slightly from west to east, are cut by many shallow streams whose valleys contain a variety of timber. West of the Rolling Plains, and in many places separated from them by "badlands" or "breaks" and an escarpment, are the level and treeless High Plains reaching elevations of from three thousand to five thousand feet.

In northwestern Texas and eastern New Mexico lies the most spectacular example of the High Plains environment: the Llano Estacado or Staked Plain. This vast plateau, greater in area than New England, is the largest tract of nearly level land in the United States. Its western and northern rims are regular, but the eastern edge is rough and deeply cut by canyons. Of these the most important are the Palo Duro, the Tule, the Quitaque, and the Yellowhouse.

The Staked Plain was a favored refuge for the red man of the Southwest, for its vast and almost waterless surface long repelled the pursuer. In 1852, while exploring the course of Red River, Captain R. B. Marcy, Fifth United States Infantry, climbed the precipitous bluffs and reached the top of the Staked Plain. He described the geological phenomenon as follows:

> Its elevation above the sea is two thousand four hundred and fifty feet at the head of Red River. It is very level, smooth, and firm, and spreads out in every direction as far as the eye can reach, without a tree, shrub, or any other herbage to intercept the vision. The traveler ... sees nothing but one vast dreary, and monotonous waste of barren solitude. It is an ocean of desert prairie . . . absence of water causes all animals to shun it; even the Indians do not venture to cross it except at two or three points, where they find a few small ponds of water.[1]

Such an area imposed the harshest conditions upon contending military forces and upon those who proposed to dwell there.

Climatically the Southern Plains suffer a deficiency of water and are buffeted by wild, capricious winds. The average annual rainfall

---

[1] Randolph B. Marcy, *Thirty Years of Army Life on the Border*, 169.

is less than twenty inches, with the heaviest precipitation in the months of April, May, and June. During the summer months, particularly in July and August, hot southwesterly or southerly winds can sometimes turn these Plains into a literal furnace, blighting plants and causing extreme discomfort to man and animal. From early fall until well into the spring cold north winds or "northers" can sweep across the Plains, causing amazingly rapid drops in temperature.

Most fearsome, however, are those winds that bring the blizzard, "the grizzly of the Plains."[2] Woe betide the traveler, war party, or column of troops caught in the open and buffeted by the violent winds, sleet, and snow accompanying such weather.

In the mid-1800's the thick grasses of the Plains supported an abundance of animal life, including the deer, antelope, prairie dog, jack rabbit, buffalo, wolf, coyote, and black bear. The grizzly bear was found on the western fringes of the Plains area. Of these mammals only the wolf and coyote were carnivorous; the black bear and grizzly bear were omnivorous.

The bison or American buffalo was by far the most numerous and the most important of the Plains animals. According to the naturalist W. T. Hornaday:

> Of all the quadrupeds that have lived upon earth, probably no other species has ever marshalled such innumerable hosts as those of the American bison. It would have been as easy to count or to estimate the number of leaves in a forest as to calculate the number of buffaloes living at any given time during the history of the species previous to 1870.[3]

A Plains traveler of 1834 expressed his astonishment at the size of the herds thusly:

> Toward evening, on the rise of a hill, we were suddenly greeted by a sight which seemed to astonish even the oldest among us. The

[2] Walter Prescott Webb, *The Great Plains*, 23.

[3] William T. Hornaday, "The Extermination of the American Bison," *Annual Report of the United States National Museum*, 387.

whole plain, as far as the eye could discern, was covered by one enormous mass of buffalo. Our vision, at the very least computation, would certainly extend ten miles, and in the whole of this great space, including about eight miles in width from bluffs to riverbank, there was apparently no vista in the incalculable multitude.[4]

Originally these lumbering beasts appear to have ranged from Canada to Texas and from the Rocky Mountains to the Atlantic Coast, but their true home was the Great Plains. On the Southern Plains their best feeding grounds lay between the South Platte and Arkansas rivers. Migratory by nature, the buffalo moved southward each fall from two to four hundred miles and, as weather moderated, returned northward in the spring.

Prior to 1850 they formed one tremendous herd, composed of innumerable smaller ones, but the gold rush of 1849 and the ensuing Plains traffic tended to divide them. With the completion of the Union Pacific Railroad in 1869 this separation became complete, and until their virtual extinction ten years later there were a Northern and a Southern herd.[5]

The buffalo was indispensable to the way of life of the Southern Plains Indians. Perhaps no other animal in the world exerted so great an influence upon the lives and institutions of a people. To them he yielded both fresh and dried meat, pemmican, and tallow; his hides provided clothing, tipis, robes, ropes, bowstrings, shields, and bags of various sorts. Cups, spoons, and glue were made from his horns, while his bones were a source of many tools and utensils. Even his dried droppings, the "buffalo chips," were usable: they were fuel.

The great tribal or ceremonial hunt was conducted during the late summer and early fall when the buffalo were fat and their hair thin. In this condition the meat was at its best and hides the easiest to dress. Religious rites were held throughout the hunt, and

---

[4] Quoted in M. D. Garretson, *The American Bison*, 58–59.
[5] Richard I. Dodge, *The Hunting Grounds of the Great West*, 131; Hornaday, "The American Bison," *loc. cit.*, 491–92.

strict tribal regulations governed both the method of hunting and the distribution of the kill. Such restrictions did not obtain during the winter when small parties might pursue the animal. The pelts at this time, thick and heavy, were unsuitable for fine dressing but provided excellent material for coarse clothing, warm robes, and moccasins.

Deriving the greater part of their material necessities from the buffalo, it was but natural that the Plains Indians should impart to it a religious significance and perform many ceremonies in its honor. Around the tipi fire, "myths recounted its creation, and its folk tales delighted old and young."[6] Disappearance of the buffalo would be synonymous with a disappearance of the Indians' way of life.

Overlords of the Southern Plains were the Comanches, Kiowas, Kiowa-Apaches, Southern Cheyennes, and Arapahoes. All were nomadic buffalo hunters, ranging over hundreds of miles, living in skin tipis, and practicing but little agriculture. Prior to their acquisition of the horse during the seventeenth and eighteenth centuries the dog had been their only beast of burden. Moving and hunting on foot, their ranges were restricted and their existence precarious.

All this changed with the advent of the horse. Strays or runaways from the herds of the Spanish explorers found a natural home upon the Plains and there multiplied at an astonishing rate. The exact time at which the Southern Plains tribes recognized their value, acquired and mastered these animals is uncertain, but the Kiowas and Comanches were mounted by the opening of the eighteenth century, and a horse culture had spread throughout the Plains area a few decades later.

Once possessed of the horse the Indian was relieved of those limitations imposed by foot travel. His range and mobility were vastly increased, and his proficiency in procuring food and cloth-

[6] Frederick Webb Hodge, ed., *Handbook of American Indians North of Mexico*, B.A.E. *Bulletin No. 30*, I, 169–70; Marcy, *Army Life*, 57.

7

ing rendered many times more efficient. Property could now be accumulated and transported easily, and if game proved scarce he was literally riding a commissary. On foot he would have presented no great obstacle to the white settler; mounted he became a fearsome antagonist and a formidable opponent even for trained cavalry.

The Plains warriors were among the finest horsemen that the world has produced, with the Comanches generally regarded as the best. The artist George Catlin, who observed their superb horsemanship, was amazed at the facility with which a fully armed warrior could drop his body horizontally at the side of his running horse, clinging to the animal by a heel over its back, and discharge his weapons from under its neck. He thought the Comanche awkward and unattractive while on foot, "but the moment he lays his hand upon his horse, his face even becomes handsome, and he gracefully flies away like a different being."[7]

The weapons of the Plains Indians consisted of a short bow of ash or *bois d'arc,* not more than three feet long, arrows tipped with bone, flint, or iron, a long lance, and a war-club. Increasing contacts with the whites brought the rifle and revolver into common use, particularly as weapons of war, but the bow and arrow remained a favorite hunting weapon. To protect himself in battle the Indian bore a circular shield made of two-ply buffalo hide, hardened and undressed.[8]

Indian warfare was conducted by the tribe as a whole, by bands within the tribe, or more commonly by small war parties composed entirely of volunteers. These ranged in size from half a dozen warriors to one hundred or more. Though eager to slay his enemy and recognizing no noncombatants, the Plains Indian often

[7] George Catlin, *North American Indians,* I, 74–75; Marcy, *Army Life,* 28; Hodge, *Handbook,* I, 569–71.

[8] Hodge, *Handbook,* II, 915; Dodge, *Hunting Grounds,* 330–31; Marcy, *Army Life,* 24–25. Marcy says that the Plains Indians could launch an arrow with such force as to drive it entirely through a buffalo.

raided for the sole purpose of stealing horses and cattle. At this art he was most adept. Colonel Dodge wrote:

> Where all are such magnificent thieves, it is difficult to decide which of the plains tribes deserves the palm for stealing. The Indians themselves give it to the Comanches. . . . I have known a Comanche to crawl into a bivouac where a dozen men were sleeping, each with his horse tied to his wrist by the lariat, cut a rope within six feet of a sleeper's person, and get off with the horse without waking a soul.[9]

Counting coup was also an important part of Indian warfare. This practice, which consisted of performing brave deeds such as killing an enemy, scalping him, or being the first to touch or strike him, entitled those successful to the rank of warrior. Prestige among his fellows arose from the number of coups a warrior had counted.

Military societies flourished among the Plains Indians, with from four to twelve within each tribe. At all tribal gatherings, hunts, and war expeditions these organizations took care of details, enforced regulations, and punished offenders. Typical of such societies were those of the Kiowas, who had six: the Rabbits, Young Mountain Sheep, Horse Caps, Black Legs, Crazy Horses, and Chief Dogs or Koitsenkos. The Rabbits were composed of young boys, the next four were about equal in prestige, while the Chief Dogs were restricted to ten tried and true warriors.[10]

Colonel Marcy, from long experience among the Plains Indians, aptly summarized the problem that was involved in inflicting defeat upon them:

> To act against an enemy who is here to-day and there tomorrow; who at one time stampedes a herd of mules upon the headwaters of the Arkansas, and when next heard from is in the very heart of the populated districts of Mexico, laying waste haciendas, and carrying devastation, rapine, and murder in his steps; who is every where with-

---

[9] Dodge, *Hunting Grounds,* 401; Marcy, *Army Life,* 23–24; Hodge, *Handbook,* II, 914–15.

[10] Hodge, *Handbook,* I, 354, 862; Dodge, *Hunting Grounds,* 353–54, 389–90.

out being any where; who assembles at the moment of combat, and vanishes whenever fortune turns against him; who leaves his women and children far distant from the theatre of hostilities, and has neither towns nor magazine to defend, nor lines of retreat to cover; who derives his commissariat from the country he operates in, and is not encumbered with baggage-wagons or pack-trains; who comes into action only when it suits his purpose, and never without the advantage of numbers or position—with such an enemy the strategic science of civilized nations loses much of its importance.[11]

Not one of the five Southern Plains tribes was indigenous to the region. The Comanches were of Shoshonean stock and had once dwelt in southern Wyoming. Pressure from the Sioux and other tribes had caused them to drift southward upon the Plains. Early in the eighteenth century their home appears to have been in Kansas. During the next hundred years they moved still farther south, and by 1805 they were ranging from the Brazos River to the Arkansas River.

The Comanches, like the other Plains tribes, comprised a number of bands held together in loose confederation, which made negotiation with them as a tribe difficult if not impossible. Most important of the bands were the Kwahadis, the Yamparikas, the Kotsotekas, the Nokonis, and the Penatekas. As a people the Comanches enjoyed a reputation for gallantry and courage and for a high sense of honor. They felt themselves superior to the other tribes, knowing that their language was the trade language of the Southern Plains.[12]

The earliest traditions of the Kiowas placed them at the headwaters of the Missouri River, whence they had moved to the Plains. About the year 1700 they formed an alliance with the Crows, who seem to have introduced to them the horse. Pressure from the Cheyennes and Arapahoes forced them southward upon the Comanches,

[11] Marcy, *Army Life*, 67–68.

[12] B.A.E., *Fourteenth Annual Report*, II, 1044–45; Hodge, *Handbook*, I, 327. The English equivalents of these band names are respectively Antelope-Eaters, Root-Eaters, Buffalo-Eaters, Wanderers, and Honey-Eaters.

with whom they waged war until 1795. Peace was then made, and confederation followed. Five tribal divisions were recognized by the Kiowas: the Kata, Kogui, Kaigwu, Kingep, and Kongtalyui. Though brave and warlike, they were predatory and were considered generally inferior to the Comanches.[13]

The Kiowa-Apaches, a small tribe of Athapascan stock, associated with the Kiowas from earliest historic times, and had moved to the Plains and southward with them. They have been called "Gattackas" or "Katakas" but more commonly "Kiowa-Apaches," for they were mistakenly believed to be an eastern Apache band committed to life on the Plains. Known to the Kiowas as "Semats" or "Thieves," they were generally friendly to the whites and reluctant to take the warpath.[14]

The Cheyennes and Arapahoes, both of Algonquian stock, had apparently made their earlier home in Wisconsin and Minnesota with the Arapahoes to the north. The Sioux had uprooted them and driven them westward toward the Black Hills, with the Cheyennes moving in the more southerly direction. Unrelenting, the Sioux forced the Arapahoes toward the headwaters of the Yellowstone and Missouri, and the Cheyennes were pushed toward the upper reaches of the North Platte.[15]

With the building of Bent's Fort on the Arkansas in 1832, a portion of both tribes moved southward toward that stream, engaging as they did so in a fierce war with the Kiowas and Comanches. This struggle ended in 1840 when friendly relations were established. Thereafter all four tribes were usually united in war. The separation of northern and southern branches of the Cheyennes and Arap-

---

[13] James Mooney, "Calendar History of the Kiowa," *Seventeenth Annual Report of the Bureau of American Ethnology*, 153–64; B.A.E., *Fourteenth Annual Report*, II, 1078. Respectively the English equivalents of the Kiowa bands are Biters, Elks, Kiowas, Big Shields, and Black Boys.

[14] Hodge, *Handbook*, I, 701–702; A. L. Kroeber, *Cultural and Natural Areas of Native North America*, 79.

[15] Kroeber, *Native North America*, 72; B.A.E., *Fourteenth Annual Report*, II, 1024–25; George B. Grinnell, *The Cheyenne Indians*, I, 1–46.

ahoes had become permanent within a score of years, but close relationships continued.[16]

Of eleven tribal divisions or bands among the Cheyennes as a whole, six appear in the southern branch, with the Hevhaitanios or Fur-Men the most important. A brave, proud, and contentious people, they were excellent warriors. Their Dog Soldiers, a military society, were the most feared and respected on the Southern Plains.

The Arapahoes were the most peacefully disposed of the wild tribes of the Southern Plains. Normally friendly toward the whites, amiable and accommodating, they exerted a moderating influence upon the more turbulent Cheyennes. They were much given to ceremony, with their principal observance an annual sun dance.

The colonization of Texas by Stephen F. Austin and other *empresarios* gave the Comanches and Kiowas their first experience with the aggressive expansionism of the Anglo-American settler. Long implacable enemies of the Spaniard and the Mexican, they were at first inclined to be friendly with the newcomers from the United States.

In the spring of 1822, Austin and two companions were surrounded near the Nueces River by a band of fifty Comanches who seized all their belongings. But when the Indians learned that their victims were Americans they returned nearly all their property and released them unharmed.[17]

The rapid development of the Texas settlements, particularly after independence had been won, slowly changed this attitude, although a conciliatory policy by President Houston during his first term (1836–38) forestalled major trouble. Depredations along the frontier were increasing, however, and the inauguration of President M. B. Lamar in December, 1838, brought a change in policy.

[16] B.A.E., *Fourteenth Annual Report,* II, 1025–27; Hodge, *Handbook,* I, 72; Mooney, "Calendar History," *loc. cit.,* 172; Kroeber, *Native North America,* 81; Grinnell, *Cheyenne Indians,* I, 1.

[17] Rupert N. Richardson, *The Comanche Barrier to South Plains Settlement,* 89; Eugene C. Barker, ed., *History of Texas,* 71.

Unlike Houston, Lamar had no faith in the peaceful solution to the Indian problem, and advocated expulsion or extermination of the Indians. The time had come, he said, for "an exterminating war upon their warriors; which will admit of no compromise and have no termination except in their total extinction or total expulsion."[18]

This declaration of war was soon returned by the Comanches. In January, 1840, a small delegation of them visited Colonel H. W. Karnes, commanding the post at San Antonio. They informed him that their people desired peace and wished to sign a treaty to that effect. In reply Karnes indicated the government's willingness to make such a treaty if all captives and property were returned and future raiders brought in for punishment. When the Indians agreed, arrangements were made for a council.

On March 19 sixty-five Comanche men, women, and children and one white captive reached San Antonio. Two Texan commissioners met with twelve chiefs in a council house, while the remainder of the Indians loitered about the rear of the house. Near by Lieutenant Colonel W. S. Fisher was holding two companies of troops in readiness for any trouble that might occur.

In the council room an argument developed over apparent failure of the Comanches to bring in all their captives. Fisher sent a detachment of his men inside, and the chiefs were then informed that they were prisoners and hostages pending the safe return of the captives. One of them, making a dash for the door, stabbed a guard barring the way. This precipitated a wild melee in which all the chiefs were slain.[19]

Outside, the Comanches engaged the troops in a bitter fight which ended in the death or capture of all but one of the Indians. Such a sanguinary affair cost the Comanches thirty-five dead, in-

[18] Mirabeau Buonaparte Lamar, *Papers*, ed. by Charles Gulick, Jr., and Katherine Elliott, II, 352–53.

[19] Anna Muckleroy, "The Indian Policy of the Republic of Texas," *Southwestern Historical Quarterly* Vol. XXVI (October, 1922), 143; Louis J. Wortham, *A History of Texas*, IV, 65; Barker, *History of Texas*, 353.

cluding three women and two children. Twenty-seven women and children and two old men were taken prisoner. Eight Texans were killed and seven wounded.

In two years of warfare which followed the "Council House Fight" the Comanches were badly worsted, so the Texas frontier had a measure of relief from raids and depredations. Nevertheless, the Indians neither forgot nor forgave their losses at San Antonio. Thereafter a Texan received no more consideration than a Mexican or a Spaniard.[20]

Annexation of Texas to the United States in 1845 transferred the problem of controlling the Comanches and their Kiowa allies to the federal government. Over the course of fifty years Congress had established, by 1849, the principal instrumentalities whereby Indian affairs were administered. In 1789 the War Department had been assigned the supervision of the Indians, and in March, 1824, an Office of Indian Affairs had been established within that department. In July, 1832, there was authorized a Commissioner of Indian Affairs who would, under the Secretary of War, manage all Indian affairs and all matters arising out of Indian relations.

Two years later, in June, 1834, Congress provided for a field force of agents and subagents, interpreters, and other employees. Provisions were also made for the payment of annuities and the purchase of supplies. In addition the act provided for a reorganization of the various superintendencies and agencies. The final major development until well after the Civil War came in 1849 with the transfer of Indian affairs from the War Department to the Department of Interior.

Early federal relations with the Comanches and Kiowas had been fairly satisfactory. Treaties had been concluded with the Comanches at Camp Holmes on the Canadian River in August, 1835, and with the Kiowas and Kiowa-Apaches in May, 1837. Terms of these agreements were similar. Both tribes consented to the passage

---

[20] Muckleroy, "Indian Policy," *loc. cit.*, 144–45; Wortham, *History of Texas*, IV, 65–66; Joseph C. McConnell, *The West Texas Frontier*, 237–57.

of American citizens across their lands, agreed to cease their depredations along the Santa Fe Trail, and accepted the Cross Timbers as an eastern limit of their hunting range. There was to be a perpetual peace between them and the Civilized Tribes of the Indian Territory.[21]

Unfortunately, a peaceful solution of the Texas Indian problem was rendered virtually impossible by that state's retaining control of its public domain and refusing to recognize Indian land claims. Thus, with the frontier moving rapidly westward, plagued with increasing Indian hostility, the federal government was powerless to effect a boundary settlement with the tribes or to afford them any protection from white encroachment. Furthermore, the change in relationship between Texas and the United States was not understood by the Indians. Disposed to maintain friendly relationships with Americans, they considered Texans their mortal enemies. When the federal government complained of their raids, they would insist that they were at peace with the United States and merely at war with Texas.

In the spring of 1847, Major R. S. Neighbors, a former army officer and Indian agent for the Republic of Texas, was appointed federal special agent to the Texas Indians. His principal efforts were directed toward the establishment of reservations where his charges might settle, farm, and live at peace with the whites. His projects were unfortunately not popular in Texas, and for many years little success attended his labors. Meantime the westward surge of the whites had pushed the embittered Comanches and Kiowas ever farther north and west until they menaced the Santa Fe trade and the settlements in western Kansas and eastern Colorado.[22]

---

21 Charles J. Kappler, *Indian Affairs: Laws and Treaties,* II, 322–23, 363–64; Mooney, "Calendar History," *loc. cit.,* 173. The Cross Timbers is a belt of hardwood trees from five to thirty miles wide extending from the Arkansas River southwestward to the Brazos, a distance of some four hundred miles. Ralph H. Brown, *Historical Geography,* 377; Marcy, *Army Life,* 166–67.

22 U.S. Congress, Senate, *Sen. Exec. Doc. No. 171,* 30 Cong., 1 sess., 1–3; *Annual Report of the Commissioner of Indian Affairs for the Year 1850,* 137–39; Richardson,

An inevitable increase in raids and depredations brought insistent Texan demands for federal protection. Between 1848 and 1853 the frontier was buttressed by two lines of army posts forming an inner and outer chain of defense. The inner line, completed in 1849, consisted of Fort Duncan on the Río Grande; Fort Lincoln at D'Hanis; Fort Martin Scott, two miles south of Fredericksburg; Fort Croghan, fifty miles northwest of Austin; Fort Gates on the Leon River sixty-five miles northeast of Croghan; Fort Graham on the Colorado River in Hill County; and Fort Worth on the Trinity River fifty-four miles north of Graham.

Six posts formed the outer chain composed of Fort Belknap on the Brazos in Young County, Fort Phantom Hill on the Clear Fork of the Brazos near present Abilene, Fort Chadbourne on Oak Creek in Coke County, Fort McKavett on the San Saba River in Menard County, and Fort Clark about forty-five miles north of Eagle Pass. A band of some two hundred miles' width separating these two lines afforded the terrain for an elastic and fairly adequate scheme of defense, but swift-striking war parties still managed to penetrate far into the settlements.

In 1853 the government again sought to ease the threat to the Santa Fe trade by peaceful means. On July 27 the Comanches, Kiowas, and Kiowa-Apaches were persuaded to sign a treaty at Fort Atkinson, Kansas, wherein they agreed to permit the construction of roads and military posts in their country, to stop their raiding both in Mexico and in the United States, and to pay either nation for damages inflicted. In return they were promised $18,000 per annum for ten years and received assurances of government protection.

Meanwhile Major Neighbors' untiring efforts were about to pro-

---

Comanche Barrier, 260–66; Mooney, "Calendar History," *loc. cit.,* 132. Only 36 Texas counties had been organized prior to 1846. By 1860 the number had risen to 119. In 1843 the population was estimated at 140,000, and had risen to 602,000 by 1860. Lena Clara Koch, "Federal Indian Policy in Texas," *Southwestern Historical Quarterly,* Vol. XXVIII, No. 3 (Jan., 1925), 231.

duce results, though somewhat meager ones. On February 6, 1854, the Texas legislature provided for Indian reservations which the federal government might select and survey. Unfortunately, however, with more than 100,000,000 acres at their disposal, they made a niggardly grant of but twelve leagues (55,728 acres).

The work of location and survey, under Neighbors and Captain Marcy, was undertaken and completed before the end of that year. Two sites were chosen: one, known as the Brazos Agency, comprising eight leagues (38,152 acres) on the river of that name a few miles south of Fort Belknap; the other, called the Comanche Reserve, of four leagues (18,576 acres) on the Clear Fork of the Brazos about forty-five miles west of the other agency.[23]

By 1858 upward of eleven hundred of the more peaceful and civilized tribes—including the Caddoes, Wacoes, Anadarkoes, Kichais, and Delawares—had been settled at the Brazos Agency and were making good progress. Few of the Comanches, however, had shown interest in their reserve, and after three years less than four hundred had established themselves there.

Moreover, even these modest beginnings were doomed to failure, for there was an undisguised and growing hostility among near-by white settlers, and the continued marauding of vengeful Comanches and Kiowas kept public opinion inflamed beyond the point of reason. That the Texans made no distinction between peaceful and warlike Indians and desired to be rid of both was proved in December, 1858—if, indeed, proof were needed—when a group of citizens from Erath County stole upon a party of seventeen Indians from the Brazos Agency and murdered them all while they slept.

Three months later nearly 1,000 men from Erath, Jack, Palo Pinto, and Comanche counties threatened to attack the Comanche reserve, and Neighbors feared that a massacre was imminent. Late in May a force of 250 Texans actually attacked. Quick action by federal cavalry from Camp Cooper drove them off before much

[23] Marcy, *Army Life*, 170–223; R. S. Neighbors to E. M. Pease, Feb. 20, 1855, in *Texas Indian Papers, III*, 209–10; U.S. Congress, *H.R. Exec. Doc. No. 2*, 35 Cong., 1 sess., 558.

damage had been done, but this was enough for Neighbors. Aided by four companies of troops, he moved his threatened wards to the vicinity of Fort Cobb, Indian Territory, where they arrived on August 8, 1859.[24]

A generation of relentless pressure had thus culminated in a forced removal of the more peacefully inclined tribes, had driven the main body of the Comanches and Kiowas northward and westward, and had imbued them with a bitter hatred of the Texans. In his report to the Commissioner of Indian Affairs at the close of 1859, William Bent, agent of the Upper Arkansas Agency, thus summarized the result:

> The Kiowa and Comanche Indians have, for two years, appeared in full numbers and for long periods upon the Arkansas, and now permanently occupy the country between the Canadian and the Arkansas rivers. This is in consequence of the hostile front opposed to them in Texas by which they are forced towards the north and is likely to continue perpetual. . . . A smothered passion for revenge agitates these Indians, perpetually fomented by the failure of food, the encircling encroachments of the white population, and the exasperating sense of decay and impending extinction with which they are surrounded.[25]

Outbreak of the Civil War afforded these tribes an opportunity to slake their thirst for revenge. When federal troops abandoned her frontier posts, Texas was able to create only an inadequate patchwork through which war parties moved with ease. For many miles the frontier was driven eastward, and its reclamation by the whites awaited the close of the war.[26]

Meanwhile the Cheyennes and Arapahoes did not long remain

[24] U.S. Congress, *Sen. Exec. Doc. No. 2*, 36 Cong., 1 sess., 383, 639–99. Neighbors' efforts to help the Indians incurred the wrath of many fellow Texans. In September, 1859, he was shot and killed in a dispute over the treatment of reservation Indians. See Koch, "Federal Indian Policy," *loc. cit.*, Vol. XXIX, 122–23.

[25] *Annual Report of the Commissioner of Indian Affairs for the Year 1859*, 138.

[26] Letters and documents in *Texas Indian Papers*, IV, 1–90, show clearly the impact of Indian depredations along the Texas frontier between 1860 and 1865. According to Carl Coke Rister, the frontier had been driven in for a distance of 150 to 200 miles. See his "Fort Griffin," *West Texas Historical Association Yearbook*, Vol. I (June, 1925), 16.

in undisturbed possession of their lands north of the Arkansas. White traffic, crossing the Plains to Oregon, California, and Salt Lake, steadily increased from the late 1830's and, after the discovery of gold in 1848, became a human tidal wave. In September, 1851, anxious to maintain peace and to keep the great roads open, the government negotiated with these tribes and some of the Sioux the Treaty of Fort Laramie.

By its terms the Cheyennes and Arapahoes were assigned a large domain along the foothills of the Rocky Mountains between the Arkansas River and the North Platte. They agreed to the establishment of roads and military posts in their country and accepted a sum of $50,000 per annum for fifty years. Furthermore, they received the promise that the government would preserve their rights against white intrusion.

This treaty was never ratified, however, and in any case its effect would have been short-lived. The discovery of gold in Colorado in 1858, and the Pike's Peak rush which followed, brought in thousands of aggressive whites who mined, farmed, and settled with complete disregard for Indian rights. In 1859, Agent William Bent reported:

> I estimate the number of whites traversing the plains across the central belt to have exceeded sixty thousand during the present season. The trains of vehicles and cattle are frequent and valuable in proportion. Post lines and private expresses are in constant motion. The explorations of this season have established the existence of precious metals in absolutely infinite abundance and convenience of position. A concourse of whites is, therefore, constantly swelling an incapability of control or restraint by the government.[27]

Indian resentment rose as their lands were overrun and as game became scarce, but trouble was temporarily averted by a new agreement. At Fort Wise (formerly Bent's Fort) on February 18, 1861, United States Commissioners A. G. Boone and F. B. Culver con-

---

[27] Kappler, *Indian Affairs*, II, 440; *Annual Report of the Commissioner of Indian Affairs for the Year 1859*, 137–38.

cluded a treaty with the Cheyennes and Arapahoes which reduced their holdings to a small triangle of land in southeastern Colorado. In return the Indians were for fifteen years to receive an annuity of $30,000 minus the expenses of fencing, building houses, and purchasing livestock, agricultural implements, and other equipment.[28]

For the next three years only minor incidents marked the intercourse of whites and Indians, but in the spring of 1864 the inevitable happened. On the evening of April 11 a man named Ripley came to Camp Sanborn and reported that his cattle and those of his neighbors along Bijou Creek had been stolen by a party of Indians. Next day Lieutenant Clark Dunn, First Colorado Cavalry, with forty men, went in pursuit with Ripley acting as guide.

A march of sixty miles brought them upon a band of about seventy Indians driving a herd of horses. As Ripley claimed some of the stock belonged to him, Dunn stopped the herd, demanded the animals, and, when the Indians refused, attempted to disarm them. A hot skirmish resulted, and Dunn retired with four of his men badly wounded.

He was not certain of the identity of the Indians but thought them to be Cheyennes, and Colonel John Chivington, First Colorado Cavalry, commanding the District of Colorado, ordered, in effect, that all Cheyennes be "chastised severely."[29] Late in April, Major Jacob Downing of the First Colorado, with a force of sixty men, began a hunt for any Cheyennes that he could find. On May 1, after ten days of fruitless search, he captured a lone Indian whom he at first proposed to shoot, but then "I concluded to spare him if he would lead me to a Cheyenne camp."[30]

[28] *Annual Report of the Commissioner of Indian Affairs for the Year 1861*, 17; Kappler, *Indian Affairs*, II, 614–17.

[29] Chivington to Maj. Gen. S. R. Curtis, Commanding the Department of Kansas, Apr. 13, 1864, in *War of the Rebellion: A Compilation of the Official Records of the Union and Confederate Armies* (hereinafter cited as *O.R.*), Vol. XXXIV, Pt. 3, 149; *Annual Report of the Commissioner of Indian Affairs for the Year 1868*, 34. Colorado Territory formed one military district in the Department of Kansas. The other districts were those of Nebraska, North and South Kansas, and Upper Arkansas. *O.R.*, Vol. XLI, Pt. 4, 989–92.

The captive led him to a Cheyenne village at Cedar Bluffs about sixty miles north of the South Platte River. Although there was little evidence that these Indians had engaged in any hostile act, the troops attacked at daylight on May 3, effected a complete surprise, killed or wounded sixty, and destroyed all their lodges and property. Downing's loss was one man killed and one wounded.

This irresponsible act brought war to the Colorado settlements, for the Cheyennes were quick to exact revenge, and with the aid of the Arapahoes, Kiowas, and Comanches they had virtually isolated the territory from the east by midsummer. Mail and stage service was disrupted, some small communities were plundered, over fifty Coloradoans were killed, and a number of women and children were captured.[31]

Late in June, with the Indians utterly beyond control, Governor John Evans of Colorado Territory ordered all the Cheyennes and Arapahoes to come in to Fort Lyon or else face a war of extermination. The Indians were at first slow to comply. On September 3, however, three Cheyenne emissaries came to the fort and told the commanding officer, Major E. W. Wynkoop, First Colorado Cavalry, that many Cheyenne and Arapaho chiefs, along with their people, were assembled for mutual protection on the headwaters of the Smoky Hill River. They held there some white captives whom they were willing to return if a peace could be arranged.[32]

Wynkoop was a courageous officer, and with a small force he accompanied the messengers to the rendezvous on the Smoky Hill, where he was "confronted by from 600 to 800 Indian warriors drawn up in line of battle and prepared to fight." Since he exhibited none of the belligerence that had characterized too many of his

[30] Downing to Chivington, May 2, 1864, *O.R.*, Vol. XXXIV, Pt. 3, 407.

[31] *Annual Report of the Commissioner of Indian Affairs for the year 1868*, 36; Hubert Howe Bancroft, *History of Nevada, Colorado, and Wyoming, 1540–1888*, 461–62; Charles Ingersoll, Agent of the Post-Office Department, to Maj. Gen. Curtis, June 3, 1864, in *O.R.*, Vol. XXXIV, Pt. 4, 205; Mooney, "Calendar History," *loc. cit.*, 183.

[32] *Annual Report of the Commissioner of Indian Affairs for the Year 1864*, 22–23; Maj. Wynkoop to Lt. J. E. Tappan, Acting Asst. Adj. Gen., District of the Upper Arkansas, Sept. 18, 1864, in *O.R.*, Vol. XL, Pt. 3, 242.

brother officers, he soon convinced Black Kettle of the Cheyennes, Left Hand of the Arapahoes, and many of the other chiefs that he came in peace. Securing the release of four white children, he persuaded the Indians to send a delegation of chiefs to Denver for a talk with Governor Evans.[33]

Late in September, Black Kettle and six other chiefs, accompanied by Wynkoop, reached Denver and conferred with Evans, Chivington, and other territorial officials. No definite agreement could be reached, however, for Evans, refusing to treat for peace, proposed to carry on the war until the Indians should surrender.[34] Responsibility for this unfortunate decision, which was to have far-reaching consequences, rested in part upon General S. R. Curtis, commanding the Department of Kansas, who had instructed Chivington on September 28:

> I want no peace until the Indians suffer more. . . . It is better to chastise before giving anything but a little tobacco to talk over. No peace must be made without my directions.[35]

Black Kettle and the other chiefs, acting on Wynkoop's advice, now came in to Fort Lyon to surrender and shortly thereafter made their camps on Sand Creek some forty miles northeast of the post. Wynkoop, whose actions had aroused the ire of General Curtis, was on November 4, 1864, transferred to the Upper Arkansas District, and Major Scott Anthony assumed command at Fort Lyon.[36]

Anthony issued rations to the Indians and apparently gave them no reason to suspect that all was not well, yet at the same time he was urging they be punished. As General Curtis was planning an extensive winter campaign, the camps on Sand Creek made an

[33] *Ibid.*, 243.

[34] *Annual Report of the Commissioner of Indian Affairs for the Year 1864* 23; Gov. Evans to Maj. Samuel G. Colley, U. S. Indian Agent, Sept. 29, 1864, in *O.R.*, Vol. XLI, Pt. 3, 495; *Report of the Joint Special Committee on the Condition of the Indian Tribes*, 87–90. This report, on the pages indicated, carries a verbatim account of the conference.

[35] Curtis to Chivington, Sept. 28, 1864, in *O.R.*, Vol. XLI, Pt. 3, 462.

[36] Special Orders No. 13, Headquarters, District of the Upper Arkansas, Fort Riley, Kansas, Nov. 4, 1864, in *ibid.*, Pt. 4, 433.

inviting target. From Salt Lake City, Brigadier General P. E. Connor telegraphed Chivington: "Can we get a fight out of the Indians this winter?"[37] It is perhaps significant that Connor, prior to the Civil War, had commanded Texas volunteer troops in Indian campaigns.

The result was a Chivington-led expedition, composed of 1,000 men, mostly of the Third Colorado Cavalry, which reached Fort Lyon on November 28. Reinforced by the eager Anthony and 125 men of the post garrison, he made a forced march to the village on Sand Creek, arriving just at daybreak. Without warning he loosed his troops upon the unsuspecting Indians, and the butchery which followed is unparalleled in the annals of Plains warfare.[38]

Even though Black Kettle raised first the American flag and then a white flag, Indian men, women, and children were shot and sabered, their bodies scalped and otherwise mutilated. According to an official government commission:

> Fleeing women holding up their hands and praying for mercy were brutally shot down; infants were killed and scalped in derision; men were tortured and mutilated in a manner that would put to shame the savage ingenuity of interior Africa.[39]

Of some 700 Indians encamped on Sand Creek, Chivington reported that he had slain 500. He had destroyed 130 lodges and captured 500 horses and mules.[40]

The Sand Creek massacre colored United States–Indian relations for a generation. According to one officer of long Plains experience:

[37] Gen. P. E. Connor to Chivington, Oct. 22, 1864, in *ibid.*, 259; Curtis to Brig. Gen. J. H. Carleton, Commanding the Department of New Mexico, Nov. 28, 1864, in *ibid.*, 709; *Annual Report of the Commissioner of Indian Affairs for the Year 1868,* 35.

[38] Maj. S. J. Anthony to the Acting Asst. Adj. Gen., Fort Riley Kansas, Nov. 28, 1864, in *O.R.*, Vol. XLI, Pt. 3, 708; *Report of the Joint Special Committee on the Condition of the Indian Tribes.* 41.

[39] U.S. Congress, *H.R. Exec. Doc. No. 97,* 40 Cong., 2 sess., 9.

[40] Chivington to Evans, Dec. 7, 1864, in *O.R.*, Vol. XLI, Pt. 4, 797. Chivington's report of Indian losses is open to question. Other estimates are as low as 150. Maj. S. G. Colley to Col. Thomas Moonlight, in *O.R.*, Vol. XLVIII, Pt. 1, 511; J. E. Tappan to D. C. Nettleton, in *ibid.*, 597.

But for that horrible butchery it is a fair presumption that all subsequent wars with the Cheyennes and Arapahoes and their kindred tribes might possibly have been averted.[41]

Colonel Jesse Leavenworth, formerly of the Colorado cavalry, and from the summer of 1864 agent to the Kiowas and Comanches, was of the opinion that this atrocity destroyed the last vestige of confidence between red man and white.[42]

Whatever the long-term consequences, the immediate result of Sand Creek was an Indian war of unprecedented scope and violence. The survivors, among them Black Kettle, sought and obtained aid from the Northern Cheyennes and Arapahoes and from the Comanches and Kiowas. This combination set the Plains aflame from the Red River to the Canadian border, slew scores of whites, and fought off all troops sent against them. Connor and Chivington had gotten their "fight," but, by midsummer of 1865, $40,000,000 and 8,000 troops had not sufficed to stop it.[43]

Although the army planned an even more extensive campaign, further expenditure of men and money was now halted by a growing public indignation over the Chivington massacre and by an accompanying demand for some more humane solution to the Indian troubles. This development was materially assisted by peace overtures from the warring tribes. They made known their desires through Agent Leavenworth, who, since the fall of 1864, had worked assiduously for a comprehensive settlement.[44]

The result was a meeting at the mouth of the Little Arkansas River on August 15, 1865, between Leavenworth, assisted by Major

[41] Nelson A. Miles, *Personal Recollections*, 139.

[42] *Annual Report of the Commissioner of Indian Affairs for the Year 1865*, 387; C. W. Whitney to Commissioner of Indian Affairs, July 11, 1864, Office of Indian Affairs, Letters Received, Kiowa Agency.

[43] Mooney, "Calendar History," *loc. cit.*, 183; U.S. Congress, *Sen. Exec. Doc. No. 13*, 40 Cong., 1 sess., 2.

[44] Maj. Gen. G. M. Dodge, Commanding the Department of the Missouri, to the Hon. James Harlan, Secretary of Interior, June 22, 1865, in *O.R.*, Vol. XLVIII, Pt. 2, 971–72; *Annual Report of the Commissioner of Indian Affairs for the Year 1865*, 388–89; U.S. Congress, *Senate Rep. No. 156*, 39 Cong., 2 sess., 38.

General John B. Sanborn, commanding the District of the Upper Arkansas, and some sixteen chiefs of the Comanches, Kiowas, Kiowa-Apaches, Arapahoes, and Cheyennes. There were made arrangements for a cessation of hostilities and for a full-scale peace conference to be held on October 4 at Bluff Creek, forty miles below the mouth of the Little Arkansas.

At the appointed time a United States commission composed of Leavenworth, Sanborn, William S. Harney, Thomas Murphy, Kit Carson, William W. Bent, and James Steele arrived to negotiate with the assembled Indians. The Cheyennes and Arapahoes were dealt with first. General Sanborn opened the proceedings by apologizing for the many wrongs done them, repudiating Colonel Chivington's action, and offering reparations. He then urged the two tribes to accept lands south of the Arkansas River away from the main lines of travel. In this way the whites might be kept from penetrating their country, and future difficulties would be avoided.[45]

Black Kettle and Little Raven, speaking for the Cheyennes and Arapahoes respectively, expressed their desires for peace and asked for new agents, preferably Colonel Bent or Major Wynkoop; but they were reluctant to sign any agreement in the absence of many of their people who were away in the north.[46] Bent removed this objection by promising that their absent kinsmen would be given plenty of time to come south and receive the proposed benefits. Thus reassured, the chiefs affixed their marks on October 14, 1865.[47]

By this treaty the Indians surrendered their old lands in Colorado and accepted a reservation lying partly in southern Kansas and partly in Indian Territory. They could not remove there, however, until the government should extinguish the titles of interested tribes in Indian Territory. Meanwhile, they were free to roam the un-

---

[45] *Annual Report of the Commissioner of Indian Affairs for the Year 1865*, 516–18.

[46] *Ibid.*, 518–21, 523. According to Black Kettle, he and Little Raven represented 270 lodges, 190 Arapaho and 80 Cheyenne. Absent were 760 lodges. These Indians averaged about 5 individuals to the lodge.

[47] Kappler, *Indian Affairs*, II, 887, 890. Prominent signatories for the Cheyennes were Black Kettle and Little Robe; for the Arapahoes, Little Raven, Big Mouth, and Spotted Wolf.

settled portions of their old reservations but were not to encamp within ten miles of any of the main traveled roads, military posts, cities, towns, or villages—not, that is, without express consent of the commanding officers or civil officials concerned.[48]

The contracting parties agreed to a perpetual peace, arbitration of disputes, and to the surrender of Indian raiders. The government would pay annuities for forty years. These would be at the rate of twenty dollars per capita until the tribes were actually on the reservation and forty dollars thereafter.

On October 17 the commissioners reached an agreement with the Kiowa-Apaches whereby they would confederate with the Cheyennes and Arapahoes and share in fruits of this treaty. Next day the Comanches and Kiowas accepted, with much grumbling, a reservation comprising most of the Panhandle of Texas and all of Indian Territory west of the ninety-eighth degree of west longitude. Terms similar to those with the Cheyennes and Arapahoes were agreed upon with respect to annuities, the settlement of disputes, and the punishment of criminals.[49]

Unfortunately, although the treaties of the Little Arkansas brought a measure of peace to the Southern Plains, they were of no lasting value. Texas' control of her public lands nullified the agreement with the Kiowas and Comanches. Moreover, a refusal by Kansas to countenance any Indian reservations within her boundaries caused the Senate to amend the Cheyenne-Arapaho treaty so as to require the President to assign them lands wholly outside that state. They were, in consequence, deprived of any home whatever for more than two years.[50]

[48] *Ibid.,* 887–88. The boundaries of this reservation were to begin at the mouth of Red Creek or the Red Fork of the Arkansas River; go up this stream to its course; westward to a point on the Cimarron River opposite the mouth of Buffalo Creek; due north to the Arkansas River; and thence down this river to the beginning.

[49] *Ibid.,* 892–95; *Annual Report of the Commissioner of Indian Affairs for the Year 1865,* 528–33. For the Kiowas, Little Mountain, the principal chief, Satanta, Lone Wolf, and Kicking Bird were signatories; for the Comanches, Milky Way, Buffalo Hump, Ten Bears, Eagle Drinking, and Horse Back signed. Poor Bear and Crow were the principal chiefs who signed for the Kiowa-Apaches.

While a solution to the Indian problem was thus projected into the future, the pressure of white settlement increased. Coming in from all sides, the settlers perceived no Indian rights they felt bound to respect. The game, whereon the red man depended for his very existence, was inevitably depleted, and a rapid construction of roads and railways accelerated this process. If the Southern Plains formed one of the last frontiers for the white man, they were equally the last home of the Indians. Here these desperate people had to make a final stand. There was nowhere else for them to go.

The task of protecting the swiftly advancing white culture fell upon a frontier army ill prepared for such a task. Right after the Civil War over 1,000,000 volunteers had been mustered out, reducing the nation's armed forces to a peacetime basis. By the end of July, 1866, the authorized strength of the Army was no more than forty-five regiments of infantry, ten of cavalry, and five of artillery, a total of but 54,641 officers and men.[51]

The normal peacetime aversion to military service and a ridiculously low pay scale within the army made it very hard to get recruits. By the close of the year the actual strength was only 38,540, and of this number many were "the off-scourings of the community." Allowing for staff, heavy artillery, and those unfit for duty, not more than 25,000 soldiers were available for field service.[52]

The arbitrary release of thousands of officers, and drastic reductions in rank for most of those who remained, created a serious morale problem. Many a Civil War general found himself reduced to the grade of colonel, major, or even captain. There developed an unhealthy rivalry for promotion, petty jealousies flourished, co-operation was often lacking, and some bitter hatreds were en-

[50] Kappler, *Indian Affairs*, II, 888–89; *Annual Report of the Commissioner of Indian Affairs for the Year 1868*, 35; Frank W. Blackmar, *Kansas*, I, 477–81; Laurence F. Schmeckebier, *Office of Indian Affairs*, 63.

[51] *Annual Report of the Secretary of War for the Year 1866*, 3–4; Gen. William T. Sherman, *Memoirs*, II, 413; Oliver Lyman Spaulding, *The United States Army in War and Peace*, 340.

[52] William Addleman Ganoe, *History of the United States Army*, 303, 307. The pay of an Army private was $16.00, less standard deductions of some $1.13.

gendered. On the frontier one heard ugly rumors that this officer or that wished to provoke a war in order to gain personal distinction.[53]

For administrative purposes the nation was divided into military divisions, departments, and districts, commanded respectively by lieutenant, major, and brigadier generals. Their boundaries were subject to frequent change, but for the greater part of the next decade the Southern Plains would lie within the Departments of Texas and Missouri. These departments, in turn, formed the southern half of the vast Military Division of the Missouri, which encompassed the whole of the Great Plains.

Commanding General of this great division from 1865 to 1869 was William Tecumseh Sherman. His principal task was to protect the advancing settlements and the transcontinental railroads then under construction. To carry out this assignment he proposed to throw a line of defense along the entire length of the Southern Plains. This involved in part a maintenance of garrisons in forts already established and in part the construction of new posts.

By 1868 his line of frontier posts began with Fort Duncan on the Río Grande and ran some six hundred miles across Texas via Forts Clark, Territt, McKavett, Concho, and Griffin to Fort Richardson in Jack County. Forts Arbuckle and Cobb in Indian Territory connected Richardson with the posts in Kansas. There Forts Zarah, Larned, and Dodge, all along the line of the Arkansas, stood guard over the Santa Fe Trail, while to the north Forts Harker, Hays, and Wallace were built to protect the Smoky Hill route to Denver.[54]

---

[53] *Ibid.*, 305. Much revealing information on these conditions may be gleaned from the letters of Colonel Benjamin H. Grierson, in the Papers of Benjamin H. Grierson, Miscellaneous Letters, 1867–1875, Illinois Historical Society, Springfield, Illinois (hereinafter cited as Grierson Letters). For reductions in rank, consult Francis B. Heitman, *Historical Register and Dictionary of the United States Army*, II.

[54] *Annual Report of the Secretary of War for the Year 1868*, 162, 211; Charles W. Ramsdell, *Reconstruction in Texas*, 137–38; William C. Holden, "Frontier Defense, 1865–1889." *Panhandle-Plains Historical Review*, Vol. II (1929), 53–54; Marvin Garfield, "The Military Post as a Factor in the Frontier Defense of Kansas," *Kansas Historical Quarterly*, Vol. I (Nov., 1931), 50–62.

Augmented by many sub-posts, this chain of defense looked impressive, but it was insufficient to protect more than a thousand miles of frontier. Furthermore, Sherman had too few troops to man adequately the defense that he had. Thus, in August, 1866, the Department of the Missouri—military custodian of all of Kansas and Missouri, Indian Territory, and the Territory of New Mexico—had only three regiments of cavalry. Two of these, except for their officers, were composed of raw recruits.[55]

Sherman had no illusions about the effectiveness of this slender barricade. In 1867 he wrote:

> Were I or the department commanders to send guards to every point where they are clamored for, we would need alone on the plains a hundred thousand men, mostly cavalry.[56]

The time would come when he might well wish for such a number.

[55] Assigned to the Department of the Missouri in August, 1866, were the following: Battery B, Fourth Artillery, the Third and Seventh Regiments of cavalry, eight troops of the Tenth Cavalry, the Third, Fifth, Thirty-seventh, and Thirty-eighth Regiments of infantry, and 150 Indian scouts. The troops of the Tenth Cavalry as well as all the infantry were colored. *Annual Report of the Secretary of War for the Year 1866*, 19.

[56] *Annual Report of the Secretary of War for the Year 1867*, 50.

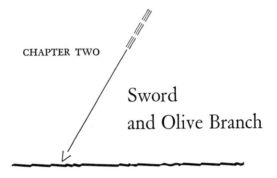

CHAPTER TWO

Sword
and Olive Branch

Winfield scott hancock, in command of the Department of the Missouri, was certain that the spring of 1867 would witness a major Indian outbreak on the Southern Plains. Once the grass grew long and green, and the war ponies were strong after their winter fast, the lance and the scalping knife would be busy. True, the preceding year had been one of comparative peace, but the trend of events had not been reassuring.

Following the treaties of the Little Arkansas in the fall of 1865, traffic flowed unmolested over the great arteries of commerce, the Santa Fe Trail, the Smoky Hill route to Denver, and along the Platte. Individual white men went among the Indians in apparent safety, and reported the red men more peaceably inclined than in many a long year. In western Kansas fingers of settlement crept steadily into the valleys of the Saline, the Solomon, and the Republican rivers. In such areas, long favored by Indian hunters, these isolated frontiersmen tilled their fields in peace.

The prairie scene was not so satisfactory as it might have been, however, for there were two fertile seed beds of trouble. The Cheyennes and the Sioux needed watching. Early in 1866 the most prolific source of worry had been the Cheyenne Dog Soldiers. This warrior society had shunned the meetings on the Little Arkansas, and had rejected every effort to effect their surrender of hunting grounds along the Smoky Hill.

In February, Major Wynkoop, now a special Indian agent, escorted by two companies of the Second Cavalry, had left Fort Larned to visit the Cheyenne camp, then on Bluff Creek, to try to reach agreement with the Dog Soldiers. When he arrived Wynkoop had held council with the principal chiefs, including Black Kettle, Medicine Arrow, and Big Head. Both the latter chiefs were Dog Soldiers, had little faith in the recent treaties, and were reluctant to make any concession on the Smoky Hill.[1]

After prolonged discussions in which Black Kettle had used his influence to aid Wynkoop, promises at last were made by the Dog Soldier chiefs to remain peaceful and to stay near the Arkansas. The agent had distributed some goods and returned to Fort Larned. He felt that his mission had been successful and that peace would prevail if the government carried out to the letter the Little Arkansas agreements.

Rumors of impending trouble from the Dog Soldiers had continued, however, and in May some outrages had occurred along the Solomon in Kansas.[2] In July, therefore, Wynkoop had again journeyed to the Cheyenne camps, where he found the Indians restless but still peaceable. They were resigned to giving up their former hunting grounds and hoped that the government would live up to its promises.

---

[1] *Annual Report of the Commissioner of Indian Affairs for the Year 1866*, 277; Post Returns, Fort Larned, Feb., 1866.

[2] *Annual Report of the Commissioner of Indian Affairs for the Year 1866*, 346–47; Daniel W. Wilder, *The Annals of Kansas*, 437; M. Winsor and J. A. Scarbrough, "Jewell County," *Collections of the Kansas State Historical Society*, Vol. XVII (1928), 391. These depredations were not directly traced to the Dog Soldiers.

Wynkoop was especially sanguine about their future behavior because Black Kettle, Little Wolf, Big Head, Roman Nose, White Beard, and Sitting Bear, all chiefs or warriors with much prestige, had earnestly expressed a desire to remain at peace. They were most anxious for the government to return two Indian children captured at Sand Creek, and to replace the ponies taken there. Wynkoop, promising to do all he could, had returned again to Fort Larned.

More disturbing, however, were events that had occurred far to the north. In July, Red Cloud and his Sioux had gone on the warpath along the Powder River road. The government was building military posts along this route to the Montana gold fields and had promised travelers on the road full protection; but this was Red Cloud's buffalo range, and he refused to give it up. Scorning the government's efforts to secure the road by treaty, he had stalked from the council tent, and, caressing the butt of his rifle, had said, "In this, and the Great Spirit I trust for the right."[3]

However, Red Cloud did not speak for all the Sioux, and some of them had seen enough of war. They were willing to surrender their hunting grounds rather than fight for them, and when hostilities broke out they sought to avoid the conflict. Breaking their camps, they had moved southward to the valley of the Republican, and then, after a time, to the vicinity of Fort Larned.[4]

Although they came in peace, their movement across the routes of travel made the freighters uneasy. Moreover the frontier settlers, ever wary of Indian attacks, feared that raids and depredations were imminent. The prevailing rumor was that the Sioux had come to arrange an alliance with the Southern tribes, and that a general Indian war was in the making. The rumors were given

[3] Quoted in George W. Manypenny, *Our Indian Wards*, 167. See also Flora W. Seymour, *The Story of the Red Man*, 292–93; George E. Hyde, *Red Cloud's Folk*, 139.

[4] U.S. Congress, *H.R. Exec. Doc. No. 97*, 40 Cong., 2 sess., 10; Manypenny, *Our Indian Wards*, 167; *Annual Report of the Secretary of War for the Year 1867*, 34; U.S. Congress, *Sen. Exec. Doc. No. 13*, 40 Cong., 1 sess., 54. These Indians appear to have been largely Brulé Sioux, accompanied by Northern Cheyennes.

substance by the Fetterman massacre in December, which sent a chill of horror and fear along the whole frontier. Now every trivial incident was magnified, and General Hancock was subjected to a barrage of reports compounded of rumor and fear.[5]

Major Henry Douglass, Third Infantry, commanding at Fort Dodge, was his most assiduous informant. Early in the winter of 1867 he wrote his superior that large bands of Sioux, Cheyennes, and Arapahoes were moving south. This movement was ostensibly to hunt buffalo, but it seemed to Douglass additional confirmation of the expected outbreak in the spring.[6]

He also informed Hancock that the Indians possessed much arms and ammunition. The weapons were being furnished not only by authorized Indian agents but in alarming amounts by unlicensed traders. This circumstance so angered the department commander that late in January, 1867, he issued an order forbidding the sale of arms and ammunition to the Indians "by any person or persons whomsoever within the limits of this Department, save at military posts to be hereafter designated."[7]

News from the South had been even less encouraging. During the summer Little Mountain (or Dohasan), great chief of the Kiowas, and an earnest advocate of peace, had died. Lone Wolf had taken his place but could not command so much respect, and many subchiefs like Satanta now followed their own inclinations.[8]

---

[5] *Annual Report of the Commissioner of Indian Affairs for the Year 1868*, 37; Hyde, *Red Cloud's Folk*, 146–49; *Army and Navy Journal*, Vol. IV (Feb. 2, 1867), 380; U.S. Congress, *Sen. Exec. Doc. No. 13*, 40 Cong., 1 sess., 62. On the morning of December 21, 1866, a wood train from Fort Phil Kearney in Wyoming was attacked by the Sioux under Crazy Horse. Colonel Carrington, commanding the post, ordered Captain W. J. Fetterman with eighty-one infantry and cavalry to rescue the wood train. Fetterman was specifically ordered not to pursue the hostiles beyond bluffs near the fort, but he saw fit to disobey this order. The result was the slaughter of the entire rescue party. Crazy Horse also had help from the Northern Cheyennes. See George B. Grinnell, *The Fighting Cheyennes*, 225.

[6] Port Returns, Fort Dodge, Jan., 1867.

[7] U.S. Congress, *Sen. Exec. Doc. No. 13*, 40 Cong., 1 sess., 53–54; *Army and Navy Journal*, Vol. IV (Feb. 23, 1867), 422.

[8] Jesse W. Leavenworth to D. N. Cooley, May 1, 1866, Office of Indian Affairs, Letters

Along with the Comanches, therefore, the Kiowas were indulging in their favorite pastime: raiding in Texas. If these tribes had not appreciated the significance of the annexation of Texas, it was hardly to be expected that they could fully comprehend the swift changes between state and nation during the period from 1861 to 1865.

The close of the Civil War and the beginning of Reconstruction had brought the collapse of Texas' frontier defense organizations. Coupled with Little Mountain's death, the result was the greatest suffering from Indian raids and depredations in the history of the Texas frontier. War parties struck hard in Jack, Wise, Erath, Montague, and Lampasas counties, killing eight persons in the month of July alone and running off thousands of head of cattle. Governor Throckmorton went so far as to telegraph President Johnson that the state would be depopulated unless radical measures were adopted.[9]

It was Satanta, however, who furnished the most fireworks. In August the burly chief led a small band of eager young warriors across Red River into Cooke County. Near the town of Gainesville the raiders found easy prey. One James Box and his family were returning from a visit to sick relatives. Three miles from home they drove virtually into the midst of Satanta and his party. Two arrows in the breast killed Box, who was twice scalped. Mrs. Box, her daughters Margaret, Josephine Maizie, Ida, and infant Laura were taken captive. After plundering the wagon, the war party moved swiftly north and fourteen days later reached the Kiowa camps near the Arkansas River.[10]

Received, Kiowa Agency; *Annual Report of the Commissioner of Indian Affairs for the Year 1867*, 2.

[9] *Texas Indian Papers*, IV, 95–105; J. W. Throckmorton to E. M. Stanton, Aug. 5, 1867, in *ibid.*, IV, 235–36; U.S. Congress, *Sen. Exec. Doc. No. 74*, 40 Cong., 2 sess., 20. Throckmorton in his final report on affairs of his administration (1867) showed that between 1865 and 1867, 162 persons had been killed by Indians, 43 captured, and 24 wounded.

[10] Statement of Mrs. Martha Box to Capt. Andrew Sheridan, Third Infantry and Brevet

In September, Satanta came to Fort Larned and informed Colonel Cuvier Grover, Thirty-eighth Infantry, commanding the post, that he had some white captives and was willing to turn them over for a consideration. Grover at once informed the Indian agent at Fort Zarah, and forwarded a report to General Hancock. The agent hurried to Fort Larned to demand of Satanta the return of the captives, warning him that his raid was a violation of the Little Arkansas Treaty.

Satanta, no whit embarrassed by the agent's lecture, coolly asked for ransom, and when this was indignantly refused, requested time to consider the matter. A short time later, however, Major Andrew Sheridan, commanding at Fort Dodge, paid two thousand dollars to secure the release of the pitiful captives.[11] The affair was thus ended, but Hancock had not heard the last of Satanta.

In February, 1867, Major Douglass kept the telegraph wire hot with reports to department headquarters. On the ninth F. F. Jones, a Kiowa interpreter, had filed a disturbing complaint. Jones, John E. Tappan, and a Major Page had gone to the Kiowa camp to trade. The Indians had responded by seizing their trade goods and threatening to kill them. Furthermore, Satanta had told Jones to inform Major Douglass that he wanted all the troops and army posts removed from the country, and that he desired all stages and railroads to stop operating in the area. As a parting shot, he said he hoped the government stock at Fort Dodge was in good shape: he would be over in a few days to round it up.

All this was bad enough, but Jones now went on to state that before he left the Kiowa camp, a war party had arrived bringing two hundred stolen horses and the scalps of seventeen Negro soldiers

Major, U.S.A., commanding post, Fort Dodge, Kansas, Office of Indian Affairs, Letters Received, Kiowa Agency. Baby Laura did not survive. She died on the way to the Kiowa camps, and her body was thrown into a ravine.

[11] *Annual Report of the Commissioner of Indian Affairs for the Year 1866*, 280; Report of Lt. G. A. Hesselburger, Company A, Third Infantry, to Bvt. Maj. Andrew Sheridan, Fort Dodge, Sept. 29, 1866, Office of Indian Affairs, Letters Received, Kiowa Agency.

and one white man.[12] Douglass accepted the complaint and sent it along to Hancock. A few days later both Tappan and Page came to Douglass and branded Jones an unmitigated liar: there was not a word of truth in his story. But for reasons best known to himself the Major failed to mention this to General Hancock.[13]

Having convinced himself that real trouble was brewing, Douglass held council with Satanta, Stumbling Bear, and other Kiowa chiefs on February 23. Satanta did most of the talking. He told Douglass that he was friendly toward the white men but that he disliked their using the grass, wood, and water about Fort Dodge for it all belonged to him. The whites had not been asked to come there, and they must leave and not run off the buffalo. Satanta then said that his people were hungry, and that he was going south to hunt. This speech puzzled Douglass: he was not sure whether Satanta meant peace or war, but he thought the latter more probable.

Douglass had not been the only source of the growing pile of reports on Hancock's desk. In the same month Captain E. L. Smith, Nineteenth Infantry, commanding at Fort Arbuckle, wrote that he understood the Comanches were raiding over a wide area. Such was the information given him by many frontier settlers; and Horace P. Jones, the post interpreter, had told him that he feared a general Indian war in the spring.

Moreover, Lieutenant George Asbury at Fort Larned informed Hancock that a small party of Cheyennes had compelled one Parker to cook supper for them, and had threatened to kill him because he had no sugar. A few days later Asbury filed a more alarming report. A band of Sioux had crossed the Arkansas heading south, and the Captain now feared that the expected alliance was a fact.

Since early in the summer of 1866, Governor Samuel Crawford

---

12 *Annual Report of the Commissioner of Indian Affairs for the Year 1868*, 37f.; Hancock to Agent Leavenworth, Mar. 11, 1867, Office of Indian Affairs, Letters Received, Kiowa Agency, 1867.

13 *Annual Report of the Commissioner of Indian Affairs for the Year 1868*, 39. Organizational Returns for Negro troops operating in the area show no such loss.

of Kansas had been bombarding Hancock with appeals for federal troops to protect his frontier. He was certain that the Indians were concentrating to make an all-out attack and to halt construction of the Pacific railroads. Nor did he stop with Hancock but telegraphed his fears to General Sherman as well. Despite his frantic urgency, however, Crawford could offer no concrete evidence to support his stories. It is perhaps significant that Governor Crawford was later charged with accepting a bribe from the Union Pacific Railroad. Even though a legislative investigating committee exonerated him, the fact remained that the railroad had given him 640 acres of land.[14]

Concerned over the Indian situation—as reflected in these reports —Sherman decided to make a personal investigation. During the fall he toured the Kansas and Colorado frontiers. But to his surprise he found no Indian trouble—only rumors—and he summed up his opinion in a letter to his brother:

> These reports are all mysterious and only accountable on the supposition that our people out West are resolved on trouble for the sake of profit resulting from the military occupations.[15]

And in his annual report of 1867 to General Grant, Sherman wrote:

> During the past year we have been infinitely embarrassed by many causes and I trust will not occur again. In the early part of the year there seemed to be a concerted and mischievous design to precipitate hostilities, by a series of false reports almost without parallel.... These false reports may have originated in a natural rivalry for business on the three great roads, the friends of each aiming to damage the others.[16]

Such was the situation in the fall and winter of 1866–67 as Sherman viewed it.

---

[14] Samuel J. Crawford, *Kansas in the Sixties*, 251; Marvin Garfield, "Defense of the Kansas Frontier, 1866–1867," *Kansas Historical Quarterly*, Vol. I (Aug., 1932), 326–27. According to Garfield, at no time during 1866 did the Indian situation offer the appearance of preparation for a general war. See also Blackmar, *Kansas*, 482.

[15] Rachel S. Thorndike, ed. *The Sherman Letters, Correspondence between General and Senator Sherman from 1837 to 1891*, 277.

[16] *Annual Report of the Secretary of War for the Year 1867*, 36–37.

General Hancock, for his part, neither visited the frontier nor held council with a single Indian. He chose to accept at face value all the welter of reports which reached him. He was, therefore, convinced that his department must face a major Indian outbreak in the spring, and his course of action seemed clear. A strong force must be assembled and marched into the Indian country to overawe the tribes if possible, or to whip them if necessary.[17]

During March, Hancock translated his convictions into action, raising a force of some 1,400 cavalry, infantry, and artillery.[18] Since the troops were to be drawn from various posts in the department, Fort Harker on the Smoky Hill River was designated as the concentration point. By April 1 all units of the expedition had arrived and were encamped on "Smoky Bottom" just west of Fort Harker.[19]

Meanwhile Hancock had informed the agents of the Kiowas and Comanches and the Cheyennes and Arapahoes, Colonel Jesse Leavenworth and Major E. W. Wynkoop respectively, of his intent to visit the tribes in their charge. He would come desirous of peace but would fight if the Indians wanted a fight. Let the Indians be told that he wanted to talk with them. If convenient, he would like both Leavenworth and Wynkoop to go with him.[20]

---

[17] New York *Tribune* (Sept. 2, 1867). Testifying before the Indian Peace Commission, Hancock admitted that up to the time he took the field he had not talked to an Indian during his administration, and further, that he based his action on the rumor that a general war was impending.

[18] U.S. Congress, *Sen. Exec. Doc. No. 7*, 40 Cong., 1 sess., 2. Hancock's force consisted of seven companies of the Thirty-seventh Infantry commanded by Brevet Major John Rziha; eleven troops of the Seventh Cavalry under Brevet Major General A. J. Smith, with Lieutenant Colonel George A. Custer second in command; a battery of the Fourth Artillery commanded by Lieutenant Colonel C. C. Parsons; some Delaware Indian scouts; and a few white scouts, the most noted being "Wild Bill" Hickok. Post Returns, Fort Harker, Apr., 1867; *Army and Navy Journal*, Vol. IV (Apr. 6, 1867), 518.

[19] Post Returns, Fort Harker, Apr., 1867. U.S. Congress, *H.R. Exec. Doc. No. 240*, 41 Cong., 2 sess., 79; *Harper's Weekly Magazine*, Vol. X (Apr. 27, 1867), 270. Hancock inspected the post on April 2. A little Indian boy, son of a chief killed at Sand Creek, also accompanied the expedition. Hancock was returning him to his people. See Agent Leavenworth to Commissioner of Indian Affairs, Apr. 9, 1867, Office of Indian Affairs, Letters Received, Kiowa Agency; Almira R. Hancock, *Reminiscences of Winfield Scott Hancock*, 114–15.

With his command ready to move, Hancock issued an official communiqué setting forth the character and purpose of his expedition. Its belligerent tone contrasted sharply with the conciliatory messages sent the Indian agents:

It is uncertain whether war will be the result of the expedition or not; it will depend upon the temper and behavior of the Indians with whom we may come in contact. *We go prepared for war, and will make it if a proper occasion presents.* We shall have war if the Indians are not well disposed towards us. If they are for peace, and no sufficient ground is presented for chastisement, we are restricted from punishing them for past grievances which are recorded against them; these matters have been left to the Indian department for adjustment. No insolence will be tolerated from any bands of Indians whom we may encounter. We wish to show them that the government is ready and able to punish them if they are hostile, although it may not be disposed to invite war. In order that we may act with unity and harmony with these views, no one but the commander present, on detachment or otherwise, will have interviews with Indians. Such interviews as may be necessary with them will be reserved, and corresponding reserve will be required from those under his command.[21]

On April 3, Hancock's long column left Fort Harker, and with ranks tightly closed, marched to Fort Zarah where Agent Leavenworth joined the expedition. The command then went on to Fort Larned on the Arkansas, arriving on April 7. There Major Wynkoop met Hancock. He declared that the Dog Soldiers and some Sioux were camped on Pawnee Fork and had agreed to assemble near Fort Larned on April 10. This arrangement seemed all right to Hancock, and he agreed to the meeting.[22]

The council was delayed, however, by a blinding snowstorm

[20] U.S. Congress, *Sen. Exec. Doc. No. 13,* 40 Cong., 1 sess., 78; Hancock to Agent Leavenworth, Mar. 11, 1867, Office of Indian Affairs, Letters Received, Kiowa Agency.

[21] U.S. Congress, *Sen. Exec. Doc. No. 13,* 40 Cong., 1 sess., 83.

[22] Henry M. Stanley, *Early Travels and Adventures in America and Asia,* I, 20; Post Returns, Fort Larned, Apr., 1867; *Annual Report of the Commissioner of Indian Affairs for the Year 1867,* 311; George A. Custer, *Wild Life on the Plains,* 39. From all indications, the Sioux mentioned here were probably Brulés.

which developed on the afternoon of the ninth. Two days later Wynkoop reported that the Indians had started into Fort Larned but had encountered a herd of buffalo and had stopped to hunt. This looked very suspicious to Hancock, but he told the agent that he would allow the Indians another day before marching to their village.

The Cheyennes still being absent on the twelfth, Hancock issued orders that evening for the column to move toward the Indian village next day. Hardly were the orders out, however, when a party of fifteen warriors led by Tall Bull and White Horse reached Fort Larned. The party, cold and hungry, insisted on warming themselves and eating before they talked.

After their needs had been satisfied, a council was held by a great fire in front of Hancock's tent.[23] The General spoke first, and in an unfortunately belligerent manner. He was disappointed, he said, that so few chiefs had come to see him. He had important things to say and preferred to say them only once. If the Indians wanted a fight, he was ready. Furthermore, on the morrow he intended to march to their village and hold council with all the chiefs.

Tall Bull replied saying that he had taken Wynkoop's hand more than a year ago, and that he had held firmly to peace. The buffalo and the antelope were fast diminishing, and soon the red man would be hungry. When the game was all gone his people would have to come in to the fort to eat. He wanted no killing of either red man or white. He had now, he concluded, spoken all he had to say, and he would have nothing more to tell Hancock though he came to the village.

The General then reiterated his intention of marching to the camps on Pawnee Fork, and the council came to an end. Later Tall Bull urged Wynkoop to dissuade Hancock. The approach of the

---

[23] Theodore R. Davis, "A Summer on the Plains," *Harper's Monthly Magazine,* Vol. XXXVI (Feb., 1868), 294. According to Agent Wynkoop, a night council was unknown to the Cheyennes and "against their medicine." See *Annual Report of the Commissioner of Indian Affairs for the Year 1867,* 311.

soldiers, he said, would frighten the women and children, who had not forgotten Sand Creek. Wynkoop, however, could not prevail upon the General to alter his plan.

On the morning of April 13, therefore, Hancock's column left Fort Larned for the Cheyenne village. After a march of some twenty-one miles the command reached Pawnee Fork, which, in midafternoon, they bridged and crossed. It was expected that the village would soon be reached. Shortly, however, Pawnee Killer, a Sioux chief, and White Horse of the Cheyennes, with a small party of warriors, intercepted the column.

Pawnee Killer said that the village was not far away, and that all the chiefs would be over next morning. As he now understood that the village was but five or six miles distant, Hancock gave orders to pitch camp, saying that he would expect the chiefs to be in for the council by 9:00 A.M. Pawnee Killer agreed to deliver this message, but said that he did not think the chiefs could get there before ten or eleven.

Early next morning, having spent the night in Hancock's camp, he left to hasten on the chiefs. About 9:30 A.M., Bull Bear, a Dog Soldier chief, arrived and reported the Indians on their way, but Hancock had grown tired of waiting and had ordered the march for the village resumed.

The column had proceeded about five or six miles when a large body of Indians was sighted moving in the direction of the camp which the army had just left. Hancock halted his command at once, formed his infantry and artillery in line, and brought up his cavalry, sabers drawn, at a gallop. The Indians formed in line also, but many in the rear began to edge away, and then to run in the direction of their village.

At this crucial moment, with a fight imminent, Major Wynkoop asked permission to ride to the Indians and reassure them. His request granted, the courageous agent rode to a little knot of warriors gathered immediately in front of their own line. Warmly greeted, he soon learned the cause for their delay. The distance from the village to Hancock's camp was nearly fifteen miles, not the five or six earlier supposed, and the Indian ponies were too weak to travel fast.[24]

The Indians wanted peace and agreed readily to talk between the lines. Soon a small band of warriors led by Roman Nose, who bore a white flag, advanced to meet with Hancock and several of his staff. To Hancock's demand whether the Indians wanted a fight Roman Nose replied that they wanted peace; that if they had desired a fight they would not have come so close to the big guns. This appeared to mollify the pugnacious general, but he told Roman Nose that it was too windy to talk and that he would move on and camp near the village. A council could then be held as soon as tents were pitched.

The column now moved up Pawnee Fork to within half a mile of the village and there encamped.[25] A little later Roman Nose, Bull Bear, Grey Beard, and Medicine Wolf, of the Cheyennes, came in reporting that their women and children had fled the village in mortal fear. The chiefs might, however, overtake their people and get them to return were it not that their ponies were so weak. Hancock lent them two horses. The Indians, unable to prevail on their people to return, brought back the horses several hours later.

Hancock was now increasingly suspicious of their sincerity. To watch their movements, he sent Ed Guerrier, a half-blood interpreter, to the village with instructions to report back every two hours. A little past 9:00 P.M., the scout returned saying the warriors too were leaving the village.

Hancock ordered Custer to take a detachment of cavalry and prevent the Indians' leaving. Custer, although he lost little time in surrounding the nearly three hundred lodges, found them empty save for one emaciated old Sioux and a sick child. Many large slices

[24] U.S. Congress, *H.R. Exec. Doc. No. 240,* 41 Cong., 2 sess., 39, 51.

[25] Custer, *Life on the Plains,* 45. At the solicitation of Bull Bear, Wynkoop tried again to persuade Hancock not to camp near the village. See U.S. Congress, *H.R. Exec. Doc. No. 240,* 41 Cong., 2 sess., 81f.; Stanley, *Early Travels,* 38; *Annual Report of the Commissioner of Indian Affairs for the Year 1867,* 312–13.

of skin had been cut from the tipis, probably for use as temporary shelters, but great quantities of camp equipment lay abandoned.[26]

Apprized that the village had been deserted, Hancock ordered Custer to move early next morning in pursuit. He was to take eight companies of cavalry and if possible to force the Cheyennes to return. Meanwhile Hancock himself would burn the village and destroy all property that could be found. The flight of the Indians had convinced him that they were hostile.

When Major Wynkoop learned of the decision to burn the village he wrote Hancock immediately to protest this course of action:

> *General:* For a long time I have made the Indian character my chief study. I regard the late movement of the Cheyennes of my agency as caused by fear alone, so far as I am able to judge. They met us at first with a determination to have a peaceful talk, at such a distance from their village as would make their women and children satisfied that no danger need be apprehended by them. Your movement toward the village terrified them, squaws and children, who left with such movable property as they could gather.
>
> I learn that you propose destroying the lodges and other property now remaining in the village. I would most respectfully request you not to do so. I am fully convinced that the result would be an Indian outbreak of the most serious nature; while, at the same time, there is no evidence, in my judgement, that this band of Cheyennes are deserving this severe punishment.
>
> I am influenced alone in thus communicating with you by what I consider a strict sense of duty.[27]

His note had the effect of staying Hancock's hand, at least temporarily, for destruction of the village was now delayed until a report from Custer should be received.

At dawn on April 15, Custer left camp with his Delawares leading the way. The trail was soon found and rapidly followed. It

---

[26] Custer, *Life on the Plains*, 47–50; *Harper's Weekly Magazine*, Vol. X (May 11, 1867), 302; U.S. Cong., *Sen. Exec. Doc. No. 13*, 40 Cong., 1 sess., 84–85.

[27] *Annual Report of the Commissioner of Indian Affairs for the Year 1867*, 313.

led the column northward across Walnut Creek and toward the Smoky Hill River. Pushing his men to the utmost, Custer was soon close on the heels of the fleeing Indians, hoping to overtake them in a short time. But as afternoon came on, the Cheyennes scattered in every direction, and by five o'clock even the Delawares could no longer track them.

Custer was on the move again at 4:00 A.M. By midmorning, however, though signal fires were observed to the north, east, and west, all efforts to pick up the trail had proved fruitless. The column then struck due north and marched to the Smoky Hill River, which was reached early on the morning of the seventeenth. Turning eastward, Custer now marched some thirteen miles to Downer's Station, arriving about dusk; there was received the first news of Indian depredations.

Custer learned that Lookout Station, farther east, had been struck by hostiles on the previous day. Three men had been killed, the station hay supply burned, and all the stock run off. He dispatched a courier with this intelligence to Hancock and next morning resumed his march down the Smoky Hill.

By midafternoon the column had covered the thirty-five miles to Lookout Station. The house, stables, and haystack were in ashes. Bodies of the three men, partially devoured by wolves, were found near by. There was little Custer could do there except bury the dead. The command proceeded on to Stony Hollow Station and then to Fort Hays, where Custer expected to obtain forage and supplies before resuming his pursuit.

Reports obtained at these two places indicated that Hancock had stirred a veritable hornet's nest. Hostile Indians were swarming all over the Smoky Hill route. Stage stations were in a state of siege, six citizens had been killed, and livestock losses were mounting hourly. It seemed imperative that Custer take the field at once.

But to his great embarrassment, he found himself stalled at Fort Hays for want of the expected supplies and forage. Until these both arrived, he would be unable to move. Inadequate planning had thus immobilized eight companies of badly needed cavalry. In summarizing his position, Custer said it was "not only embarrassing but mortifying."[28]

Meanwhile Hancock, with Custer's dispatches in hand, had ordered the destruction of the Indian village. Three companies of the Thirty-seventh Infantry pulled the lodges down and burned them together with great piles of buffalo robes and camp equipment. Since available evidence indicated that the Indians had gone north toward the Platte, the General ordered Custer now to march for that stream, and to protect the Smoky Hill as best he could.[29]

With Custer assigned to the north, Hancock turned south, fearful of a concert between the Cheyennes and the Kiowas and Comanches. Sending warnings ahead to posts along the Santa Fe Trail, he broke his camp at Pawnee Fork on April 20 and marched toward Fort Dodge.

The column, shorn now of most of its cavalry, arrived on the morning of the twenty-second. There Hancock learned that some troopers posted at Cimarron Crossing, about thirty miles distant, had intercepted six Cheyennes moving south. After a chase of some ten miles the Indians had all been killed.[30]

Next morning Hancock held council with the Kiowa chiefs Kicking Bird and Stumbling Bear, who had in fact been at the fort several days awaiting his arrival. They assured him that all the tribes south of the Arkansas wanted peace. Kicking Bird for one was glad to take the white man's hand "up to the elbow." Many of

[28] U.S. Congress, *H.R. Exec. Doc. No. 240,* 41 Cong., 2 sess., 68f., 72–75, 83; Custer, *Life on the Plains,* 54, 59; U.S. Congress, *Sen. Exec. Doc. No. 13,* 40 Cong., 1 sess., 5; Stanley, *Early Travels,* 40, 83.

[29] U.S. Congress, *Sen. Exec. Doc. No. 13,* 40 Cong., 1 sess., 85–91; New York *Tribune* (May 4, 1867). Altogether 272 lodges were destroyed, along with hundreds of buffalo robes, saddles, ropes, pots and pans, kettles, spoons, hoes, axes, and other items. Wynkoop tried again to prevent this destruction, for he did not believe the Cheyennes guilty of the Smoky Hill raids.

[30] Post Returns, Fort Dodge, Apr., 1867; *Army and Navy Journal,* Vol. IV (May 11, 1867), 605. Wynkoop said that these Indians did nothing to provoke an attack and were simply trying to get out of the way. See U.S. Congress *H.R. Exec. Doc. No. 13,* 40 Cong., 1 sess., 87.

the Kiowa underchiefs, Satanta and Satank, along with the Arapahoes under Little Raven, had indeed fled toward the headwaters of the Arkansas upon Hancock's approach, but Kicking Bird declared that he would send runners asking them back.[31]

A few days later Little Raven, Cut Nose, Yellow Bear, and several other Arapaho chiefs reached Fort Dodge to talk with Hancock. They assured him that they had been at peace since the Little Arkansas agreements, that they had had no connection with the recent troubles, and that they intended to remain south of the Arkansas.

All this pleased Hancock greatly. If he had entertained any idea of marching south of the Arkansas to "overawe" the tribes there, he now gave it up in favor of holding more councils at Fort Larned. There he proceeded with alacrity and on May 1 had a long talk with the redoubtable Satanta.[32]

This chief, his whole body colored a brilliant red, echoed the sentiments of Kicking Bird. He wanted peace too and was loath to see the prairies bloody, but he did think the destruction of the Cheyenne village was a mistake. The Cheyennes had wanted peace as much as he. So impressed was Hancock with the chief's apparent sincerity that he gave him a major general's coat and a yellow sash; and Satanta strode grandly away, a riot of barbaric color.[33]

The General now marched on to Fort Hays, arriving on May 3. There he found Custer, still unable to move. Unserviceable horses, lack of supplies, and scarcity of forage held him fast. Greatly disappointed, Hancock, two days later, marched to Fort Harker, and thence to his headquarters at Fort Leavenworth; his own active campaigning was over.[34]

[31] U.S. Congress, *H.R. Exec. Doc. No. 240,* 41 Cong., 2 sess., 101–102; Stanley, *Early Travels,* 49.

[32] New York *Tribune* (May 16, 1867). According to the *Tribune* correspondent, Hancock had intended going south of the Arkansas "to hunt up the Comanches."

[33] Stanley, *Early Travels,* 80–83; *Harper's Weekly Magazine,* Vol. XI (June 8, 1867), 357–58.

[34] U.S. Congress, *H.R. Exec. Doc. No. 240,* 41 Cong., 2 sess., 90–92; Stanley, *Early Travels,* 84–85; Post Returns, Fort Harker, May, 1867.

Less than a month before, when he had gone forth so confidently to overawe the Indians, the Plains were enjoying a period of relative peace. Now as he retired from the scene, his cavalry under Custer was shackled at Fort Hays, and the Indians were literally running wild.[35] War parties of Cheyennes, and Sioux, and some Arapahoes swarmed along the Smoky Hill route and among the settlements in the Solomon and the Republican river valleys. Settlers were abandoning their homes and seeking safety at the military posts.[36]

Late in June the Indians, growing bolder, began to attack the military posts. On the twenty-first a strong war party swooped down on Fort Wallace, ran off a team of six horses, and succeeded in killing two troopers of a detachment of cavalry defending the post. Three days later Captain Barnitz and thirty-nine men of Troop G, Seventh Cavalry, arrived to reinforce the beleaguered garrison—and none too soon. On the twenty-sixth three hundred Cheyennes struck the stage station two miles from Wallace and then moved against the fort itself.

Captain Barnitz rode out with his detachment and charged the more numerous foe. The Indians fell back toward the brow of a hill some two miles distant, with the troopers pressing them closely. Upon reaching the hill, however, the hostiles turned, and with great daring and determination, charged the cavalry. The pursuer then became the pursued, and Barnitz was driven back into the fort with a loss of six men killed and six wounded. The Indians withdrew at their leisure.[37]

Governor Crawford and General Hancock were meanwhile besieged by telegrams from officials of the Union Pacific Railroad

[35] *Army and Navy Journal,* Vol. IV (July 20, 1867), 770; Grinnell, *Fighting Cheyennes,* 256; Post Returns, Forts Wallace, Hays, and Harker, May and June, 1867.

[36] Garfield, "Defense of the Kansas Frontier, 1866–1867," *loc. cit.,* 330; U.S. Congress, *H.R. Exec. Doc. No. 240,* 41 Cong., 2 sess., 62–63. Post Returns, Fort Wallace, June, 1867, indicate fourteen attacks during the month of June on stations along the Smoky Hill.

[37] Post Returns, Fort Wallace, June, 1867; Mrs. Frank C. Montgomery, "Fort Wallace and Its Relation to the Frontier," *Collections of the Kansas State Historical Society,* Vol. XVII (1928), 209–10; *Harper's Weekly Magazine,* Vol. XI (July 27, 1867), 467–68.

demanding protection for their workers. On June 17, R. M. Shoe-maker, general superintendent of the road, telegraphed the Governor that all workmen had been driven off the line for a distance of twenty miles. A week later John D. Perry, president of the eastern division of Union Pacific, wired the Governor that hostile Indians had driven workers off seventy-five miles of line.[38]

Nor were the rampaging red men satisfied with merely attacking railroad personnel. A group of Cheyennes and Sioux, fleeing the village on Pawnee Fork, conceived the idea of wrecking a train, and proceeded at once from thought to action. Near Omaha they placed a big stick across the rails and sat down to see what would happen.

After a time a handcar came along, struck the stick, and went flying from the track. The Indians pounced upon the five passengers, killing three of them. One survivor was an Englishman named Thompson. Thrown from the handcar, Thompson picked himself up and tried to run away but was shot, lanced, and clubbed to the ground by a warrior, who then dismounted and scalped the wounded but still conscious Englishman. The pain was excruciating but he played possum, suffering it without a whimper.

As the Indian mounted his pony and rode away, the scalp slipped unnoticed from his belt. Thompson regained it, found a bucket in the wreckage of the handcar, filled it with water from a near-by stream, and in it tenderly placed the scalp. The painfully wounded man now made his way into Omaha, where surgeons vainly tried to sew the scalp back into place.

The Indians next tried for bigger game. They took levers, pried up the end of a rail, and again waited to see the results. They succeeded beyond their wildest expectations. Near midnight a train came puffing along, hit the pried-up rail, and plunged from the track. The delighted Indians killed the engineer and fireman; plundered the boxcars of calico, cotton goods, tobacco, sugar, and whisky; and burned the train.[39]

[38] Garfield, "Defense of the Kansas Frontier, 1866–1867," *loc. cit.,* 331.

Hancock filed a gloomy report to General Sherman. For a distance of ninety-five miles east and seventy-five miles west of Fort Wallace hostile Indians had attacked every stage station at least four times. Furthermore, the war was spreading, with hostile bands operating both north and south of the Platte. Sherman immediately ordered Custer from the Smoky Hill to the South Platte, and came west himself to get a firsthand view of the situation.[40]

Custer had spent a humiliating month at Fort Hays. Food supplies and forage were slow to arrive, and when they did much of the food was unfit for use. Many of his men were ill, morale was low, and desertions were frequent. Reports came in of Indian raids and depredations but there was little he could do. Not until the end of May were the animals strong enough for a campaign, and sufficient supplies on hand.[41]

On June 1 he finally marched with three hundred troopers, his scouts, and twenty wagons. He planned to move northward to Fort McPherson on the Platte, then up the south bank of that stream to Fort Sedgwick. There he was to have further orders from Sherman, and obtain rations, forage, and some fresh mounts.[42]

The column made a rapid and uneventful march to the Platte, passing many abandoned ranches and several rudely carved wooden headstones bearing the simple but significant inscription, "Unknown—Killed by the Indians."[43] At Fort McPherson, Custer telegraphed Sherman, and in turn was instructed to remain there until Sherman himself could arrive.

[39] New York *Tribune* (Aug. 14, 1867); Grinnell, *Fighting Cheyennes*, 258; Stanley, *Early Travels*, 156–61.

[40] *Annual Report of the Secretary of War for the Year 1867*, 33; U.S. Congress, *H.R. Exec. Doc. No. 240*, 41 Cong., 2 sess., 58; Post Returns, Fort Wallace, May, 1868.

[41] Custer, *Life on the Plains*, 66. Custer said that some of the bread he received had been baked in 1861. See also Davis, "A Summer on the Plains," *loc. cit.*, 298; New York *Tribune* (July 16, 1867).

[42] Davis, "A Summer on the Plains," *loc. cit.*, 299; Custer, *Life on the Plains*, 69; *Annual Report of the Secretary of War for the Year 1867*, 35. Custer's command consisted of Companies A, D, E, H, K, and M, Seventh Cavalry, Will Comstock, a Plains veteran, and some Delawares as guides. The train was in care of Lieutenant W. W. Cooke.

[43] Davis, "A Summer on the Plains," *loc. cit.*, 301.

While he waited Custer held council with Pawnee Killer and a few other Sioux who had come in. The chief professed to be delighted to see him and assured him that he earnestly desired peace. The Cheyennes were bad Indians, and he wanted nothing to do with them; he would be only too happy to bring his band to Fort McPherson and camp there. So pleased was Custer that he presented the chief with substantial quantities of sugar, coffee, and bread.

When Sherman arrived he assumed direct command of Custer's operations. The latter was to move his column to the Republican and scout the headwaters of that stream, in the hope that the Indians who had fled from Pawnee Fork had gone there. He was to come in for supplies at "Fort Sedgwick or below."[44]

On June 15, Custer marched south from the Platte over exceedingly rough and broken country under a torrid sun. Four days later the command pitched its tents on the forks of the Republican, about equidistant from Fort Sedgwick on the north and Fort Wallace on the south. There Custer proposed to remain until he had thoroughly scouted the area and had further orders from Sherman.

Supplies were, however, quickly depleted and on the twenty-third Custer sent Lieutenant W. W. Cooke with sixteen wagons, escorted by Lieutenant Sam Robbins and forty-eight troopers, to Fort Wallace to replenish the larder. At the same time Major Joel Elliott, with ten picked men, was sent to Fort Sedgwick with dispatches for Sherman.

Early next morning a large party of warriors swept past the camp, trying to stampede the animals. They failed because of quick action by the guards, but a picket was severely wounded. The Indians retired to the brow of a near-by hill and there sat their ponies in full view of the command. Soon the troopers observed signals being flashed with mirrors, and in a short time Indians appeared at a distance on all sides of the camp.

Custer decided to try talking with them and sent a scout, Gay,

[44] Custer, *Life on the Plains,* 78; Davis, "A Summer on the Plains," *loc. cit.,* 302.

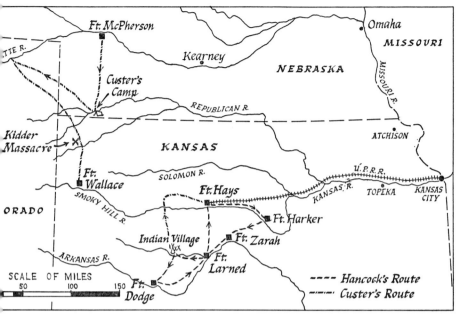

The Hancock–Custer Campaign of 1867

out to make arrangements. A small party of the hostiles detached themselves from the band on the hill and rode down to meet Gay. The leader proved to be none other than Pawnee Killer, willing to talk with the "white chief" if he were accompanied by only a few men. Gay agreed, but warned the chief that there must not be more Indians than whites at the conference.

Custer now took half a dozen men and met Pawnee Killer between the lines. Sullen and uncommunicative, the chief demanded why Custer had left the Platte. He refused to explain his own attack on Custer's camp. As other warriors soon were edging down the hill, Custer, growing fearful that treachery was planned, broke off and returned to camp. There he mounted the entire command and moved out to do any further talking with carbine and saber.[45]

[45] Custer, *Life on the Plains*, 82–83; New York *Tribune* (July 16, 1867). The *Tribune* correspondent who went with Custer listed the Indians at the council as Pawnee Killer, Pole Cat, Fire Lightening, Walks Under the Ground, and several others.

51

The Indians disappeared at once, and a vigorous pursuit proved futile. It was an angry and frustrated column of troopers who returned to their tents. A short time later, spying a small party of warriors on some bluffs near by, Custer ordered Captain Louis Hamilton to take a detachment and thrash them. Hamilton mounted his men and quickly reached the bluffs, only to find that his quarry had moved just beyond rifle range. The Indians were playing the hoary decoy game, and ancient as it was, it worked.

Hamilton continued the pursuit from hill to hill for nearly eight miles. Then the hostiles split into two groups and veered off in opposite directions. Hamilton divided his detachment so as to follow both parties, and with twenty-five men at his back continued the pursuit. Minutes later, as Hamilton was working his way over very rough ground, he found himself surrounded by a force of warriors twice his size.

The Indians had the advantage of surprise, but their fire was so inaccurate as to be ineffectual. Hamilton dismounted his men, deployed them in a circle around the horses, and beat off the attack with comparative ease. Two Indians were killed and several wounded, while the detachment sustained only the loss of a horse. Then, having inflicted the first casualties of Custer's campaign, Hamilton made his way back to camp.

The command was greatly cheered by the safe return of Major Elliott on June 27. He had made a perilous round-trip of over two hundred miles and had brought new orders from Sherman. Custer was to move back to the Platte and strike that stream somewhere west of Fort Sedgwick, where he would apply to Sherman for further instructions. He had to await, however, the arrival of his train from Fort Wallace, and, as the country swarmed with hostiles, fear for its safety daily mounted.

Cooke and Robbins had reached Fort Wallace without incident, had loaded their wagons, and on the evening of the twenty-fifth had begun their return journey. Next morning as the train moved toward Beaver Creek, Will Comstock, the veteran guide, glanced with ever-increasing frequency toward the bluffs several hundred yards away and on either side of the train. Comstock literally "smelled" Indians.

About eight o'clock his fears were realized. With the little column some fifteen miles from the Beaver, large numbers of Indians suddenly arose on all sides as if from the ground. Quickly the wagons were corralled, and then started again, with enough space left between for horses. The escort dismounted and formed as skirmishers about the train.

Cheyennes and Sioux to the number of five or six hundred completely encircled them, but a steady and accurate fire from the embattled train kept the Indians at long range except for occasional swift dashes by small parties. For several hours the fight swirled slowly toward the Beaver, but as that stream was neared, the Indians broke off and retired, having suffered five killed and a number wounded.

On reaching the Beaver, Cooke and Robbins found Captain R. M. West with Company K awaiting their arrival. With West was Theodore Davis, *Harper's* correspondent, to whom Robbins gave the following laconic account of the fight:

> I gave the Indians to understand that the forty men of Company "D" were quite as fond of coffee, sugar, etc., as they were; and inasmuch as they had it on hand, they were disposed to hold on to it.[46]

The train, with its escort, then proceeded to Custer's camp on the Republican, arriving on the morning of the twenty-eighth.

Eager to carry out his orders, Custer broke camp and moved for the Platte next morning. For seven days the column was pushed to the limit of endurance over rough and broken terrain under a broiling sun. Camps were broken before sunrise, and the march continued until long after nightfall. The dawn of July 6 found a

[46] *Harper's Weekly Magazine*, Vol. XI (Aug. 17, 1867), 513f.; Custer, *Life on the Plains*, 84–85, 93; *Army and Navy Journal*, Vol. IV (July 20, 1867), 758; Davis, "A Summer on the Plains," *loc. cit.*, 303; New York *Tribune* (July 15, 1867); U.S. Congress, *H.R. Exec. Doc. No. 240*, 41 Cong., 2 sess., 111.

worn and grumbling command at Riverside Station on the banks of the South Platte, some forty miles west of Fort Sedgwick.

Custer now telegraphed General Sherman of his arrival, and in reply received disturbing news. The previous appearance of the Seventh Cavalry on the Platte had caused the Indians to transfer their activities southward toward the Smoky Hill. On June 29, therefore, Lieutenant Lyman Kidder and a detachment of ten men had been sent from Fort Sedgwick to the camp on the Republican bearing new orders directing Custer to move toward Fort Wallace.

Since Kidder had been neither seen nor heard from by Custer's command, fears were entertained for his safety. The whole countryside was alive with hostile Indians, and woe betide so small a party unfortunate enough to run afoul of them. Custer had no choice but to turn southward at once, hoping that the Kidder party had gone in to Fort Wallace.

But as he turned south again the mounting dissatisfaction of his men found expression in mass desertions. Thirty-five absconded on the banks of the Platte, and none were apprehended. Half a day's march from Riverside Station ten more deserted, half of them mounted and the other half afoot. Angry and distressed, Custer ordered Major Elliott to take a detachment and pursue these last deserters, telling him to shoot to kill if resistance were encountered.

Elliott managed to overtake the men who had escaped afoot, but he had to shoot three of them, one fatally. After he returned, it was learned that a plot was brewing for desertion en masse that evening. All officers were alerted, but the night passed without incident. It was a sober command that took up the march next day.

Custer moved southward as swiftly as the condition of his animals would allow until the column struck the trail made by Cooke's wagons on their return from Fort Wallace, at a point some eighty miles from that place. Shortly thereafter, as the command moved down the wagon road, they came upon the trail of Kidder's party. The detachment had apparently turned toward Fort Wallace after finding Custer's camp deserted.

Farther on was the body of a dead cavalry horse, and some two miles beyond a second. Comstock, the canny old plainsman, could see from the tracks that a large body of Indians had been pursuing the Kidder party. A few miles farther, and vultures were observed circling to the left of the trail and near Beaver Creek. A hurried search in the rushes and willows bordering the stream revealed the horribly mutilated bodies of the Kidder party.[47]

After burying these pitiful remains, Custer brought his command into Fort Wallace, arriving there on July 12. If Kidder's fate had drawn a curtain of gloom over Custer's troopers, little was found at Fort Wallace to relieve it. Almost constant Indian attacks had exhausted the slender garrison, supplies were low, much of the food was rotten or molded, the stages had stopped running, and no mail had come in for some time. As if this were not enough, the dread cholera had made its appearance.[48]

Anxious to obtain supplies and to see his wife, who was at Fort Riley, Custer left Fort Wallace on the eighteenth with a picked escort of seventy-five men under the tireless Captain Hamilton. The 156 miles to Fort Hays was covered in 55 hours, although two of the escort were killed by hostiles who struck the little column at Downer's Station on the Union Pacific. There leaving Hamilton and most of the escort, Custer, with four men, went on to Fort Harker.

There he arranged for the badly needed supplies and reported to Colonel Smith, the district commander. This done, he went on to Fort Riley and to his wife. Shortly thereafter, however, he was arrested for absenting himself from his command without leave, and for needless abuse of his men and animals. Tried by court-martial at Fort Leavenworth, he was sentenced to suspension from

---

47 Custer, *Life on the Plains,* 100–101, 107; Davis, "A Summer on the Plains," *loc. cit.,* 306; New York *Tribune* (July 22, 1867); *Harper's Weekly Magazine,* Vol. XI (Aug. 17, 1867), 513.

48 Post Returns, Fort Wallace, July, 1867; New York *Tribune* (Aug. 27, 1867).

rank and command for one year and to forfeit his pay for a like period.[49]

Thus Hancock's campaign, launched with much bluster and braggadocio, had reached its dismal conclusion. Had there been any doubt of war on the plains in the spring of 1867, certainly there was none after he destroyed the Cheyenne village in April. Far from overawing or whipping the wild horsemen of the Plains, Hancock had loosed the hurricane.

The Kansas frontier by summer's end was in a state of siege; hostile Indians seemed everywhere, property damage was running into the hundreds of thousands of dollars, and the scalping knife was working overtime.[50] Indeed, the damage would have been far greater but for the energetic action of state officials. These had raised a battalion of volunteers to assist overworked detachments of federal troops in developing a partially effective, patchwork defense.[51]

[49] Montgomery, "Fort Wallace," *loc. cit.*, 219f.; New York *Tribune* (July 22, 1867); Custer, *Life on the Plains*, 112, 170; U.S. War Department, General Courts-Martial, No. 93, Adjutant General's Office, 1867.

[50] *Harper's Weekly Magazine*, Vol. XI (Sept. 7, 1867), 564; *Annual Report of the Commissioner of Indian Affairs for the Year 1868*, 9. N. G. Taylor, commissioner of Indian affairs, summarized Hancock's campaign as follows: "On the 19th of April, 1867, a military command burned the peaceful village of the Cheyennes on Pawnee Fork, Western Kansas, who had been at peace with us since the treaty of 1865, on the Arkansas, and were on lands assigned them by that treaty. The Cheyennes flew to arms and the war of 1867 followed, in which we lost over 300 soldiers and citizens, several millions in expenses and an immense amount of public and private property, and killed it is believed six Indians and no more."

[51] To assist in defending the Kansas frontier, the Eighteenth Kansas Cavalry was organized and mustered into service on July 15. Together with units of the Seventh and the newly organized Tenth Cavalry (Colored), the Eighteenth Kansas spent four months on the frontier. Even though it was of considerable assistance in affording protection to the outlying settlements, two companies of the Eighteenth, with one company of the Tenth Cavalry, all under command of Brevet Major George Armes were soundly thrashed by a large force of Cheyennes and Sioux on Prairie Dog Creek, August 21–22, 1867, losing three men killed, twenty-eight wounded, and suffering the loss of thirty-seven horses killed and three wounded. See Organizational Returns, Tenth Cavalry, 1867; Post Returns, Fort Dodge, Aug., 1867; Col. George A. Armes, *Ups and Downs of an Army Officer*, 245–46; Horace L. Moore, "The Nineteenth Kansas Cavalry," *Transactions of the Kansas State Historical Society*, Vol. VI (1900), 37; George B. Jenness, "The Battle on Beaver Creek," *Transactions of the Kansas State Historical Society*, Vol. IX (1906), 444–52.

Meanwhile, the slowly turning wheels of the federal government ground out a different approach to the Indian problem. The widespread troubles of the Civil War period and the national revulsion which attended the infamous Chivington affair had brought home to Congress that it must find a peaceful solution of the problem or else must condone a policy of extermination.

The immediate result was the creation, by a joint resolution on March 3, 1865, of a Joint Special Committee on the Condition of the Indian Tribes. Consisting of three senators and four representatives, the Commission divided itself into three groups for an intensive study of conditions along the Pacific Slope, and the Northern and Southern Plains.[52]

In January, 1867, they rendered a report of nearly five hundred pages filled with the testimony of army officers, Indian agents, state officials, frontiersmen, and just plain settlers. Taken as a whole the report painted a sorry picture of conditions among the Indian tribes. Indian wars, in most cases caused by the aggressions of lawless white men, were levying a heavy toll on the Indian population; disease and intemperance were accelerating the process. Inroads by whites upon the Indian hunting grounds were destroying the red man's livelihood.

The report scored the graft and ineptitude rampant in the Indian Bureau and took a vigorous slap at the military arm:

> While it is true many agents, teachers, and employees of the government are inefficient, faithless, and even guilty of peculations and fraudulent practices upon the government and upon the Indians, it is equally true that military posts among the Indians have frequently become centers of demoralization and destruction to the Indian tribes, while the blunders and want of discretion of inexperienced officers in command have brought on long and expensive wars, the cost of which, being included in the expenditures of the army, are never seen and realized by the people of the country.[53]

[52] *Report of the Joint Committee on the Condition of the Indian Tribes*, 3.

[53] U.S. Congress, *Senate Report No. 156*, 39 Cong., 2 sess., 3–8.

The Committee concluded that continued civilian control was preferable, but that it should be subject to frequent inspection by a group of five boards to be established for the purpose.

Congress was slow to act, but by the summer of 1867, with conditions on the Plains in a critical state and the partisans of peace and of force demanding a solution, some immediate action became essential. The decision of Congress was to extend the olive branch, not the sword. On July 20 an act was approved creating an Indian Peace Commission, "to establish peace with certain hostile Indian tribes."[54]

It was authorized to bring together the chiefs and headmen of the unfriendly Indians, to learn the reasons for their enmity, and if advisable, to make peace with them. Three objectives were to be kept uppermost: to remove, if possible, the causes of war; to secure, so far as practicable, the frontier settlements and the safe building of the Pacific railroads; and to suggest or inaugurate some plan of civilizing the Indians. If the commission found these objectives impossible of attainment, the President might call out four regiments of troops and "conquer a peace."[55]

The commission would be composed of N. G. Taylor, commissioner of Indian affairs; John B. Henderson, chairman of the Senate Commission on Indian Affairs; John B. Sanborn of Minnesota; S. F. Tappan of Colorado; and three officers of the army, not below the rank of brigadier general, to be selected by the President. President Johnson appointed Lieutenant General Sherman and Brigadier Generals Harney and Terry.

The commission lost little time in getting down to work. Their first meeting was held in St. Louis on August 6. There Taylor was elected president of the commission, and plans were laid for carrying out its prescribed duties. It was quickly agreed that the Indians

[54] *United States Statutes at Large*, XV, 17.

[55] *Ibid.*, 17; Sherman, *Memoirs*, 434; U.S. Congress, *H.R. Exec. Doc. No. 97*, 40 Cong., 2 sess., 1. Military estimates indicated that to conquer a peace would require 25,000 men and five to ten years of fighting. See U.S. Congress, *Sen. Exec. Doc. No. 13*, 40 Cong., 1 sess., 55.

must be removed from around the great roads of the Plains and placed on reservations with liberal provision for their maintenance. Sherman through his post commanders and Taylor through his agents and superintendents were to notify the Northern tribes to assemble at Fort Laramie on September 13, while the Indians south of the Arkansas were to gather at some point near Fort Larned on or about October 13. Pending the outcome of negotiations, Sherman notified his subordinates, all military movements would be purely defensive in nature.[56]

The meeting with the Northern tribes was abortive. Many of the Northern Cheyennes were absent, and any agreements reached without their consent would have been worthless. The council was adjourned, therefore, with plans for a second meeting in the following spring. The commissioners returned to Omaha, where General Sherman learned that his presence was required in Washington. Brevet Major General C. C. Augur took his place on the commission.[57]

From Omaha they journeyed to Fort Harker, where they learned, by letter from Thomas Murphy, superintendent of the Central Superintendency, that the Indians were assembling on Medicine Lodge Creek some eighty miles south of the Arkansas. Murphy expected some five thousand and requested the commissioners to meet him at Fort Larned so that he might escort them to the council site.

It was an impressive two-mile-long cavalcade that left Fort Larned on October 11 and marched for Medicine Lodge Creek. Accompanying the commissioners were prominent state officials, Indian agents, representatives of the press, and many bummers along for the excitement. Major Elliott with five hundred troopers

[56] U.S. Congress, *H.R. Exec. Doc. No. 97*, 40 Cong., 2 sess., 2–3; Sherman, *Memoirs*, 434; *Annual Report of the Commissioner of Indian Affairs for the Year 1867*, 28; *Annual Report of the Secretary of War for the Year 1867*, 37.

[57] Sherman, *Memoirs*, 434; Alfred A. Taylor, "Medicine Lodge Peace Council," *Chronicles of Oklahoma*, Vol. II (Mar., 1924), 99. Young Taylor, son of the Commissioner of Indian Affairs, attended the council as a secretary.

of the Seventh Cavalry furnished the escort, and protected the nearly one hundred wagons filled with supplies and gifts for the Indians.[58]

When the long column arrived in the valley of the Medicine Lodge they found more than five thousand Indians awaiting their arrival. To keep the red men in a proper mood, the commissioners arranged to have huge kettles of coffee and plenty of food always on hand. There were gifts in the form of clothing, cloth, tobacco, and utensils of all sorts. Not to be outdone, the Indians gave a great feast at which the native delicacy was served—cold, fat dog.[59]

These amenities concluded, the way was clear to begin the councils. The one flaw up to this point was the absence of many of the Cheyennes, who, exceedingly wary of gathering in the presence of white troops, had remained some forty miles away. Sand Creek and Hancock's burning of the village on Pawnee Fork were of recent and bitter memory. Nor was it easy for them to understand the abrupt change of front. Troops of this same Seventh Cavalry had but recently sought to destroy them.

In a great clearing, made in the center of an elm grove, the councils began on October 19. Chief after chief arose and addressed the commissioners citing the wrongs done his people, asking for redress of their grievances, and expressing a desire to live in peace with the white man.[60] It was a hard heart that was not stirred by the pathos and dignity of this Indian oratory. Typical and worth repeating was the speech of old Ten Bears of the Comanches:

> You said you wanted to put us upon a reservation to build us houses and make us medicine lodges. I do not want them. I was born upon

[58] Stanley, *Early Travels,* 225, 229–30; Taylor, "Medicine Lodge Peace Council," *loc. cit.,* 113; New York *Tribune* (Oct. 23, 1867).

[59] Stanley, *Early Travels,* 230; New York *Tribune* (Oct. 21, 1867); Taylor, "Medicine Lodge Peace Council," *loc. cit.,* 109–11. Commissioner Taylor was the object of special attention at the feast. One young chief approached Taylor, softly stroked his arm, and gently murmured, "Heap big damn son of a bitch."

[60] Taylor, "Medicine Lodge Peace Council," *loc. cit.,* 114; U.S. Congress, *H.R. Exec. Doc. No. 97,* 40 Cong., 2 sess., 6; New York *Tribune* (Oct. 6, 1867).

the prairie where the wind blew free and there was nothing to break the light of the sun. I was born where there were no enclosures, and where everything drew a free breath. I want to die there and not within walls. I know every stream and every wood between the Rio Grande and the Arkansas. I have hunted and lived over the country. I lived like my fathers before me, and like them I have lived happily. When I was at Washington the Great Father told me that all of the Comanche land was ours, and that no one should hinder us in living upon it. So, why do you ask us to leave the rivers, and the sun, and the wind, and live in the houses? . . . Do not speak of it more. . . . I love to carry out the talk I get from the Great Father. When I get goods and presents I and my people feel glad, since it shows that he holds us in his eye. If the Texans had been kept out of my country, there might have been peace. . . . The white man has the country we loved, and we only wish to wander on the prairie until we die. . . . I want no blood upon my land to stain the grass.[61]

Also Little Raven of the Arapahoes and Satanta of the Kiowas impressed the assemblage with their oratory.

The commissioners listened patiently and settled each case as it arose. In this fashion agreement was quickly reached with the Kiowas and Comanches, a treaty being signed on October 21. On the same day the Kiowa-Apaches, who wished to confederate again with the two former tribes, agreed to similar terms.

Meanwhile, Black Kettle, who had met the commissioners on their arrival, and who earnestly desired peace, had been working ceaselessly to get the more reluctant Cheyennes to come in. After more than two weeks of tireless effort he could report that the remainder of his people had consented to hold council. The barrier thus removed, a treaty was signed with the Cheyennes and Arapahoes on October 28.[62]

These treaties were all similar in content. The Kiowas, Coman-

[61] Stanley, *Early Travels*, 252–53.

[62] Taylor, "Medicine Lodge Peace Council," *loc. cit.*, 105–106; New York *Tribune* (Oct. 23, 1867). The *Tribune* correspondent wrote that Black Kettle had worked so earnestly for peace that he had alienated many of his own people.

ches, and Apaches were assigned a reservation of some 3,000,000 acres between the Washita and Red rivers, and the ninety-eighth and one hundredth meridians. North of this the Cheyennes and Arapahoes received a grant of about 4,300,000 acres. In return for surrendering former claims to a much greater area the Indians were now to be provided with food, clothing, and other equipment. An agency with a resident agent was to be established on the reservations, schools were to be provided for the children, as were physicians, carpenters, blacksmiths, and a farmer. The Indians retained a right to hunt buffalo anywhere south of the Arkansas. They in turn agreed to keep the peace, to stay away from the great roads, and not to molest the whites in any manner. Further, they were to drop all opposition to the construction of railroads crossing the Plains.[63]

With these final concessions the councils came to an end. The Indians departed in a relatively happy mood, and the commissioners felt that long strides had been made toward an enduring peace. But neither the mood of the Indians nor the hopes of the commissioners were to be of long duration. Circumstances which could not then be foreseen would remove the olive branch and raise the sword. Old Ten Bears would yet live to see the stain of blood upon the prairie grass.

[63] Kappler, *Indian Affairs,* 980–81, 984–89; Charles C. Royce, "Indian Land Cessions in the United States," *Eighteenth Annual Report of the Bureau of American Ethnology, 1896–1897,* 846, 852. Prominent chiefs party to this agreement were Satanta, Satank, Black Eagle, Woman's Heart, Stumbling Bear, and Kicking Bird for the Kiowas; Ten Bears, Painted Lips, Silver Broach, and Little Horn for the Comanches; and Poor Bear of the Kiowa-Apaches. Chiefs Bull Bear, Black Kettle, Gray Head, Little Rock, Tall Bull, and Little Robe signed for the Cheyennes, as did Little Raven, Yellow Bear, and Storm for the Arapahoes.

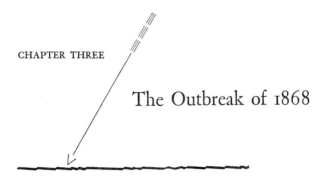

CHAPTER THREE

The Outbreak of 1868

I

N AUGUST, 1867, HANCOCK WAS transferred to the District of the Cumberland and relieved of any further responsibility for Indian affairs in the Department of the Missouri. His successor was Major General Philip H. Sheridan, whose iron-fisted administration of the Fifth Military District had aroused the displeasure of President Johnson. Hence his exile to the frontier.[1]

Sheridan reached Fort Leavenworth early in September and found his new command enjoying a period of comparative quiet because of the activities of the Peace Commission. Seizing this opportunity for a long rest he arranged for a leave of absence, so that it was not until the following March that he assumed active command of the department.

---

[1] *Annual Report of the Secretary of War for the Year 1867,* 25–26; New York *Tribune* (Aug. 21, 1867). Hancock was later transferred to the Fifth Military district. See Philip H. Sheridan, *Personal Memoirs,* II, 281.

During his absence, the bright hopes of the treaty-makers at Medicine Lodge for a lasting peace had gradually faded. The treaties had struck a Congressional snag. The Senate and House differed on financial items in the treaties, and neither house was inclined to compromise. Ratification would evidently be long delayed. And while Congress debated, conditions on the Indian frontier steadily worsened.

As weeks and then months passed, with little indication that the government intended carrying out its promises at Medicine Lodge, the Indians grew increasingly restless. Although no arrangements had been made to move them to their new reservations, white settlers were already moving in on the old tribal lands. For the red man the worst result of this influx was a rapid depletion of game, especially of the buffalo. He could see his means of livelihood evaporating before his very eyes.

During the winter and early spring of 1867–68 the Cheyennes and Arapahoes were encamped some sixty miles south of Fort Dodge. Agent Wynkoop, sincerely concerned for those Indians under his care, made frequent visits to their villages. He found them peaceful but in an increasingly destitute condition. Deplorable as it was, the agent did not consider the situation dangerous so long as the Indians could be liberally rationed.

One matter, however, gave him cause for real anxiety. In the late spring and early summer the tribes would move northward to Pawnee and Walnut creeks around Fort Larned and Fort Dodge. There they would be within easy striking distance of their ancient enemies the Kaws and Osages. Try as he might, Wynkoop could not persuade them to make peace with these tribes, for as the aggrieved parties, they felt they must strike their enemies at every opportunity.[2]

If Wynkoop had his worries, they paled to insignificance when compared with those of his fellow agent Colonel Leavenworth.

[2] U.S. Congress, *Sen. Exec. Doc. No. 13,* 40 Cong., 3 sess., 2, 4; Post Returns, Fort Dodge, Mar., 1868.

In February, following the Medicine Lodge councils, Leavenworth had journeyed south to Indian Territory, in order to be near the Kiowas and Comanches, and had established a temporary agency at Eureka Valley. He found affairs in a critical state, for his wild charges were raiding and plundering with abandon.[3]

The Civilized Tribes of the territory, especially the Chickasaws and Choctaws, were suffering heavily from these depredations. Governor Harris of the Chickasaws told Leavenworth that his people and the Choctaws had lost not less than four thousand head of horses, and that unless the raiding ceased he was prepared to declare war. The agent complained to Commissioner Taylor and in March was informed that the Secretary of Interior had written President Johnson about possible military protection for the offended tribes.

It was along the Texas frontier, however, that the red raiders were most active. Early in 1868 war parties literally swarmed across Red River to kill, scalp, and steal horses and mules. On January 5, Heap of Bears, a noted Kiowa marauder, led a strong band into Denton County. The swift-striking warriors killed eight persons, captured two women and eight children, and ran off a large number of horses. A posse of citizens pursued them and recovered the women, but the hostiles killed one of the children and made good their escape with the remaining seven.[4]

In February, Kiowa bands under Lone Wolf, Timbered Mountain, and Big Bow all launched successful forays into Texas, and every Comanche camp saw the departure of war parties on similar missions.[5] Worst of all were the implacable Kwahadis, who had ignored the proceedings at Medicine Lodge, and who now raided in small parties over hundreds of miles of frontier. Frantic efforts

[3] Leavenworth to Commanding Officer, Fort Arbuckle, Mar. 26, 1868, Office of Indian Affairs, Letters Received, Kiowa Agency.

[4] Leavenworth to Commissioner Taylor, May 21, 1868, Office of Indian Affairs, Letters Received, Kiowa Agency; U.S. Congress, *H.R. Misc. Doc. No. 139,* 41 Cong., 2 sess., 5f.

[5] Interpreter Philip McCusker to Maj. Gen. W. B. Hazen, Dec. 22, 1868, in the Sherman-Sheridan Papers, transcript in Phillips Collection, University of Oklahoma (hereinafter cited as the S.-S. Papers), 118.

by federal cavalry and state militia to pursue and punish the raiders rarely succeeded.[6]

Agent Leavenworth, working energetically to check these raids and to recover captives and stolen stock, was only partially successful. He had, to persuade the Indians to remain peacefully in their camps, neither a military force nor adequate money and supplies at his disposal. Although in April and May his burdens were somewhat lightened—by a movement of many Kiowas and Comanches northward toward Fort Larned, where they hoped to receive liberal supplies of goods and rations—he felt he had had enough and departed never to return.[7]

Thus it was that when Sheridan finally took up his duties, he faced conditions fraught with the danger of an Indian outbreak. Learning that the tribes were congregating on Pawnee and Walnut creeks near Fort Larned and Fort Dodge, he decided to visit those posts to acquaint himself firsthand with affairs on the frontier; he might then, he hoped, devise measures which would mitigate Indian unrest.[8]

At Fort Dodge a large delegation of chiefs called on him and requested a council. Even though, as he admitted later, he thereby made the Indians more reckless and defiant, Sheridan refused their request, fearing that any talk might compromise the work of the Peace Commission. Instead of indulging in the councils which his predecessor, General Hancock, had so enjoyed, he decided to issue the Indians rations from army supplies and to send emissaries

[6] Post Returns, Fort Richardson, May 1868; *Annual Report of the Secretary of War for the Year 1868*, 711–16. In the period from January, 1868, to September, 1868, twenty-seven military expeditions against hostile raiders returned with the report that no Indians could be found.

[7] U.S. Congress, *H.R. Misc. Doc. No. 139*, 41 Cong., 2 sess., 7; Leavenworth to Commissioner Taylor, May 21, 1868, Office of Indian Affairs, Letters Received, Kiowa Agency; *Annual Report of the Secretary of War for the Year 1868*, 16; U.S. Congress, *Sen. Exec. Doc. No. 60*, 40 Cong., 2 sess., 2; Marvin Garfield, "Defense of the Kansas Frontier, 1868–1869," *Kansas Historical Quarterly*, Vol. I (Nov., 1932), 451; Leavenworth to Commissioner Taylor, June 18, 1868, Office of Indian Affairs, Kiowa Agency. The Agent was under fire as well for profiteering on annuity goods.

[8] Post Returns, Fort Dodge, Apr., 1868; Sheridan, *Personal Memoirs*, II, 284.

among them. These should try to allay suspicions and to smooth over such irritations as might arise.[9]

For the delicate role of "peace mediators" Sheridan chose three veteran plainsmen, William Comstock, Abner S. Grover, and Richard Parr. All had trapped and hunted with the various tribes, knew the chiefs and principal men, and enjoyed their confidence. They were to work under the supervision of Lieutenant F. H. Beecher, Third Infantry, who would keep in constant touch with the commanding general on affairs in the Indian camps.

Sheridan's policies, however, plainly born of expediency, offered no real solution to the problem. Meanwhile Congress continued its leisurely debate over the treaties. As summer approached conditions on the Indian frontier became critical. With Indian Bureau funds practically exhausted, a worried Commissioner Taylor wrote the Secretary of Interior, O. H. Browning, that unless $1,000,000 were made available immediately to subsist the Indians, he feared real trouble. The tribes, now destitute, would begin stealing from the whites, and these would be sure to retaliate. Then war must certainly sweep the Plains.

But Congress refused to be hurried, and it was not until July 20, 1868, that it approved an appropriation of $500,000 for implementing the Medicine Lodge treaties. Furthermore, General Sherman, and not the Indian Bureau, was to disburse the money.[10]

Sherman, acting with his customary energy, on August 10 created a northern and a southern military superintendency, under Major General W. S. Harney and Brigadier General W. B. Hazen respectively. These officers were to supervise removal of the In-

[9] Sheridan, *Personal Memoirs*, II, 285–86. Sheridan's superior, General Sherman, was opposed to making any promises to the Indians. He wrote his brother Senator Sherman that the Indians were getting restless, and "this is natural for the department has been unable to fulfill any of the promises we held out to them of ploughs, seed, cattle, etc., to begin their new life of peace." See Thorndike, ed., *Sherman Letters*, 318–19; Post Returns, Fort Dodge, Apr., 1868.

[10] *Annual Report of the Commissioner of Indian Affairs for the Year 1868*, 85; *Annual Report of the Secretary of War for the Year 1868*, 6; U.S. Congress, *H.R. Exec. Doc. No. 239*, 40 Cong., 2 sess., 1–2.

dians to their reservations, to aid them in establishing homes, to furnish them with provisions, and to provide them with limited quantities of tools and farming equipment.

Congressional action had, however, been too long delayed, for as spring merged into summer Indian restlessness grew, and in June, 1868, Agent Wynkoop's worst fears materialized. Tall Bull led a great war party of Cheyennes from the camps on Pawnee Fork to fight the Kaws. The Kaw village was near Council Grove, and the citizens of that little town were frightened half out of their wits when three hundred gaudily painted Cheyennes rode down the main street en route to the attack.[11]

The Kaws were ready for their old enemies, and a long-range, four-hour battle, filled with dazzling displays of horsemanship, ensued. Not one Indian had been killed when the fight ended, but honor had been satisfied, and the exuberant Cheyennes, again visiting Council Grove, this time tarried long enough to ransack a few homes, kill a dog, and steal some flour. The only white casualty was a recently arrived Tennessean who was dozing by a quiet campfire. Startled from his nap by the noise, he roused himself so suddenly that he kicked over a kettle and scalded his feet.

A few days later Little Robe, a prominent Cheyenne chief, came and admitted to Wynkoop that his people had made the attack on the Kaws and that, finding the country nearly devoid of game, they had appropriated eleven head of cattle from white settlers. He was sorry that the raid had occurred, and he offered to pay for the cattle.

Despite this effort to make amends, Commissioner Taylor instructed Wynkoop, through Thomas Murphy, to withhold the issue of arms and ammunition to the Cheyennes when they came in for their annuity goods. He was to tell them that, if they could

11 Post Returns, Fort Dodge, May, 1868; Garfield, "Defense of the Kansas Frontier, 1868–69," *loc. cit.,* 454; Thomas F. Doran, "Kansas Sixty Years Ago," *Collections of the Kansas State Historical Society,* Vol. XV (1923), 491.

show the government they meant to keep their treaty pledges in good faith, they would receive the promised issue later.

Wynkoop carried out these instructions. He wrote Murphy on July 20 that when the Cheyennes had come in and were told they were not to receive arms and ammunition they had refused to take any goods whatsoever. Much disappointed, they had declared they feared "the hand given them at Medicine Lodge was being taken away." The agent, himself very upset, urged that a full issue be made at an early date, for he feared the result of a failure to do so.[12]

Meanwhile relations with the Kiowas and Comanches had also taken an ominous turn. Early in July these tribes had congregated near Fort Larned to collect their annuities, but shipment of the goods from the depot at Lawrence, Kansas, had been delayed by transport difficulties. Now thousands of hungry and idle red men were milling about the fort, a ready market for the wares of unscrupulous whisky dealers.

Under such conditions trouble was inevitable, and minor clashes between Indians and whites occurred with alarming frequency. At 3:00 A.M. on Sunday, July 9, two drunken young Kiowas, mounted on a single horse and dashing through a white man's camp yelling at the top of their lungs, were fired on and one of them seriously wounded. When they reached the Kiowa camp and told their story, a large band rode to the vicinity of Fort Larned and wounded a Mexican. Only the persuasive oratory of Satanta averted a serious clash with the troops.

On the same day a government wagonmaster came to the post to report that his train had been stopped by the Kiowas and robbed of flour, sugar, and coffee. A squadron of cavalry and a detachment of infantry were ordered to recover the stolen goods. When the troops came within sight of the Kiowa camp on the Arkansas, fearful women and children fled to the river and began swimming across. Grim warriors lined the banks to protect their people, and

[12] *Annual Report of the Commissioner of Indian Affairs for the Year 1868*, 64–67.

a fight seemed imminent. Suddenly frightened at the prospect of bloodshed, the wagonmaster admitted that he had lied and that actually he had given the goods to the Indians. His confession came just in time to stop the attack.

Brevet Brigadier General Alfred Sully, commanding the District of the Arkansas, which included Fort Larned, on reporting to Sheridan that the situation looked ugly, was ordered to move to the post with a sufficient mounted force. He brought eight companies of the Seventh Cavalry.

On his arrival he found the Indians hungry but peacefully inclined. The chiefs blamed the sporadic troubles on a few bad young men who were difficult, if not impossible, to control. Sully, feeling that either they must be rationed or the Plains must have a war, prevailed on Sheridan to authorize issues of food in small quantities.

Meanwhile reports of mounting Indian dissatisfaction had caused Commissioner Taylor to change his mind. On July 23, 1868, he wrote to Murphy that Wynkoop had been telegraphed to exercise his discretion about issuing the tribes all their annuity goods. Murphy was to proceed to Fort Larned without delay and consult with Wynkoop on the proper course to follow. He was also to arrange for delivery of goods to the Kiowas and Comanches.[13]

Murphy and Wynkoop held council with the Arapahoes and Kiowa-Apaches on August 1. The Indians gave assurances of their peaceful intentions, and Little Raven, principal chief of the Arapahoes, promised that if the arms and ammunition were issued to his people, they would never be used against the whites. Convinced of their sincerity, Murphy allowed Wynkoop to deliver rifles, pistols, powder, and lead to both tribes.

Eight days later Wynkoop made a similar issue to the Cheyennes.

[13] Taylor wired Wynkoop as follows: "If you are satisfied that the issue of arms and ammunition is necessary to preserve the peace, and that no evil will result from their delivery, let the Indians have them." *Annual Report of the Commissioner of Indian Affairs for the Year 1868*, 63–64, 67–68; U.S. Congress, *Sen. Exec. Doc. No. 13*, 40 Cong., 3 sess., 6; Records of the Office of Indian Affairs, Letters Sent, Vol. LXXXVII, 153.

He then wrote Taylor that the Indians were delighted and that he had never before seen them so pleased and contented. There need be no fear of trouble on the Plains for this season at least.[14]

Yet even as he penned these cheerful tidings a large war party from the Cheyenne camps was moving northward to find and fight the Pawnees. Moreover, in a council of war held on the Saline River, the bolder and more aggressive warriors urged an attack instead upon the whites. Although this proposal met considerable opposition, a majority of the band finally turned down-river toward the white settlements.[15]

At the first home encountered they professed to be friendly and were given food and sweet coffee, of which they were very fond. Then, after eating and drinking their fill, the warriors dropped their friendly mask, seized their host, and raped his wife into insensibility. It was the beginning of a reign of terror in the river valleys of central and western Kansas.

Moving rapidly from the Saline to the Solomon, the war party struck like a hurricane the settlements along that stream. Fifteen persons were killed, five women were outraged, several homes were burned, and a large number of horses were stolen. A small band then moved on northward as far as the Republican to kill and pillage, while the main body turned back to the Saline to do a more thorough job in that locality.[16]

Upon again approaching these settlements, however, they met a detachment of the Seventh Cavalry under Captain F. W. Benteen, who had marched out from Fort Zarah to intercept them. In a

[14] *Annual Report of the Commissioner of Indian Affairs for the Year 1868,* 68–70. To the Arapahoes, Wynkoop delivered 160 pistols, 80 rifles, 12 kegs of powder, and 1½ kegs of lead.

[15] *Ibid.,* 72; Sheridan, *Personal Memoirs,* II, 290; *Annual Report of the Secretary of War for the Year 1868,* 3. The war party consisted of two hundred Cheyennes, twenty Sioux, and four Arapahoes.

[16] Post Returns, Fort Harker, Aug., 1868; U.S. Army, Military Division of the Missouri, *Record of Engagements with Hostile Indians within the Military Division of the Missouri 1868–1882* (hereinafter cited as *Record of Engagements*), 8; New York *Tribune* (Aug. 15, 1868).

running fight of ten miles Benteen drove off the raiders and recovered two captive women, but he was unable to inflict any casualties.

Wynkoop was astounded to learn of the Saline and Solomon
raids. Sending immediately for Little Rock, a Cheyenne chief, he
demanded an explanation. Little Rock denied any knowledge of
the depredations but promised to investigate. On August 19 he
reported that the war party had left the Cheyenne camps on the
second or third of the month led by Red Nose, Tall Wolf, Oh-E-
Ah-Mohe, Porcupine Bear, and Bear That Goes Ahead. The chief
feared further depredations and begged the agent to tell him what
to do. Most of his people, he declared, had taken no part in the raids.

Wynkoop demanded that the leaders be turned over to him for
punishment and told Little Rock that such a course would prevent
harm from befalling his people. But anxious as he was to avoid
trouble, the chief was powerless to assure the surrender of the warriors; he could only try.

Garbled reports of the outrages had, meantime, reached Lieutenant Beecher and his scouts encamped on Walnut Creek. In an
effort to prevent further trouble, and to make explanations if the
whites had been at fault, Beecher sent Comstock and Grover to the
village of the Cheyenne chief, Turkey Leg, then located on the
headwaters of the Solomon River.

The two scouts anticipated a friendly talk, for they had known
Turkey Leg for years, but he received them coldly and ordered them
to leave the village. Their disappointing reception seemed offset a
little when an escort of seven young warriors was provided to keep
them from harm; but as the little party rode slowly over the prairie,
chatting in friendly fashion, the escort suddenly pulled up and
opened fire.

Though veteran plainsmen, Comstock and Grover were taken
completely by surprise. The former, struck by several balls, died
instantly; Grover, although badly wounded, managed to use the
body of his fallen comrade as a shield and to hold off his assailants

until nightfall. Then he crawled away and made good his escape to Fort Wallace.[17]

The raids along the Saline and Solomon, and the shooting of Sheridan's scouts, proved but the prelude to more devastating attacks. Roving war parties lashed at the Kansas and Colorado frontiers, killing, burning, and raping. On August 17, Governor Crawford telegraphed President Johnson:

> I have just returned from northwestern Kansas, the scene of a terrible Indian massacre. On the thirteenth and fourteenth instant, forty of our citizens were killed and wounded by hostile Indians. Men, women and children were murdered indiscriminately. Many of them were scalped, and their bodies mutilated. Women, after receiving mortal wounds were outraged and otherwise inhumanly treated in the presence of their dying husbands and children.[18]

Acting Governor Frank Hall of Colorado wired General Sherman that hostile Indians were attacking within twelve miles of Denver. The red warriors, he said, were better armed, mounted, and disciplined than ever before, and "the prospect was never so dark as now."[19]

The army, like the frontier settlers and Indian agents, was caught off balance by the suddenness and scale of these attacks. In the whole of his vast department, east of New Mexico, Sheridan had only 2,600 men about equally divided between cavalry and infantry. Until reinforcements could be obtained, supplies and equipment gathered, and a comprehensive campaign devised, he would have to be content merely to defend the settlements with the limited means at his disposal.[20] And he was hard pressed to do even this

---

[17] *Annual Report of the Secretary of War for the Year 1868*, 11; Sheridan, *Personal Memoirs*, II, 292; *Harper's Weekly Magazine*, Vol. XII (Sept. 19, 1868), 606.

[18] Crawford, *Kansas in the Sixties*, 291; Garfield, "Defense of the Kansas Frontier, 1868–1869," *loc. cit.*, 457; New York *Tribune* (Aug. 18, 1868).

[19] Sept. 24, 1868, S.-S. Papers, 2; *Annual Report of the Secretary of War for the Year 1868*, 4–5.

[20] Sheridan, *Personal Memoirs*, II, 297. General Sully put several detachments of cavalry to work building blockhouses to protect outlying settlements. Post Returns, Fort Harker, Aug. 1868.

for the red warriors showed no reluctance in meeting their blue-clad opponents.

Hostile red men attacked a wagon train near Fort Dodge on August 18, wounded five men, and tarried long enough to skirmish with a relief force sent out from the post. Three wood choppers were killed at Twin Butte Creek near Fort Wallace on the nineteenth, and twenty-five of their animals were stolen. On the twenty-third the Denver stage escaped capture only after a running fight of four miles, and the stage to Cheyenne Wells had a similar experience. On the same day two men were killed and scalped on Pond Creek.[21]

Detachments of the Seventh and Tenth Cavalry scouted for and pursued the red phantoms along the Saline, Solomon, Smoky Hill, and their tributaries with little to show for their efforts. Interceptions were rare and even when effected imposed few casualties. Scouting operations by six troops of the Tenth Cavalry in the month of August alone covered more than a thousand miles with no indications of having killed a single Indian.[22] Additional troops were needed immediately, and Sheridan authorized his aide, Brevet Colonel George A. Forsyth, to "without delay, employ fifty (50) first class handy frontiersmen, to be used as Scouts against the hostile Indians and to be commanded by yourself with Lieut. Beecher, 3rd Infantry, as your subordinate."[23]

At Forts Harker and Hays, Forsyth had little difficulty in recruiting his scouts, most of whom though not all were veteran Indian fighters. Once organized, they comprised a small but formidable body of fighting men, well mounted, and armed with

[21] Post Returns, Fort Dodge, Aug., 1868; Post Returns, Fort Wallace, Aug., 1868; *Record of Engagements*, 9.

[22] Organizational Returns, Tenth Cavalry, Aug., 1868.

[23] George A. Forsyth to Bvt. Brig. Gen. C. M. McKeever, Asst. Adj. Gen., Department of the Missouri, Mar. 31, 1869, "Report of the Organization and Operation of a Body of Scouts Enrolled and Equipped at Fort Harker and Hays, Kansas, August 24, 1868," MS, Phillips Collection, University of Oklahoma (hereinafter cited as Forsyth, "Report").

Spencer repeating rifles and Colt revolvers. "Sharp" Grover, but recently recovered from his wounds, was made chief scout, while Dr. J. H. Mooers accompanied the command as surgeon.

On the morning of August 29, 1868, Forsyth received his marching orders, and on that day his little column left Fort Hays. They scouted the headwaters of the Solomon River as well as the valley of the Beaver, but saw no Indians so turned toward Fort Wallace, arriving there on September 5. There Forsyth proposed to await further orders from Sheridan.

On the night of September 9, however, he received a telegram from Governor Hunt of Colorado, urging him to come to the aid of settlers between Bijou Basin and Hardingens Lake, now under constant Indian attack. Forsyth had determined to move toward the headwaters of the Republican, in an effort to bring these settlers some relief, when word came that hostiles had struck a freighters' train near the town of Sheridan some thirteen miles east of Fort Wallace.

The scouts moved swiftly to the scene but found that the Indians had fled. Wasting no time, Forsyth took up the trail of the marauders and followed it until darkness forced a halt. Next morning he resumed pursuit, following a faint trail in the general direction of the headwaters of Beaver Creek. Hopes were low, however, until on the morning of September 14 the scouts found a small but fresh trail leading up the Arikaree Fork of the Republican River.

As they followed the trail up the south bank, it gradually broadened into a large well-beaten path over which many horses had trod. Some of the scouts now began to doubt the wisdom of following the trail farther, but Forsyth silenced them, asking if they had not after all enlisted to fight Indians.

On the afternoon of the sixteenth the command moved into a small valley with a rolling plain to the south and a range of hills to the north. They camped that night beside the Arikaree, just across from a small island around which flowed some five inches of water. Rations were low, but there was plenty of salt, and Forsyth was determined to push on next day, relying for food on whatever game might be encountered.

Then, in the early dawn of the seventeenth, a small band of warriors tried to stampede the horses. They were easily driven off, but seven animals were lost. Shortly thereafter, as the command saddled up, the whole valley seemed suddenly to come alive with Indians. From all sides, on foot and on horseback, the hostiles pressed toward the little band of scouts.

Forsyth's position on the bank of the Arikaree was untenable. Unless he could find a strong defensive position, the Indians would slaughter his command. The best available cover would be the little island. About two hundred feet long by forty feet wide, a little below the level of the riverbanks, and about ninety feet distant from either bank, it bore a few stunted trees and bushes.

There he ordered the men to take their position, lie down in a circle, and entrench themselves in the sand with their hands and knives. At once they scrambled for the island, tied their horses to the trees and bushes, and began digging in as swiftly as they could. And not a moment too soon, for as the scouts worked frantically at the sand, the Indians fell upon them singly and in groups.

They drove the first attackers off handily and a lull ensued. Then about 9:30 A.M. three hundred painted warriors made a gallant charge. Working the levers of their seven-shot Spencers as rapidly as possible and firing volley after volley, the scouts managed to split the charge, the warriors streaming past on both sides of the island. The Indian loss was heavy, and lying among the dead only a few paces from the entrenchments was the great war chief Roman Nose who had led the charge.[24]

---

[24] *Ibid.*; Grinnell, *Fighting Cheyennes*, 276–77; Sheridan, *Personal Memoirs*, II, 302. Roman Nose had taken no part in the earlier fighting. A few days before the fight he had eaten in a Sioux camp. After finishing his meal he learned that the bread had been taken from the frying pan with an iron fork. This violated a taboo and took away the protective powers of his war bonnet. He had not had time to go through the necessary purification ceremonies and knew that he would be killed. But when he learned that his people were

Throughout the rest of the morning and during the whole of the afternoon the beleagured scouts and their red antagonists maintained a heavy rifle fire. At two o'clock and again at five o'clock came efforts to ride over the hard-pressed men on the island. Both charges were repulsed handily, but not until nightfall, when the Indians ceased firing, could Forsyth take stock of his situation.

And a desperate situation it was. Early in the fighting Forsyth had been shot through both legs, one ball shattering the bone of his left leg between knee and ankle. Lieutenant Beecher had been hit in the side and after hours of agony had died; Surgeon Mooers had also been mortally wounded, as were two of the scouts. Sixteen others had been wounded, some of them dangerously.

But this was not the end of Forsyth's woes, for all his rations were exhausted, his medical supplies had been lost in the rush for the island, and all his animals had been killed. Help could be had only from Fort Wallace, some eighty-five miles away; and between that oasis of safety and his beleagured command were several hundred hostile Cheyennes and Sioux.

A courageous officer, Forsyth lost no time in bemoaning his fate. There was water just for the digging, meat on the carcasses of his horses, and plenty of ammunition. Even though a drizzling rain had set in, and the night was very dark, he put all his able-bodied men to work improving the position. They deepened the rifle pits and connected them by a series of trenches; scooped out a large depression in which they placed the wounded and made them as comfortable as possible; and cut a generous supply of meat from the dead animals.

These necessary tasks accomplished, Forsyth called a council and asked for volunteers to go to Fort Wallace for aid. Sharp Grover protested. It would be suicide for anyone to attempt to get through the encircling lines. But despite Grover's pessimism, two scouts, Jack Stilwell and Pierre Trudeau, volunteered.

dying, he donned the war bonnet and led the charge which resulted in his death. Grinnell says that he was hit in the back just above the hips.

About midnight, after donning moccasins made from boot tops and taking some strips of horse meat, the two scouts slipped out from the island and made their way toward the southwest. Their comrades listened with bated breath for some sound to indicate that they had been intercepted, but as the hours passed and nothing was heard, hopes for their safety rose.

All through the next five days the Indians maintained their siege, firing from daylight until dark at the men huddled in the rifle pits. On the second night Forsyth sent out two more scouts, but they were unable to get through and had to return. When the third day had passed, with still no sign of relief, two more volunteers, A. J. Pliley and Jack Donovan, crawled away and disappeared in the darkness. They did not return, and again hopes ran high that they would reach Fort Wallace.

By dawn of the seventh day the Indians had disappeared, but the scouts were in a pitiful condition. The wounded, lacking all but the most primitive treatment, were in agony. Maggots were busy in the gaping wounds of Forsyth's legs. Hunger was acute, for the horse meat had been putrid since the fourth day, and not even sprinkling it with gunpowder could then make it palatable. By the sixth day they had exhausted even this dubious nourishment, and in his diary one of the scouts recorded with evident relish, "Kilt a Coyote and eat him all up."[25]

But rescue was now near at hand, for Stilwell and Trudeau had made good their escape. After leaving the island, they had carefully avoided ravines and other rough terrain, keeping to the open prairie where their keen-eyed foe would least expect to find them. Although they had made only a few miles the first night, they had eluded several small parties and had found a safe hiding place in which to spend the day.

That night they made good progress, and dawn of the nineteenth

[25] Sigmund Shlesinger, "The Beecher Island Battlefield—Diary of Sigmund Shlesinger," *Colorado Magazine,* Vol. XXIX (July, 1952), 169; Forsyth, "Report."

found them on the South Fork of the Republican—virtually in the midst of a large Indian village. They quickly took refuge in a near-by swamp, and even though warriors rode to and from the village constantly, their hiding place was not discovered.

At dark they were on their way again, and as the night passed without incident, they decided to continue after sunrise. Then, about 7:00 A.M., while walking across open ground, they sighted a large body of Cheyennes coming directly toward them. A frantic search for cover disclosed the near-by carcass of a buffalo surrounded by a small patch of yellow weeds. The ribs were still covered by enough hide to offer a scanty and odorous sanctuary, and into it they crawled.

Scarcely daring to breathe, the scouts watched as one Indian warrior approached within a few yards of their hiding place before turning away. Then as danger lessened from one quarter another arose, for uncoiling its length within the carcass, a rattlesnake hissed its warning. Stillwell, however, equal to the occasion, routed this new enemy with an accurate spray of tobacco juice.

Trudeau was now weak and sick, but the journey was resumed that night and continued through a light rain and snow the next day. About noon on the twentieth they reached a wagon road which they recognized as leading to Fort Wallace. A short time later they met two colored troopers bearing dispatches from the post to Brevet Lieutenant Colonel Louis Carpenter, who was on a scout along the Denver road with Company H of the Tenth Cavalry. After apprising the soldiers of Forsyth's plight, the scouts turned toward Fort Wallace; arriving there in the evening, they reported to Brevet Colonel Henry Bankhead, the commanding officer.[26]

Bankhead telegraphed Sheridan and was ordered to go at once to Forsyth's relief. He acted promptly, and at midnight led a col-

[26] Winfield Freeman, "The Battle of the Arickaree," *Transactions of the Kansas State Historical Society*, Vol. VI (1900), 354, 356; Miles, *Personal Recollections*, 147ff.; Post Returns, Fort Wallace, Sept. 1868.

umn from the fort, marching for the Arikaree with all possible speed.

Meanwhile, when Carpenter learned from his couriers of the situation on the island, he decided to move to the scene and render aid, even though neither he nor any of his men were familiar with that part of the country. On this account, although he pushed his force to the utmost, much valuable time was lost through the necessity of scouting widely in a strange area.[27]

On the morning of the twenty-fifth, however, by the sheerest of luck, Jack Donovan and a party of four men from Fort Wallace met Carpenter and his command. Donovan and Pliley had also managed to reach the post, only to find that Bankhead had already left. Pliley was exhausted but Donovan secured four volunteers and was now on his way back. A short time later, nine days after the initial attack, Forsyth welcomed Carpenter and his rescuers. The following morning Colonel Bankhead also arrived, and next day the return to Fort Wallace began.

Forsyth's engagement was not decisive, for it did not check the marauding red men, but it remains one of the most spectacular fights in the history of Plains warfare. The scouts had fought an estimated 750 Cheyennes and Sioux, inflicting a loss of 32 killed and several times that number wounded. Forsyth's casualties were but 6 killed and 15 wounded.[28]

Hostile Indians had also been busy along the Arkansas, with Cimarron Crossing the favored point of attack. There early in September they had struck two large wagon trains, killed seventeen men, and run off a large number of cattle. And as Sheridan's hard-pressed cavalry proved unequal to the task of fending off the raid-

[27] Organizational Returns, Tenth Cavalry, Sept. 1868.

[28] Forsyth, "Report"; Chauncey B. Whitney, "Diary," *Collections of the Kansas State Historical Society,* Vol. XII (1912), 298. This estimate of Indian casualties is disputed, however. Grinnell says that their loss was only nine killed: six Cheyennes, Dry Throat, White Thunder, Weasel Bear, Killed by a Bull, Little Man, and Roman Nose; one Arapaho, Prairie; and two Sioux whose names are unknown. See Grinnell, *Fighting Cheyennes,* 281.

ers, they became bolder. Even General Sully's camp near Fort Larned was not immune, for a band of warriors attempted to stampede his horses.

While it is certain that the Cheyennes were involved in these depredations, there is room for doubt that the Kiowas and Comanches were guilty of hostilities in the Department of the Missouri. Most of them had broken their camps near Fort Larned after Wynkoop's issue of annuities and had gone south of the Arkansas. Nevertheless, Sully decided to march against these Indians, for he felt them badly in need of a whipping.

His expedition, organized at Fort Dodge, consisted of nine companies of the Seventh Cavalry, Major Joel Elliott commanding, and three companies of the Third Infantry under Captain J. H. Page. Three veteran plainsmen, John Smith, Ben Clark, and Amos Chapman, who were familiar with the country to be traversed, were employed as guides.

On the afternoon of September 7 the column moved from Fort Dodge, with two companies of the Seventh leading the advance, two on each flank, and two more forming a rear guard. The remaining cavalry acted as a headquarters guard and escort, while the infantry traveled in the wagons which formed the long train.

Sully led them up the Arkansas to Cimarron Crossing, and as he forded the stream was heard to remark, "Now we have crossed the Rubicon." Anxious to deceive the Indians, whom he believed to be watching his every move, he continued to march after dark and ordered the column to move with the greatest possible silence. Even smoking was forbidden.

Some two hours' march from the river, he sent word to the advance to halt. Commanding it was Captain William Thompson, former territorial delegate to Congress from Iowa, and possessor of a great foghorn voice in which he took much pride. Upon receiving Sully's order Thompson bellowed, "Battalion, Halt!" Whereupon a mule brayed lustily. The General was furious, for he had marched in silence and at night to confuse the Indians, "but Balaam's ass has thwarted my scheme."[29]

The column moved on in a southwesterly direction and on the evening of September 8, camped at the foot of some bluffs near the Cimarron River. Not an Indian had yet been seen, but now the tired troopers had hardly closed their eyes when arrows flew into the tents, and a small band of warriors tried unsuccessfully to stampede the horses. The attack was not pressed and no casualties resulted.

The next night found the command a few miles south of the Cimarron encamped near a deep, dry arroyo. On the following morning, after the train had laboriously crossed the arroyo, Captain Louis Hamilton mounted his squadron of the rear guard and prepared to follow. Noticing that a cook and his helper were lagging, he warned the two men not to delay and rode on ahead.

Hardly had he gone a few hundred yards when a piercing scream reached his ears. Turning in the saddle, he was astonished to see a party of hostiles carrying off the tardy troopers. Giving chase at once, Hamilton was jointed by Captain A. E. Smith with a detachment from one of the flank guards. So closely were the Indians pressed that one of the captives, superficially wounded, was dropped, and rescue of the second appeared imminent.

At this juncture, unhappily, a courier on foaming horse reached Hamilton with Sully's orders to give up the pursuit and return to the column at once. A good soldier, he obeyed reluctantly and upon rejoining the rear guard was dumbfounded to learn that Sully had placed both himself and Smith under arrest for leaving the command without orders.[30]

---

[29] E. S. Godfrey, "Some Reminiscences, Including an Account of General Sully's Expedition against the Southern Plains Indians," *Cavalry Journal*, Vol. XXXVI (July, 1927), 421–23; Post Returns, Fort Dodge, Sept., 1868; *Record of Engagements*, 8, 10.

[30] Custer, *Life on the Plains*, 152–53; Godfrey, "Reminiscences," *loc. cit.*, 424ff. Godfrey, a young lieutenant in the Seventh Cavalry, said that the command was completely demoralized by this incident; that the cavalry had always operated on the principle that no risk was too great to rescue a comrade. Custer was severely critical of Sully's conduct in this campaign.

For the next five days, as the command moved slowly southwestward, skirmishes with the Indians were constant, the red men fighting a determined rear-guard action to allow their families to get safely away. Then, as the soldiers approached the forks of Beaver and Wolf creeks, they found the Indians entrenched in strong positions. Sully dismounted a portion of the cavalry, sent them forward as skirmishers, and succeeded after a two-hour fight in driving the warriors into near-by sand hills.[31]

In the face of stiff resistance, he now, unaccountably, made only the most timid efforts to push the Indians from their positions. With but one man killed and four wounded he gave up the attempt and retired, declaring that "these sandhills are interminable."[32] For several miles the warriors followed his retreating column, thumbing their noses and slapping their buttocks, but Sully stubbornly resisted the pleas of his officers who longed to strike the contemptuous Indians.[33]

It was a humiliated command that reached Fort Dodge on September 18. There Sully telegraphed Sheridan a report of his activities and asked for reinforcements, requesting that Custer be recalled to lead the Seventh Cavalry. His sole accomplishment seems to have been to instill his Indian antagonists with confidence in their ability to cope with the blue-clad cavalry.

As the Indian attacks gathered momentum over a wide area, and while Forsyth and Sully sought with such little success to stem the tide, Sheridan requested General Sherman to send him more cavalry. Sherman approved and forwarded the request to General Grant at Washington. The result was a transfer to Kansas, from

---

[31] During one of these skirmishes Captain Keogh's horse was shot in the rump. Keogh christened him Comanche on the spot. Comanche became one of the most famous horses in the history of the cavalry, surviving the Custer disaster at the Little Bighorn though seven times wounded.

[32] Godfrey, "Reminiscences," *loc. cit.*, 426; *Record of Engagements*, 8. The Indian loss was estimated at ten killed and twelve wounded.

[33] It is hard to account for Sully's behavior. He was a veteran Indian fighter with an excellent record, but throughout the campaign he was overly cautious.

posts in various Southern states, of seven companies of the Fifth Cavalry.

By September 29 these reinforcements had concentrated at Fort Harker, where they were temporarily placed under the command of Brevet Colonel W. B. Royall, until such time as an officer of greater rank, Brevet Major General Eugene A. Carr, could secure his release from staff duties in the Department of Washington and join the regiment.[34] Royall's force received equipment immediately, and only two days after its arrival was ordered to scout for Indians along Beaver Creek in western Kansas.

The column swept a broad area between Forts Harker and Hays, and then marched north of the Kansas Pacific Railroad as far as Prairie Dog Creek, which point they reached on October 11. There they pitched tents while two detachments of three companies each scouted along the Beaver and north to the Republican River. Royall remained in camp with Company L.

Three days later, while the detachments were still out, Tall Bull with a strong war party struck Royall's camp. It was a near disaster, costing the troopers two killed and twenty-six horses run off before the Indians tired of this sport.

Royall, vastly relieved when his detachments returned, made an extensive search for Tall Bull and his band to repay them their effrontery; but his efforts availed him nothing, and he turned back to the railroad to encamp at Buffalo Tank.

Meanwhile General Carr had arrived at Fort Hays and reported to Sheridan. His orders were to proceed to Fort Wallace, secure a sufficient escort, and join his command. He arrived at the post on October 12, and next day, escorted by Brevet Lieutenant Colonel Carpenter with two companies of the Tenth Cavalry, he left to find his regiment which was thought to be on Beaver Creek.[35]

---

[34] *Annual Report of the Secretary of War for the Year 1868,* 5, 19; U.S. War Dept., Office of the Adjutant General, "The History of the Fifth Cavalry from March 3, 1855, to December 31, 1905," File No. 1102491 (hereinafter cited as "Fifth Cavalry"), 78. The regiment was comprised of Companies A, B, F, H, I, L, and M.

[35] Report of Bvt. Maj. Gen. E. A. Carr, Commanding Expedition from Fort Lyon, of

The Chief Talks to a War Party
Painting by J. H. Sharp; Photo by Kemoha
Woolaroc Museum

Pioneers Defending a Wagon Train
Painting by William R. Leigh
Woolaroc Museum

Indian Attack

Painting by Gollings; Photo by Kemoha
Woolaroc Museum

Indians Escaping after the Burning of Their Camp
Painting by Frederic Remington; Photo by Kemoha
Woolaroc Museum

Lone Wolf's Camp (Kiowa), about 1867–74
Photograph by William S. Soulé
Smithsonian Institution, Bureau of American Ethnology

An Arapaho Camp, about 1867–74
Photograph by William S. Soulé
Smithsonian Institution, Bureau of American Ethnology

General William Tecumseh Sherman
U.S. Signal Corps Photo (Brady Collection)
National Archives

General Philip Henry Sheridan
U.S. Signal Corps Photo (Brady Collection)
National Archives

Carr reached the creek on the seventeenth and early the following morning turned downstream seeking Royall's camp. Only a short time later several hundred Cheyenne warriors opened fire on his men at long range. The troopers returned the fire and a lively skirmish followed, with Carr turning northward, crossing the stream, and moving toward high ground some distance away.[36]

About 2:00 P.M., with the hostiles pressing the engagement, he reached the slope and turned at bay. Corralling the wagons in the form of a horseshoe, the troopers dismounted and tied their horses inside the corral, then leveled a heavy fire toward their now charging foe. Superb Cheyenne horsemen dashed within a few paces of the wagons to discharge bow and gun but were driven back and forced to leave five of their number on the ground near the corral.[37]

The Indians retired to a near-by hill and held an animated council while the men in the corral watched and waited. Soon, however, the warriors began to disappear, and by nightfall not a one was to be seen. Carr then moved back to the Beaver and encamped, although it is doubtful if any of the command slept soundly for "wolves" howled around the camp all night.

The hostiles had appeared in such numbers that Carr next morning decided discretion was the better part of valor, and, breaking his camp, returned to Fort Wallace, where he arrived on the afternoon of October 21. There he received a dispatch from Sheridan giving him the true whereabouts of his command. Further, he would be joined by Lieutenant Silas Pepoon with fifty scouts and furnished with forage and rations sufficient for a campaign of fifteen days.

Carr left Fort Wallace immediately and joined his command at

the operations of His Command during the Late Campaign against Hostile Indians, April 7, 1868, S.-S. Papers (hereinafter cited as Carr, Report), 233; Post Returns, Fort Wallace, Oct., 1868; "Fifth Cavalry," 79.

[36] Carr, Report, 234–35; Organizational Returns, Tenth Cavalry, Oct., 1868.

[37] Carr, Report, 237; Maj. E. N. Glass, *History of the Tenth Cavalry*, 16. Carpenter received the Medal of Honor for his role in this engagement, and General Sheridan commended personally Troops H and I of the Tenth Cavalry.

Buffalo Tank on October 22. He found his troopers tired and their horses leg weary after previous scouts, but within two days he was again on the move. His column marched toward Shortness Creek, a tributary of the Beaver, where informants reported seeing a large Indian village.

On Sunday, October 25, the column reached the creek and turned northward following its course. They had traversed but two miles when they saw Cheyennes and Sioux in large numbers on hills to the south and west. The advance charged immediately and by late afternoon had driven the Indians to the Beaver, where the remainder of the command caught up and joined the fight. Even though the number of warriors had steadily increased, they preferred to fight a rear-guard action and at nightfall broke off the engagement, having lost some thirty killed and wounded.[38]

The army encamped on the spot but got little rest, for the hostiles occasionally fired into the tents and at intervals filled the air with wolf calls.

To close with his elusive foe Carr now decided to abandon all his camp equipment and to put eight mule teams on his remaining wagons. It was a swift-moving column that resumed the pursuit at daybreak on the twenty-sixth, but try as they might they could not come to close quarters with the splendid Indian horsemen: a swirling skirmish advanced steadily northward to the Republican, which was reached on the evening of the twenty-seventh.

The Indians now turned southward to the Beaver and then down that stream, using all their Plains lore to shake off the tenacious foe at their heels. And at long last they succeeded, for on the thirty-first they vanished completely, leaving a baffled Carr to return to Fort Wallace, where he arrived on November 2.

His campaign marked the end of Sheridan's policy of defense. Intended merely to meet the demands of the moment, it had

---

[38] George F. Price, *Across the Continent with the Fifth Cavalry*, 132f. Price placed the number of Indians at five hundred. See also Carr, Report 237ff., 242; and "Fifth Cavalry," 79.

served until a better military solution could be devised. In the minds of Sherman and Sheridan that solution had now been found, and the hour was at hand to apply it.

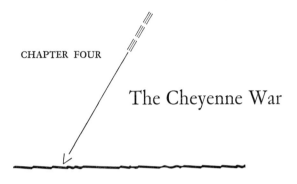

CHAPTER FOUR

The Cheyenne War

THE ACHILLES' HEEL OF THE PLAINS
Indian was winter weather. During the spring and summer, when
his war ponies were nourished on rich Plains grass, the roving red
man was a mobile, swift-striking, cunning, and dangerous foe.
He raided and destroyed without warning, could inflict great damage, and retreated skillfully. That he could seemingly vanish into
thin air many a worn-out cavalry detachment would readily attest.
But winter starved his pony and rendered it unserviceable for any
but the most limited use, while the sleet, ice, and snow sent him
scurrying for some sheltered retreat and the warmth of his tipi
fire. Normally it was spring before he could again emerge to harry
the frontier and return with the scalps of a successful mission.

The plan of Sherman and Sheridan was to launch an extensive
and carefully prepared campaign to drive the tribes into the reservations set aside at Medicine Lodge, and to pursue and kill those
who refused to go. The drive would come at the approach of winter

so as to place the Indian at the greatest possible disadvantage.[1]
Sherman, in a letter to his brother, summed up his thoughts in
this way:

> Our troops are now scattered and have daily chases and skirmishes,
> sometimes getting the best and sometimes the worst, but the Indians
> have this great advantage; they can steal fresh horses when they need
> them and drop the jaded ones. We must operate each man to his own
> horse and cannot renew except by purchase in a distant and cheap
> market. I shall keep this thus, and when winter starves their ponies
> they will want a truce and shan't have it.[2]

There would be a winter campaign then, if the necessary approval
could be had from higher headquarters.

On August 21, 1868, Sherman telegraphed both the War and Interior Departments that he had ordered General Sheridan to remove the Indians south of the Kansas line and in so doing to kill
them if necessary. Sherman requested that he be notified at once if
the President did not approve such a policy. Delay was encountered,
however, for the Interior Department insisted that some means
be found to protect the innocent from suffering the same fate as
the guilty. Plans were then made to escort the friendly Indians to
Fort Cobb, Indian Territory, so as to be out of harm's way, and
it was not until October 9 that Sherman could order his impatient
subordinate to proceed with preparations.

Separating the innocent from the guilty was no easy task. Sherman was determined on war with all the Cheyennes and Arapahoes,
even though he admitted that some of them, especially among the
latter, had committed no hostile acts. Nevertheless, they should be
punished along with the rest: they had not restrained the guilty,
nor had they given them up under terms of the Medicine Lodge

[1] It is worthy of note that at the time this decision was made no preparations of any
kind had been made for receiving the Indians at the reservations, and that many months
would be required before any facilities whatever could be installed. Mooney, "Calendar
History," *loc. cit.,* 186; *Annual Report of the Commissioner of Indian Affairs for the Year
1868,* 62.

[2] Thorndike, ed., *Sherman Letters,* 321.

treaties. To Sherman, then, only the Kiowas, Comanches, and Kiowa-Apaches were innocent.

In September most of the Kiowas and about one-third of the Comanches were encamped along the Arkansas between Fort Larned and Fort Zarah. Sherman instructed General Hazen to go to the former post, hold council with the Indians, and arrange to conduct them to Fort Cobb. He also asked the Interior Department to send an agent to Fort Cobb to care for the Indians after their arrival.

On September 20, accompanied by General Sheridan, Hazen held council with the Kiowa chiefs and with Ten Bears of the Comanches. Arrangements were made for Hazen to conduct them to the reservation, and Sheridan agreed to provide rations for the journey. However it would require some ten days to collect the rations, and the Indians were told to hunt buffalo during that time.

They failed to return, and it was at first assumed that they had thrown in their lot with the Cheyennes. But Hazen decided to go to Fort Cobb in the event they had made the journey on their own. However the war on the Plains was now in full swing, every trooper was urgently needed, and no escort could be provided. Hazen, therefore, had to take a long, roundabout route. Fearing some bands might reach Fort Cobb before him, he asked Major James Roy at Fort Arbuckle, Indian Territory, to send an officer to handle affairs until he could arrive.

In response to this request, Captain Henry Alvord appeared at Fort Cobb in mid-October. There he found several hundred Indians and learned that many more were on their way. Able and energetic, he set to work at once, issuing rations from the slender stores at his disposal, holding council with various chiefs, listening to their grievances, and ascertaining the location of many tribal encampments.[3]

When November 1 had come and passed with Hazen still absent,

[3] Capt. Henry Alvord to Gen. Hazen, Oct. 30, 1868, S.-S. Papers, 23–25.

Alvord became worried. His supplies of flour, sugar, and coffee were at the point of exhaustion, and if the issues ceased, he feared the Comanches might leave or else use the fort as a base for raiding into Texas. These worries ended a week later when Hazen finally arrived.

Alvord, who had worked at a difficult task with singular efficiency, was able to give the tardy General a detailed report on the movements not only of the Kiowas, Comanches, and Kiowa-Apaches but of most of the Cheyennes and Arapahoes as well. Warned by a trusted interpreter that Sheridan was up to some trick, the Kiowas, Comanches, and Kiowa-Apaches had moved directly to Fort Cobb without waiting for Hazen. Alvord was certain that they had engaged in no hostilities.[4]

The Kiowas had grown tired of waiting and, accompanied by the Kiowa-Apaches, had moved their camps to an area between the upper Washita and the Canadian near the one-hundredth meridian. About the time of Hazen's arrival they were again on the move, this time down the Washita, intending to camp some thirty miles above Fort Cobb. There were prominent absentees, however, for the troublesome Satanta was paying a short "visit" to Texas with a raiding party and Kicking Bird was away fighting the Utes.[5]

Most of the Comanches were near Fort Cobb, except for the Yamparikas who were on the Canadian, the Kotsotekas who were some sixty miles up the Washita, and the Kwahadis who were beyond the Kotsotekas. The main body of the Cheyennes were encamped near the Antelope Hills, with the Arapahoes near by.

News of Hazen's arrival spread quickly among the tribes, and within a few days delegations from all of them started coming in to talk with him. Acting under Sherman's instructions to make Fort Cobb a place of refuge for innocent tribes, Hazen issued ra-

[4] Hazen to Sherman, Nov. 10, 1868, in *ibid.*, 42.
[5] Alvord to Hazen, Nov. 5, 1868, in *ibid.*, 28, 34.

tions to the Kiowas, Comanches, and Kiowa-Apaches, telling them to stay close to the post, out of the way of Sheridan's punitive columns.

On November 20 there arrived delegations from the Cheyennes and Arapahoes. Speaking for the former was Black Kettle, who expressed a strong desire for peace. He had tried to prevent some of his young men from taking part in the recent hostilities, but they had refused to listen to him. At present he was encamped on the Washita some forty miles east of Antelope Hills with 180 lodges. If allowed to move nearer Fort Cobb, he was sure he could keep his people quiet. Big Mouth, who spoke for all the Southern Arapahoes, said that he wanted peace and wished to do right.

Hazen felt that the chiefs were sincere, but he had no authority to make peace. Sherman had branded their tribes as hostile and was even then preparing to punish them. Summarizing his thoughts a few days later, Hazen wrote:

> To have made peace with them would have brought to my camp most of those now on the warpath south of the Arkansas, and as General Sheridan is to punish those at war, and might follow them in afterwards, a second Chivington affair might occur, which I could not prevent.[6]

He therefore told the chiefs that they must return to their people and not come in again unless he sent for them. He could not have known, however, as he watched the chiefs depart, that he had sent Black Kettle to his death.

Meanwhile Sheridan had completed his plans and organization for the winter campaign. Four columns were to be used. One, under Major Andrew W. Evans, was to march eastward from Fort Bascom, New Mexico, while a second, commanded by General Carr, would move southeastward from Fort Lyon, Colorado. These columns were to act as "beaters in" for a third force moving south from Fort Dodge under General Sully. Augmenting the regular

[6] Hazen to Sherman, Nov. 22, 1868, in *ibid.*, 51–52, 55.

troops, and acting in conjunction with Sully, would be a regiment of volunteer Kansas cavalry.

Sheridan, planning a six months' campaign, left nothing to chance. He secured the services of a dozen Osage scouts, headed by the noted trailers Little Beaver and Hardrope, and sent out from Fort Cobb a few Penateka Comanches to locate the families and property of the hostiles. While vast supplies were accumulating at Forts Dodge, Lyon, and Arbuckle, he pored over available maps of the area south of the Arkansas and talked with old plainsmen about the weather he might encounter.

Meantime, troops of the various columns were being put through a rigorous training schedule. This was especially true in the camps of the Seventh Cavalry near Fort Dodge. A comparatively new regiment, plagued by a rapid turnover of personnel primarily because of large-scale desertions, its morale was low and the men inexperienced.[7]

An additional complication was the activity of the Indians themselves. Encouraged by their previous experience with Sully, they enlivened the training period with almost daily forays against the camp. As the ever-cautious commander was not disposed to attempt pursuit, conditions soon approached a state of siege. Eventually, however, Custer, who had now rejoined the regiment persuaded Sully that a column moving at night might surprise the hostile camp and put an end to the humiliation.[8]

Late one evening a strong detachment moved out guided by the recently appointed chief of scouts, "California" Joe. If anyone in the area could find an Indian village at night it was this tall, loquacious, and unkempt man, who possessed an unsurpassed knowledge of the Plains and its red inhabitants. Riding his mule and smoking

---

[7] Custer, *Life on the Plains,* 190; *Godfrey,* "Reminiscences," *loc. cit.,* 417. Godfrey says that these desertions were appalling and ran to hundreds at a time.

[8] Post Returns, Fort Dodge, Oct., 1868; War Department, Adjutant General's Office, Letters Received, "Engagements and Casualties during the War of 1868 and '69 against Hostile Indians in the Department of the Missouri"; Custer, *Life on the Plains,* 175.

an ever-present pipe, "California" rode well ahead of the column and after a time disappeared from view entirely.

The march had proceeded without incident for several hours when the advance sent back word that Indians were believed near at hand. The officers halted the command and after a conference decided to send "California" with a few picked men to investigate. This worthy was, however, nowhere to be found, and a search revealed that he had not been seen for hours. At this point, far to the front, a single rifle shot shattered the night air, and the troops heard wild screams and yells and the pounding of hooves. The column, immediately alert, made ready to receive an attack. Then, riding out of the night and directly toward them, came "California" shrieking at the top of his lungs and striking out wildly on all sides.

He charged right in among the troopers, several of whom were required to subdue him and tie him to his mule. And now was learned the cause of it all: "California" was gloriously drunk. Having filled his canteen with a potent brand of whisky, he had quaffed the whole of it while scouting ahead of the column. Superb plainsman that he was, his knowledge of the terrain was at least equalled by his acquaintance with every "ranche" on the frontier.[9]

The expedition ended forthwith, for every Indian within miles was now undoubtedly alert. "California," returned to camp in disgrace, had his rank as chief scout withdrawn abruptly.

Perhaps amusement over the incident had raised morale a little, but positive measures did more. To improve notoriously poor marksmanship, Custer was carrying out an intensive program of target practice. As incentive the men were told that a record would be kept of every shot and that the highest scorers would be formed into an elite group. The results justified his effort, for the competition raised spirits and produced forty sharpshooters. These were relieved from extra duties and placed under the command of Lieutenant Cooke.

[9] *Ibid.*, 177–82. In Sheridan's opinion, "Joe was an invaluable guide and Indian fighter wherever the clause of the statute prohibiting liquors in Indian country happened to be in full force." Sheridan, *Personal Memoirs*, II, 319.

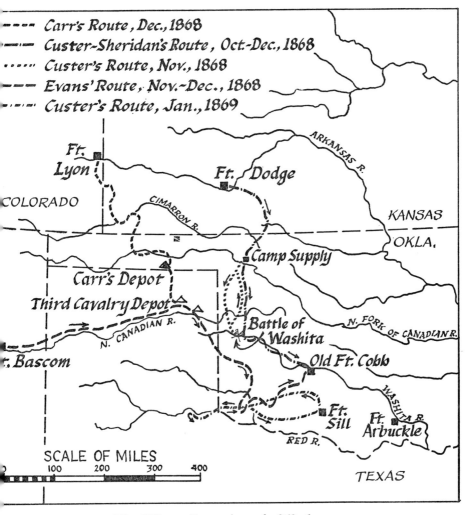

The Winter Campaign of 1868–69

By November 1, Sheridan, now ready to move, issued marching orders to his subordinate commanders. Evans, with six troops of cavalry and two of infantry, was to operate east along the line of the main Canadian and remain out as long as his supplies permitted. Carr would lead seven troops of the Fifth Cavalry from Fort Lyon, unite with Brevet Brigadier General W. H. Penrose, already in the field with five troops, and scout toward the Antelope Hills.[10]

The main column, under Sully, whom Sheridan proposed to accompany, was to march into the western part of Indian Territory toward the headwaters of Red River. They would establish a supply depot at the junction of Wolf and Beaver creeks in order to facilitate operations south of that point.[11]

Sully's command was composed of eleven troops of the Seventh Cavalry under Custer, five companies of infantry commanded by Captain Page, and the Nineteenth Kansas Volunteer Cavalry led by Colonel Samuel Crawford, who had resigned his governorship to take part in the expedition. The Kansans would, however, march to the supply camp by a different route.[12]

On November 12, Sully's long column, with a train of more than four hundred wagons, left Fort Dodge. Cavalry formed the advance and rear guards, while other mounted detachments screened the flanks. Infantry were distributed throughout the train, sometimes walking, and at other times climbing into the wagons to ease their aching feet.

The chary commander kept his column well closed, for he believed that spies were watching his every move, but no incident worthy of notice occurred until, on the fifth day's march, they reached the valley of the Beaver. Then, while moving slowly downstream, they struck the north-bound trail of a large war party. Custer asked to take the cavalry on the back trail of the party, hoping to strike their village, but to his great disgust the request was

---

[10] Sheridan, *Personal Memoirs*, II, 309; *Record of Engagements*, 15.

[11] Sheridan, *Personal Memoirs*, II, 308; De Benneville R. Keim, *Sheridan's Troopers on the Borders*, 101; Sheridan to Sherman, Nov. 23, 1868, S.-S. Papers, 57.

[12] Sheridan, *Personal Memoirs*, II, 308; James A. Hadley, "The Kansas Cavalry and the Conquest of the Plains Indians," *Collections of the Kansas State Historical Society*, Vol. X (1908), 433; E. S. Godfrey, "Some Reminiscences, Including the Washita Battle," *Cavalry Journal*, Vol. XXXVII (Oct. 1928), 3. Page's infantry consisted of three companies of the Third, one company of the Fifth, and one company of the Thirty-eighth regiments. See also Keim, *Sheridan's Troopers*, 101.

denied: Sully feared the village would be on the alert and the troopers ambushed.[13]

Next day the command reached the site of the intended cantonment, which was to be named Camp Supply. The men were put to work at once constructing buildings, erecting a stockade, and digging wells.[14]

Harmony was now threatened, however, by a dispute between Sully and Custer. The Articles of War specified that when volunteers and troops of the regular army were acting together, brevet rank should take effect. The Kansas volunteers had not yet arrived, but Crawford was a full colonel whereas Sully and Custer were merely lieutenant colonels. Neither Sully nor Custer, who cordially detested each other, was inclined to take orders from a volunteer colonel. Sully, therefore, began issuing orders over his signature as brevet brigadier general, and Custer replied by trying to assume command under his own brevet rank of major general.

Sheridan, escorted by two troops of the Nineteenth Kansas, arrived on November 21—after marching for five days in sleet and snow—and quickly settled the dispute in Custer's favor. The disgruntled Sully returned to Fort Dodge. Although concerned over the continued absence of the remaining eight troops of Kansas cavalry, the impatient Sheridan ordered Custer to proceed without them.[15]

It now became increasingly colder, and a heavy snow fell throughout the day and night of the twenty-second. Snow was still falling at three o'clock next morning when reveille roused the troopers, but despite darkness and the numbing cold, preparations were completed by daybreak. Then to the tune of "The Girl I Left

[13] Custer, *Life on the Plains*, 194; Godfrey, "Washita Battle," *loc. cit.*, 5. The Osage trailers estimated the strength of the party at one hundred warriors.

[14] Godfrey, "Washita Battle," *loc. cit.*, 5; Sheridan to Sherman, Nov. 23, 1868, S.-S. Papers, 57. Sheridan gave the location of Camp Supply as 105 miles from Dodge, 100 miles from Fort Cobb, 35 miles from Antelope Hills, and 25 miles from the eastern line of the Panhandle of Texas.

[15] Sheridan, *Personal Memoirs*, II, 311–12; Post Returns, Camp Supply, Nov., 1868; Post Returns, Fort Dodge, Nov. 1868.

Behind Me," Custer moved out with his scouts and all eleven companies of the Seventh Cavalry.

The day grew warmer, but it continued to snow, and a thick white blanket, obliterating every trail and landmark, obliged Custer to lead the way, compass in hand. Early in the afternoon Wolf Creek was reached and crossed, and the march continued up its right bank. Deep snow hampered the movement, and nightfall found the command only fifteen miles from Camp Supply.

When on the morning of the twenty-fourth the snow stopped and the sun came out, this proved a mixed blessing, for the glare caused some snow blindness. Pushing slowly on through mud and slush, the command made its way up the valley of the Wolf until near noon of the twenty-fifth and then turned southward toward the Canadian, which was reached that evening.

There Custer, after talking with the Osage scouts and "California" Joe, decided to send a strong force upriver to look for the trails of any war parties that might have been in the vicinity since the storm. Major Joel Elliott, given this assignment, on the morning of the twenty-sixth left camp with troops G, H, and M, some white scouts, and a few of the Osage trackers. Should he discover a trail, he was to follow it at once and send word to Custer, who would overtake him as quickly as possible. Meantime, the main column would cross the river and continue southward.

Fording the icy Canadian proved a time-consuming task, and the rear guard had just struggled across when a courier arrived from the scouting force. Only twelve miles upstream, and scarcely twenty-four hours old, he reported, was a trail leading in a southeasterly direction. It was being followed at all possible speed. On a fresh mount the courier returned to Elliott with orders to press the pursuit vigorously while Custer would seek to catch up. Should he not have done so by 8:00 P.M., Elliott was to halt and wait for him.[16]

[16] Godfrey, "Washita Battle," *loc. cit.,* 8; U.S. Congress, *Sen. Exec. Doc. No. 18,* 40 Cong., 3 sess., 27; Custer, *Life on the Plains,* 201; Custer to Sheridan, Nov. 28, 1868, S.-S. Papers, 60.

Rapid-fire orders now sent men and officers of the main column scurrying to prepare for a swift march. Lieutenant James M. Bell was to accompany the command with seven wagons carrying a few supplies and some ammunition, while the rest of the train, guarded by eighty men, would follow as best it could. Each trooper was ordered to carry one hundred rounds of ammunition for his Spencer carbine and his Colt revolver. A little coffee, some hard bread, and a small amount of forage was also to be taken.

Just as the command was ready to move, Captain Hamilton, charged with protecting the train, came to Custer and begged to accompany the troopers. He was told he might if he could find an officer willing to trade places. Hamilton hurried away only to return in a few minutes and exultantly report that Lieutenant E. G. Mathey, who was snow-blind, had agreed to remain with the train.

Even though Custer pushed his column to the limit, foot-deep snow and bitter cold made progress difficult, and not until 9:00 P.M. was Elliott overtaken. After an hour's rest, during which the men were allowed hot coffee and a little bread, the march continued.

In order to move as silently as possible, any gear that might rattle was tied down, the men were instructed to talk only in whispers, and under no circumstances were they to strike a match. With little sound to mark its progress, save the creak of leather and the crunch of hoofs in the snow, the column followed a trail which, plainly visible in the light of a rising moon, led into the valley of the Washita.

About midnight two Osage scouts, some four hundred yards in advance, smelled smoke, and a short time later they found the dying embers of a fire. They believed it had been made by Indian boys tending a pony herd and reasoned that a village must be near at hand. A few minutes later, as their cautious advance continued, one of them reached the crest of a long ridge, peered intently over it, and then came back to report, "Heaps Injuns down there."

Custer and his scouts went to the crest and with straining eyes tried to penetrate the gloom. All they could see was an indistinct mass of animals, but soon a dog was heard to bark, and there followed the tinkling of a bell. Evidently a pony herd was in the vicinity, but there was little else to indicate the presence of an inhabited village. Then, borne by the cold night air to the silent watchers on the crest, came the unmistakable wail of an infant. All doubts vanished; an Indian encampment had been found.

Custer returned and assembled his officers, had them remove their sabers to prevent noise, and led them to the ridge. In the pale moonlight they tried to discover the exact position and extent of the village. From their vantage point it appeared to be some two miles to the southeast in a heavy strip of timber bordering a great bend in the Washita. Its size was uncertain, but "California" Joe opined "thar's a mighty sight in the draw."[17]

The meagerness of Custer's information did not for a moment deter him. He would divide his command into four columns, surround the village, and attack at sunrise. Elliott, with three troops, was to make a wide circuit to the left and strike from the northeast or east; Thompson would lead two troops well to the right, make contact with Elliott, and attack from the southeast; Lieutenant Colonel William Myers would move about a mile to the right with two troops and close in from a southerly direction; Custer himself would make a frontal assault with four troops under Hamilton and West, with the Osage scouts and Cooke's sharpshooters. Lieutenant Bell would remain well to the rear.[18]

It was now nearly 2:00 A.M. and bitter cold. Elliott and Thompson had a considerable distance to march, and Custer gave them until first daylight to get into position. For the others there remained several chilly hours of enforced silence. Smoking was forbidden, and they were not allowed even to stamp their numbed feet

---

[17] Quoted in Custer, *Life on the Plains*, 215–17; Godfrey; "Washita Battle," *loc. cit.*, 9; U.S. Congress, *Sen. Exec. Doc. 18*, 40 Cong., 3 sess., 28; F. S. Barde, "Battle of the Washita—Death of Captain Hamilton," MS, Cheyenne-Arapaho Files, Oklahoma Historical Society, 5.

[18] Custer, *Life on the Plains*, 315; Godfrey, "Washita Battle," *loc. cit.*, 10. Elliott's troops were G, H, and M; Thompson's, B and F; Myers', E and I; and Custer's, A, C, D, and K.

in the snow. Conversing in whispers, shivering officers and men impatiently scanned the eastern horizon for the first signs of dawn.[19]

The Indian camp below was none other than that of Black Kettle and his Cheyennes. All were slumbering peacefully, for a timely warning had been ignored. On the night of the twenty-fifth a band of Kiowas, returning from a foray against the Utes, had struck a trail near the Antelope Hills which led south toward the Washita. When they had reached the Cheyenne camp they had told them what they had seen and warned that soldiers might be near, but the Cheyennes had laughed at them—weren't the Kiowas aware that the bluecoats didn't operate in such weather?[20]

At dawn Custer ordered his men to remove their overcoats and haversacks to gain more freedom of movement. Then the column advanced slowly toward a ridge farther down the slope whence the attack would be launched at sunrise. Unfortunately the muffled thud of many hooves aroused the dogs in the village, and they began barking furiously. A lone Indian emerged from his tipi, rifle in hand. One startled glance at the ridge sufficed, and the sound of his shot echoed and re-echoed down the valley.

Immediately Custer turned and ordered the trumpeters to sound the charge. Then to the strains of "Garry Owen" the command rushed the village, now a bedlam as old men, women, and children sought to escape, while from under the riverbanks in icy, waist-deep water the warriors opened a heavy fire.

Captain Hamilton, riding by Custer's side, was hit and instantly killed, but few other casualties were suffered as the troopers swept into the village and drove its desperate defenders to the outskirts. There, in ravines and hollows, the Cheyennes rallied and made a valiant stand to the accompaniment of the death chant from many women who had remained in the village.

In the face of such resistance, the cavalry dismounted and fought on foot, with Cooke's sharpshooters doing notable execution, pick-

19 *Record of Engagements,* 16; Custer, *Life on the Plains,* 215.
20 Report of Philip McCusker, U.S. interpreter, S.-S. Papers, 78–80. McCusker interviewed Black Eagle, a Kiowa.

ing off warriors as they raised their heads to fire. In this manner seventeen Indians died in a single depression. Thirty-eight others took up positions in a deep ravine and fought to the last man. Nor had they died in vain, for their stubborn defense gave many women and children time to make good their escape.

A large number of these, together with a few warriors, leaped into the river and began wading downstream. About two miles below the village, the Washita formed a horseshoe bend with deep water and steep banks. There the fugitives had to leave the river and emerge into the open to cross the neck of land. Elliott, in the thick of the fighting near the village, saw them and, calling for volunteers, rode to cut off their escape. Sixteen men followed him.[21]

Screening the flight of the Indians were three warriors, two Cheyennes and a Kiowa, the latter a visitor in the camp when the attack came. As Elliott came within range, one of the Cheyennes, Little Rock, fired and killed the horse of Sergeant Major Walter Kennedy. His fire was returned, and Little Rock was killed, but the two remaining warriors made good their escape while continuing to shield the fleeing Indians.

A woman and three children, however, overcome by exhaustion, suffered capture.[22] Kennedy, now afoot, started back with the captives while the pursuit continued. He had traveled but a short distance when a large body of warriors, retreating from the village, rode out of the timber along the river and bore down upon him. On his third shot his carbine jammed, and as he worked frantically at the lever he was tomahawked and killed.

The band then moved up on Elliott's rear while swarms of Cheyenne and Arapaho warriors, from camps downstream alerted by the firing, suddenly appeared on his front and flanks. Completely surrounded, his only hope was to hold them off until aid could reach him. Dismounting his troopers, Elliott ordered them to lie in a

[21] Godfrey, "Washita Battle," *loc. cit.*, 11; Grinnell, *Fighting Cheyennes*, 291f.; Hadley, "Kansas Cavalry," *loc. cit.*, 441. Hadley's account is taken from a letter written by George Bent, who lived with the Cheyennes and got it from participants.

[22] This woman was Buffalo Woman.

circle in the tall grass. This was a fatal mistake, for the grass obscured their line of sight, and their aim was high. Crouching low, the Indians crept within point-blank range. It was all over in a moment, and women came up from the river bed to mutilate the bodies.[23]

Meanwhile Custer had ordered Lieutenant E. S. Godfrey to take a platoon and round up the pony herd. In doing so he charged through the village and some distance below it. Seeing Indians bent on escape, he pursued them for more than two miles and eventually topped a high ridge. There he reined in suddenly, his eyes wide with astonishment: in the valley beyond he saw hundreds of tipis, and a large number of warriors moving rapidly toward him. Godfrey beat a hasty retreat and reported his discovery.[24]

As Custer pondered this information, there came a report that the number of his antagonists was steadily increasing. About 10:00 A.M. a captured woman was questioned, and for the first time it was learned that the winter camps of the Cheyennes, Arapahoes, Kiowas, and Comanches, in that order, stretched for ten miles down the Washita: there was now a distinct possibility that the command might be overwhelmed. Custer immediately re-formed and consolidated his troops, while with the Indian ranks receiving constant reinforcement, sharp skirmishing "broke out all around."[25] Despite their growing numbers, however, the warriors did not choose to press the attack and near midafternoon broke off the engagement.

Custer had nonetheless struck the Cheyennes a heavy blow. One hundred and three had been killed, including Black Kettle, whose scalp was claimed by the Osage trailers. Fifty-three women and children, among them Mah-wis-sa, sister of the dead chief, were captives. Fifty-one lodges had been pulled down and burned with

---

[23] Grinnell, *Fighting Cheyennes*, 293; Hadley, "Kansas Cavalry," *loc. cit.*, 441. These accounts are remarkably similar, and both indicate that troopers shot wildly and that few warriors were killed.

[24] Godfrey, "Washita Battle," *loc. cit.*, 11. This seems to have been the first intimation that Custer had that additional villages were below the one he had attacked.

[25] Custer, Life on the Plains, 222, 224.

all their contents, including great piles of buffalo robes, blankets, clothing, camp equipment, food, and weapons. Nearly nine hundred animals had been caught in the troopers' net, and all had been shot.[26]

The army had, of course, not escaped unscathed. Besides Captain Hamilton, three enlisted men had been killed, and three officers and eleven men were wounded. Furthermore, there were fears for the safety of Major Elliott and his detachment, last seen in pursuit of a party of Indians down the valley. Custer, expressing a hope that they were merely lost, made no effort to search for them.[27]

Discretion now indicated a retirement, for morning might well bring attack by the combined strength of the tribes, and this could run into thousands. The men were cold and hungry, for the Indians had found and carried away their discarded overcoats and haversacks. They might also have discovered the supply train with its slender escort, and fears mounted for its safety.

Before sunset, therefore, the column with its prisoners was formed for a return march. To confuse the red watchers on the hills and ridges, Custer ordered a feint of several miles toward the villages downstream. Then, in darkness, his shivering command was countermarched back to the battlefield, thence on, with all possible speed, toward the Canadian and, it was hoped, toward the supply train.

Not until well past midnight did Custer halt and allow the exhausted troops a cold and cheerless respite. They were in motion again before daylight and continued until near ten o'clock on the morning of the twenty-eighth, when, to the great joy of all, the supply train was reached. The united command then pushed on

[26] U.S. Congress, *Sen. Exec. Doc. No. 18,* 40 Cong., 3 sess., 28f.; Godfrey, "Washita Battle," *loc. cit.,* 13–14; *Record of Engagements,* 15; Custer, *Life on the Plains,* 224; *Annual Report of the Board of Indian Commissioners for the Year 1869,* 43. This was the army's official report, but the Indians have always disputed it. The greatest loss they have ever admitted is thirteen men, sixteen women, and nine children.

[27] Brevet Lieutenant Colonel Albert Barnitz was seriously wounded, while Brevet Lieutenant Colonel T. W. Custer, brother of the commanding general, and 2nd Lieutenant T. J. March were slightly wounded.

until evening before going into camp. "California" Joe was sent ahead to Camp Supply with dispatches, while the troopers resumed the march at a more leisurely pace.[28]

When the column reached Wolf Creek, Custer sent a courier to Sheridan requesting a formal review, to which the latter agreed. On the afternoon of December 2, when the command reached Camp Supply, it passed in review before the commanding general and the assembled populace of the fort. To the tune of "Garry Owen" the painted, chanting Osages led the parade, followed in order by the scouts, the guarded prisoners, and the long line of troopers.[29]

Even though Sheridan congratulated Custer on the success of his expedition, he questioned him sharply about Elliott, whose absence threw a pall over the whole celebration. Many of the missing man's brother officers were also critical of Custer's failure to make a search and thereafter accorded him scant respect. Indeed the hot criticism of one such found its way into public print.[30]

Sheridan, eager to follow up the strike on the Washita, was now delayed by the condition of the Kansas cavalry. Twelve volunteer companies had been mustered into service and had completed organization at Topeka by November 4. Two companies, D and G, had escorted the commanding general to Camp Supply, while

[28] Godfrey, "Washita Battle," *loc. cit.,* 14; Custer, *Life on the Plains,* 232. While Custer claimed a victory the Indians felt that they had held their own and were still masters of their camps. See A. G. Boone to N. G. Taylor, Commissioner of Indian affairs, Mar. 3, 1868, Office of Indian Affairs, Letters Received, Kiowa Agency.

[29] Keim, *Sheridan's Troopers,* 121–23; Custer, *Life on the Plains,* 239–40; Sheridan, *Personal Memoirs,* II, 320. A formal funeral was held the same day for Captain Hamilton, while that evening the Osages held a well-attended scalp dance.

[30] Sheridan, *Personal Memoirs,* II, 317. This officer was Captain F. W. Benteen, whose bitterly critical letter to a friend was published without his permission in the St. Louis *Democrat* of February 9, 1869. The letter was not signed, and Custer was furious when he read the article. He summoned his officers and with a dog-whip in one hand and the newspaper in the other demanded to know if any of them had written the account. He added that if he ever found the culprit he would whip him publicly. Benteen asked to see the article and then admitted authorship, and advised the angry general that if he wished to start whipping he could begin right there. Custer strode away. See Carl Coke Rister, *Border Command,* 114.

others had marched for that point via Camp Beecher on the Little Arkansas.

The regiment had been promised both rations and forage at Beecher but upon arriving there had found no such supplies on hand. They had departed, therefore, on November 14 with rations for but five days and with even less forage. Moreover, their guides were not familiar with the country south of Beecher, and by November 21, near the Cimarron River, they found themselves thoroughly lost and with supplies exhausted. Worse still, a howling blizzard had deposited a deep blanket of snow, and with their mounts growing steadily weaker, their every movement had become difficult.

Four days they had wandered in a maze of box canyons near the Cimarron with the specter of starvation hovering over them. Then on November 25 it had been decided to split the command. Five hundred of the strongest, under Lieutenant Colonel Horace L. Moore, would make a desperate effort to reach Camp Supply. The remaining six hundred would stay in camp and await rescue. Moore managed to reach the fort on November 28, but it was December 1 before the second group straggled in.

Seven hundred horses had been lost from starvation and exposure, and the surviving animals were in no condition for service. Unhappily, they could not be replaced and most of the Nineteenth Kansas had to serve out the campaign as "foot" cavalry. Thus a full week was lost while the Kansans rested and refitted.

Sheridan used this time to complete his plans for the next phase of operations, which he proposed to observe in person, although Custer would continue as field commander. As interrogation of the prisoners had indicated that there were other villages below Black Kettle's, Sheridan now planned to march to the battlefield on the Washita, and thence downstream to Fort Cobb, striking the tribes, if he could, a devastating blow and bringing them to terms.

On December 7, Custer led out his battle-sharpened Seventh Cavalry and ten companies of the Nineteenth Kansas. Three hundred wagons formed the supply train carrying thirty days' rations and forage. With the column were three of the Indian women captured in the Cheyenne village. These had been detained at Camp Supply when the rest of the prisoners were sent on to Fort Hays. They were Mah-wis-sa and a Sioux woman of whom she was fond, and a lovely young daughter of the slain Little Rock, Mo-nah-se-tah. Custer believed they might be of service in establishing contact with hostile camps.[31]

In deep snow and sub-freezing temperatures the column made a slow and uncomfortable march to the Washita, reaching a point near the battlefield on the evening of December 10. Next morning, while they rested, Sheridan, Custer, and a small party rode to the scene of the fight and combed it carefully. Elliott's trail was easily found and was followed down the south bank for about two miles, where lay the naked and mutilated body of Sergeant Kennedy.[32]

After marking this spot, the group went on a short distance, crossing a narrow ravine, and just beyond found the gashed and riddled bodies of Elliott's detachment. All were carried back to camp and buried there except the officer himself, who was interred later at Fort Arbuckle.

On the morning of the twelfth, the column began their march down-river toward Fort Cobb. Soon they were passing through the hastily abandoned camps of the Arapahoes and Kiowas. Lodge-poles, kettles, pots, cups, and other equipment littered the sites, while in one of the erstwhile villages were found the body of a young white woman, identified as a Mrs. Blynn, and that of her small child.[33]

---

[31] Sheridan, *Personal Memoirs*, II, 324; Keim, *Sheridan's Troopers*, 128; Custer, *Life on the Plains*, 247. The force numbered about 1,700 men. Five companies of infantry garrisoned Camp Supply, and two companies of the volunteers were assigned to escort trains moving between Supply and Fort Dodge.

[32] Custer, *Life on the Plains*, 253; Keim, *Sheridan's Troopers*, 144. Kennedy's body bore nineteen bullet holes, and his head was partly cut off.

[33] Sheridan to Sherman, Dec. 19, 1868, S.-S. Papers, 91; Keim, *Sheridan's Troopers*, 150. Sheridan was quick to blame Satanta for this tragedy, but Hazen said that Mrs. Blynn and her child were held by the Arapahoes and killed by them on the morning of the

Sleet, snow, and chilling winds pursued the column down the valley and made progress slow. Thick timber and underbrush kept several hundred men constantly at work cutting a passage for the train. However the area redeemed itself somewhat, in the eyes of the miserable troopers, by offering an abundance of game, and men dined sumptuously on wild turkey, quail, deer, and antelope.

There was little to interrupt the monotony of their march until the morning of the seventeenth, when the Osage scouts reported a large force of Indians on the column's immediate front. With the scouts was a courier from General Hazen with this message to Custer:

HEADQUARTERS SOUTHERN INDIAN DISTRICT, FORT COBB,
9 A.M., December 16, 1868
To the Officer Commanding Troops in the Field.

Indians have just brought in word that our troops today reached the Washita some twenty miles above here. I send this to say that all the camps this side of the point to have been reached, friendly, and have not been on the warpath this season. If this reaches you, it would be well to communicate at once with Satanta and Black Eagle, chiefs of the Kiowas, near where you now are, who will readily inform you of the position of the Cheyennes and Arapahoes, also our camp.

Respectfully,
W. B. HAZEN
Brevet Major General.[34]

The courier declared that the Indians ahead were Kiowas under Lone Wolf and Satanta and that they were holding hostage a companion who had accompanied him from Fort Cobb.

Hazen's communication displeased both Custer and Sheridan, for they believed the Kiowas just as guilty as the Cheyennes and wished to punish them accordingly. The word of Sherman's per-

---

Washita battle, and further, that he was in correspondence with her and was trying to effect her release at the time. See William B. Hazen, "Some Corrections of Life on the Plains." *Chronicles of Oklahoma*, Vol. III (Dec., 1925), 305.

[34] Custer, *Life on the Plains*, 257.

sonal appointee could not, however, be lightly brushed aside, and they reluctantly decided that the message must be honored.

A small party of warriors bearing a white flag now approached and signaled for a parley. Custer, with a few officers and some fifty scouts, rode forward to meet them, acutely conscious of hundreds of warriors in full war paint watching from near-by ravines and hills. Two interpreters advanced a few paces to meet a pair of Indians. A talk was quickly arranged, and Satanta and Lone Wolf came up and met with Custer.

Brusquely refusing their proferred hands, the officer told them that Hazen's letter would be respected. If the whole tribe would move to Fort Cobb and encamp there, no harm would befall them. These terms were acceptable, and to show their good faith Satanta and Lone Wolf, with several of their warriors, agreed to go along with the column. Their villages must follow by easy stages, for their animals were in poor condition.[35]

Satanta had some difficulty in making himself understood and signaled to the group at his back for "the man who spoke English." This was Walking Bird, who had picked up a few words around the army posts. Walking Bird's English was insufficient but he made a mighty effort by walking up to Custer, stroking his arm and saying, "Heap big nice sonabitch. Heap sonabitch." Needless to say, the General was not flattered and Walking Bird was in disgrace.[36]

The march was now resumed, but the number of Indians with the command steadily declined. Warrior after warrior moved off on pretense of helping their families to reach Fort Cobb. By the morning of the eighteenth only Satanta and Lone Wolf remained. A suspicion grew that they had no intention of keeping their agreement but rather were attempting to send their people to some remote haunt on the headwaters of Red River.

[35] *Ibid.*, 258; Sheridan, *Personal Memoirs*, II, 334; Keim, *Sheridan's Troopers*, 156. Custer's refusal to shake hands angered Satanta, who drew back, struck his breast, and exclaimed, "Me Kiowa!"

[36] Wilbur Sturtevant Nye, *Carbine and Lance: The Story of Old Fort Sill*, 95.

This suspicion was confirmed when, near midafternoon, Satanta suddenly put spurs to his pony and tried to escape. Already under close watch, he was overtaken within a few hundred yards and returned to the column where, with Lone Wolf, he was arrested and put under guard. Sheridan now proposed to hold them as hostages until their people complied with the agreement. Without further incident the command made its way to Fort Cobb, arriving on the afternoon of December 20 and going into camp on Pond Creek some half-mile from the post.[37]

In conference with Hazen, Sheridan was able to establish with some certainty the movements of the various tribes since the Washita battle. The Cheyennes and Arapahoes, about one-half of the Kiowas under Satanta, Satank, and Timbered Mountain, and Mow-way's Kotsotekas had broken their camps and moved rapidly southward. By November 30 they had all encamped together on the North Fork of Red River at the mouth of Sweetwater Creek. The other Kiowas under Lone Wolf, Black Eagle, Little Heart, and Kicking Bird, and most of the Comanches and Apaches, had remained on the Washita sending Hazen assurances of their peaceful intent.[38]

On December 1 a great council had been held on the Sweetwater, with Kicking Bird and Little Heart in attendance as representatives for those on the Washita. The Cheyennes and Arapahoes, with little choice but to declare themselves hostile, had tried to induce the others to remain with them. In this they had been disappointed, for the Kiowas had declared they intended moving toward Fort Cobb, while Mow-way, neither desiring war nor trusting the whites, had pronounced in favor of remaining out on the prairie. The hostiles had then expressed their friendship for those desiring peace,

[37] Sheridan, *Personal Memoirs*, II, 335; Custer, *Life on the Plains*, 262–63; Keim, *Sheridan's Troopers*, 157–61. Fort Cobb was located on Pond Creek about one mile from its junction with the Washita.

[38] Alvord to Hazen, Dec. 7, 1868, S.-S. Papers, 81–82. The powerful Kwahadis, however, were on the Staked Plain.

asking the "friendlies" to send them what goods they could spare from government issues.

Thus many of the Comanches were on hand when Sheridan reached Fort Cobb, and within a short time all of them had come in except the Kwahadis, the Kotsotekas, and a small band of irreconcilables who had fled to the headwaters of Red River. The Kiowas, however, were nowhere to be seen, even though both Satanta and Lone Wolf insisted these would arrive at any moment. Sheridan, after waiting two days, ordered Custer to tell the chiefs that, unless the tribe came in and submitted within forty-eight hours, he would hang them both.[39]

At first the captives begged for more time, but when Sheridan proved adamant, they requested, and were allowed to send, a runner to their people. By the afternoon of the second day the Kiowas were beginning to arrive, and all were in at nightfall except Woman's Heart and his band, who had fled to the Staked Plain.

Thus by the end of December the Kiowas and Comanches, with but few exceptions, had been corralled. Yet Sheridan did not believe they fully appreciated the significance of this submission. They must be made to realize that their freedom would henceforth be severely circumscribed and that they would be held strictly accountable for their misdeeds. He therefore continued to hold Satanta and Lone Wolf and refused to take council with any of the Indians, although, as he remarked, they sent him many earnest requests "in which they eat dirt."[40]

Sheridan had also decided to abandon Fort Cobb. Ill situated with respect to the Kiowa-Comanche reservation, it was also too far north to afford protection to the Texas frontier. A new military post, well within the reservation, must be established so that a close watch might be kept upon the tribes. Accordingly, Colonel Benjamin H. Grierson, Tenth Cavalry, commanding the District of

[39] Sheridan, *Personal Memoirs,* II, 335; Custer, *Life on the Plains,* 270. Sheridan mentioned only the latter band, but neither the Kwahadis nor the Kotsotekas were in.

[40] Sheridan to Gen. W. A. Nichols, Asst. Adj. Gen., Military Division of the Missouri, Jan. 23, 1869, S.-S. Papers, 194.

the Indian Territory, already familiar with the country south and west of Fort Cobb, was ordered to conduct an exploring party in search of a suitable location.[41]

On a previous visit Grierson had been favorably impressed with the site of an old Wichita village at the junction of Medicine Bluff and Cache creeks, some thirty-six miles south of the fort. Escorted by a detachment of the Tenth Cavalry, and accompanied by General Hazen and Colonel Forsyth, he now returned to that place. When his careful survey revealed an abundance of water, grass, and building material, he submitted a report recommending the location.[42]

Sheridan decided to make the movement at once. Despite cold, stormy weather and swollen streams, all troops were on hand at the new site January 10, and work began. The post, at first called Camp Wichita, was later named in honor of Brigadier General Joshua W. Sill, a classmate of Sheridan's, killed at Stone River in the Civil War.[43]

Hazen, with the assistance of Leavenworth's replacement, Agent A. G. Boone, who had now arrived, also moved the Indians, and late in the month Sheridan relaxed his hitherto unyielding attitude toward them.[44]

At a series of councils extending into February the chiefs of both tribes were lectured on their behavior since the Medicine Lodge treaties. They were warned that future violations would meet with a punishment swift and severe. At present, however, since they had assured him of a wish to hold firmly to the white man's road, Sheridan was willing to let them live in peace.[45]

[41] Organizational Returns, Tenth Cavalry, May, 1868.

[42] *Ibid.*, June, 1868; S.-S. Papers, 185.

[43] Post Returns, Camp Wichita, Aug., 1869; Sheridan, *Personal Memoirs*, II, 339.

[44] Sheridan, *Personal Memoirs*, II, 339; U.S. Congress, *H.R. Exec. Doc. No. 240*, 41 Cong., 2 sess., 4–5; *Annual Report of the Commissioner of Indian Affairs for the Year 1868*, 80. Wynkoop was also ordered to Fort Cobb, but he had resigned when he learned of the winter campaign. The Indians had trusted him before, and it had led to Sand Creek. He now feared another massacre, and said he did not wish to be a party to it.

[45] Proceedings of a Council held with Chiefs of the Kiowa Nation by General Sheridan

And on February 16 were released Satanta and Lone Wolf after abject promises, on their part, that all their bad deeds were behind them. The former was especially emphatic:

> Whatever you tell me I mean to hold fast to it. I will pick it up and hold it close to my breast. It don't alter my opinion a particle if you take me by the hand now, or take and hang me. My opinion will be just the same. What you have told me today has opened my ears, and my heart is open also. All this ground is yours to make the road for us to travel on. After this, I am going to have the white man's road, to plant corn and raise corn. You can send the same reports to Washington. You will not hear of the Kiowas killing any more whites. . . . I am not telling you a lie now. It is the truth.[46]

Sheridan was well pleased. He could now turn his full attention to the hostiles, and already circumstances pointed to a victory complete and final.

and General Custer at Medicine Bluff Creek, Indian Territory, Feb. 16, 1869, S.-S. Papers, 214–18.

[46] Interview between General Sheridan and the Kiowa Chiefs Satanta and Lone Wolf, Feb. 15, 1869, S.-S. Papers, 209–10.

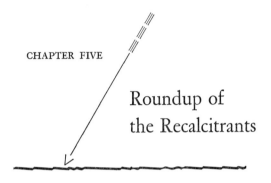

CHAPTER FIVE

Roundup of the Recalcitrants

T HE BATTLE OF THE WASHITA AND
Sheridan's sweep from Camp Supply to Fort Cobb had resulted in
the tribal submission of the Kiowas, Comanches, and Kiowa-
Apaches, and the settlement of nearly all their number upon a reservation set aside for them at Medicine Lodge. The primary targets
of the winter campaign, however, the Cheyennes and Arapahoes,
had fled south and then west toward the headwaters of Red River.
So it remained for Sheridan to secure their surrender and to drive
in, if he could, those scattered bands still on the loose.

The supporting columns of Evans and Carr solved part of the
problem. With six troops of the Third Cavalry, a company of the
Thirty-seventh Infantry, a battery of mountain howitzers, and a
large complement of guides and scouts, Evans left Fort Bascom on
November 18 and began a movement down the Canadian River.[1]

---

[1] Bvt. Lt. Col. A. W. Evans to the Asst. Adj. Gen., Headquarters, District of New
Mexico, Report of the Canadian River Expedition, Jan. 23, 1869, S.-S. Papers (hereinafter

Two days later a howling blizzard assaulted the column, causing great suffering to both men and animals. With deep snow now covering the ground grazing became impossible, and the supply of forage was quickly exhausted. Five days were lost while a slow-moving ox train brought more in.

Then in bitter cold, sleet, and snow, the march proceeded down-river until the column reached Monument Creek. Here Evans sent out scouting parties to the northeast and southeast while a depot for his stores was constructed between two sand hills. The search brought no results, and on December 15 the command, leaving their depot, moved down the left bank of the Canadian. Captain Arthur B. Carpenter, Thirty-seventh Infantry, with a detachment of twenty men, remained behind to guard the supplies.

A few miles west of the Antelope Hills they struck a south-bound trail, less than a week old, of fifty to sixty Indian lodges. Evans took up the pursuit immediately, followed a well-beaten path to the North Fork of Red River, and reached it on December 23. Now the trail led southeastward down-river and finally entered a canyon which the stream had cut through the Headquarters Mountains.

This gave Evans pause. The water of the North Fork, heavily impregnated with gypsum and salt, was nauseous and unpalatable. Furthermore, the Indians were evidently aware of pursuit, for they had burned off the grass over a wide area. Early on the morning of the twenty-fourth, therefore, he crossed the river and marched south and southeast skirting the mountains, hoping to pick up the trail beyond the canyon.

There, however, an all-day search, in frigid weather, failed to reveal any sign of the Indians, and on Christmas Day, Evans felt obliged to turn northward to the right bank of the North Fork, there to find shelter from the cold and encamp. No sooner was the river attained than scouts came in to report that they had seen two

cited as Evans, "Canadian River Expedition"), 165. The command consisted of Troops A, C, D, G, F, I, Third Cavalry, Company I, Thirty-seventh Infantry, an infantry detachment to man the howitzers, and 72 scouts, guides, and citizen employees—a total of 526 men and officers.

Indians near by, apparently spying on the column. While Captain Elisha W. Tarlton took his company and gave chase, the rest of the command, moving upriver a short distance, found a suitable campsite.

The troopers were busily unpacking the animals when word arrived from Tarlton that he needed help. In the canyon he had struck a large party of hostiles, who had promptly charged him. He had repulsed the charge but had lost two of his horses and was now hard pressed. Evans immediately sent off Captain Deane Monahan and his company and soon ordered a section of artillery under Lieutenant Edward Hunter, along with another company of cavalry, to follow Monahan. Meanwhile the remaining troops packed up and moved to join in the fight.

With his reinforcements, Tarlton drove the stubbornly resisting Indians through a strip of timber and thence to an area some two miles from the point of first contact. There the river broadened, and at the far end of a bend, nestling in a grove of trees at the base of a mountain, lay their village. Bringing up his howitzers, Hunter fired two shells among the lodges, where the Indians were desperately trying to remove their belongings. The first was a dud, but the second exploded, frightening the Indians off into the trees.

The troops, pressing forward through the village, drove the hostiles out of the grove and over a ridge beyond. As their warriors, nothing daunted, contested every foot, Tarlton decided to halt on the ridge until Evans came up. This, however, proved impossible, for the Indians had gained the rocks about the ridge and now poured down such a hot fire that the troops were forced to retreat to the village.

Evans, meanwhile, who had marched to the scene as fast as the state of his animals allowed, arrived at the village just in time to drive off a strong force who had slipped around the bend to strike Tarlton's rear. Then, while skirmishing continued, there began the destruction of the village. As nightfall found the task far from complete, the troops were formed in a hollow square around the village to repel an expected assault.

Before midnight sixty lodges, over ten tons of dried buffalo meat, hundreds of sacks of meal, and large quantities of sugar, coffee, tobacco, lead, powder, and camping equipment had been either burned or thrown into a near-by spring. The Indians, prowling around camp all night, occasionally fired on the pickets but made no effort to press an attack.

Next morning Evans crossed the river and moved out northward over the bluffs, stopping only long enough to throw a few shells back into the village when some Indians were seen re-entering it. The command had suffered one trooper killed and two slightly wounded. The Indians, however, had sustained a damaging blow, for in addition to the loss of all their property twenty-five had been killed and many wounded.[2]

Marching a little east of north, still plagued by the bitter cold, Evans' column on December 30 reached the Washita at a point some twenty miles above Fort Cobb. With a small escort Lieutenant Hunter went down to the post with dispatches for Sheridan, while Evans made ready to return to his base. From hunger and exposure the men were in wretched condition, while the animals were dying at a rate of more than ten a day.[3]

The command left the Washita camp on January 3 and, toiling at a snail's pace, took ten days to reach the depot on Monument Creek, their back trail littered with over two hundred dead horses and mules.

Although Evans' campaign ended thus dismally, much had been accomplished. The village he had destroyed was that of the Nokoni chief Horseback. Members of his band had been leading spirits in raids along the Texas frontier that summer and fall, with his own son among those who had made a particularly brutal strike at

[2] *Record of Engagements,* 17.
[3] Evans, "Canadian River Expedition," 166, 170–73, 176–82, 184, 188–90.

Spanish Fort on September 1.[4] So impressed were they by the sudden appearance of the soldiers that many had made the long trek to Fort Bascom, and there surrendered, even before Evans returned.[5]

Carr, meanwhile, had moved from Fort Lyon on December 2 with seven troops of the Fifth Cavalry, one company of the Third Infantry, 100 pack mules, and 130 wagons. His orders were to effect a junction with Penrose, who had taken the field from Fort Lyon with five troops of cavalry on November 10, and then to establish a supply base on the headwaters of the North Canadian whence to launch his squadrons.[6]

The column made good progress southeastward until the fifth, when a raging snowstorm overtook them. Sheridan Canyon provided a bleak shelter for the next two days while the storm spent its fury. Resuming his march on the seventh, Carr reached the Cimarron next day and found Penrose's trail leading downstream. In the bitterly cold weather and deep snow the trail proved difficult to follow, despite an occasional discovery of dead animals and the yeoman service of scouts William F. (Bill) Cody and Ed Guerrier.

Not indeed until December 23 did the command reach Penrose, awaiting them near the North Canadian some one hundred miles west of Camp Supply. His camp was in a sad state, with supplies nearly exhausted and forage at the vanishing point. His men were suffering intensely from the cold, and many whose mounts had died and put them afoot were badly frostbitten.

There Carr established his supply base, even though he disliked the site, for he was anxious to proceed with operations. From it he advanced southward with scouting parties flung wide, reaching

[4] Lt. William E. Doyle, Tenth Cavalry, Company D, to Bvt. Maj. Gen. Hazen, Mar. 1, 1869, Office of Indian Affairs, Letters Received, Kiowa Agency. A band of thirty-four warriors hit Spanish Fort, Texas, and killed eight persons, including one woman whom thirteen warriors raped before killing and scalping her. See L. J. Walkley to Hazen, Dec. 23, 1868, S.-S. Papers, 121–22; *Annual Report of the Secretary of War for the Year 1868*, 53.

[5] Sheridan, *Personal Memoirs*, II, 337. Other members of the band came into Fort Cobb.

[6] Carr, Report, 243–45; "Fifth Cavalry," 81; Organizational Returns, Tenth Cavalry, Nov., 1868.

on December 28 the main Canadian some twenty miles above Evans' depot on Monument Creek. A loan of supplies and of some forage for the half-starved animals was now obtained from Captain Carpenter, and when grass was found along the river, Carr decided to remain where he was and sent out detachments to search the region.

After Cody made a lonely and daring ride to Camp Supply for maps, small columns inaugurated the hunt for Indian hideaways. In this, however, they had scant success. Almost constant storms dogged their steps, and the severe cold killed dozens of their animals. While some forty of Carr's teamsters quit and forfeited their pay rather than endure the icy weather, his unfortunate troopers were reduced to utter misery.

On January 8, 1869, Carr gave up the struggle and returned to Fort Lyon, where he arrived on February 19. No Indians had been found, 2 men had died from exposure, and 181 animals had been lost.[7] Winter had administered a lesson and a defeat.

Carr's movement along the Canadian, combined with Evans' operations, had, however, frightened the Cheyennes and Arapahoes and kept their camps in constant motion. As a result the women and children suffered and sickened, and many of the ponies died. With soldiers constantly in pursuit, hunting was unsafe and the people grew hungry. Under such conditions, peace with the white man would perhaps be good, and swift runners told Kiowa and Comanche friends that an end to the war would be welcomed.

When this intelligence came to Sheridan's ears, he decided to give up coercion and attempt persuasion. Even should such an effort come to nothing, he would benefit by the delay, for his animals were weak, and his supplies were insufficient for a long campaign. Therefore, a few days prior to the move from Fort Cobb to his new post at the foot of the Wichitas, he authorized Custer to open negotiations and seek the peaceful submission of the two tribes.

To establish contact, Custer secured the services of an Apache

7 Carr, *Report*, 247, 250, 252–56; "Fifth Cavalry," 81–82.

chief, Iron Shirt, and of Black Kettle's sister Mah-wis-sa, who volunteered to seek out the hostile camps and try to persuade them to come in and make peace. The mission proved a failure, for Mahwis-sa remained with her people, and Iron Shirt reported that only two chiefs, Little Robe of the Cheyennes and Yellow Bear of the Arapahoes, had urged their people to come to Fort Cobb and submit.

On January 1, however, these two chiefs themselves arrived and sat down for a long talk with Sheridan. They had urged their people to follow them but were not sure they would do so. In any case they would be slow, for their ponies were in poor condition. The General replied that if the tribes stayed out, he would make war on them winter and summer until they were annihilated, but if they would come in and make peace, "I will not be a bad chief to you."[8]

When several days of waiting failed to produce the Indians, Custer became impatient. He requested permission to act as a peace commissioner, go to the tribes in person, and make a final appeal for their submission before again taking the field against them. To reassure the Indians of his intentions, he proposed limiting his escort to forty men. Sheridan gave his consent reluctantly, for he doubted the merits of the venture, and feared for the safety of so small a group in hostile country.

To accompany him Custer selected two score of Cooke's sharpshooters, his brother, Lieutenant Tom Custer, a medical officer, a Blackfoot Indian named Neva, who had guided John C. Frémont, and the two chiefs, Little Robe and Yellow Bear. A last-minute addition to the party was a young Kansan named Brewster, who had arrived at Fort Cobb in search of a sister the Indians had carried away that summer.

With Neva leading the way, the little column marched nearly due west along the northern edge of the Wichitas, where it was expected the villages would be found. The westernmost peak was

8 General Sheridan's Interview with Little Robe and Yellow Bear, Jan. 1, 1869, S.-S. Papers, 137.

reached, however, with no trace of the Indians, and even though Little Robe and Yellow Bear climbed to the summit and sent up smoke signals, no response was observed. Undiscouraged, Custer sent a courier to Sheridan, now at Fort Sill, asking additional supplies, and then pushed on westward across the North Fork of the Red and into the Panhandle of Texas.

It was a punishing march on leg-weary mounts, but persistence was at length rewarded, for the Arapahoes were found encamped on Mulberry Creek, a tributary of Red River. Little Raven, the principal chief, gave the party a warm welcome, and immediately accepted the offer of peace. He promised within three days to start for Fort Sill with all his people, and he proved to be as good as his word.[9]

While Little Robe went on to look for his Cheyennes, Custer remained on Mulberry Creek until Lieutenant Cook, "California" Joe, and a dozen men arrived with fresh supplies. The chief did not return. Moreover, a march toward the headwaters of Red River, embracing several days, convinced the group that the Cheyennes were still far to the west and that further search was useless. Apparently these Indians preferred to be driven into the reservation, and Custer returned to Fort Sill anxious to lead a punitive column against them.

However a shortage of supplies and the poor condition of the animals delayed this campaign, so that not until March 2 was the expedition ready to move. It consisted of eleven troops of the Seventh Cavalry, ten companies of the Nineteenth Kansas, white scouts, and the Osage trailers. Having learned from Little Robe that white prisoners were in the Cheyenne camp, young Brewster went along, and so too did the beautiful Mo-nah-se-tah, who might be useful in locating her people.[10]

9 Custer, *Life on the Plains*, 277–79, 281–84, 288; Agent Boone to N. G. Taylor, Mar. 3, 1869, Office of Indian Affairs, Letters Received, Kiowa Agency.

10 Sheridan, *Personal Memoirs*, II, 344; Custer, *Life on the Plains*, 289–90, 298–99; David L. Spotts, *Campaigning with Custer and the Nineteenth Kansas Volunteer Cavalry on the Washita Campign*, 1868–69, 156; Report of Operations of Troops Operating South

Custer was not in full command. Sheridan, gone to Camp Supply to speed preparations, had there got notice of his promotion to lieutenant general and found orders summoning him to Washington at once. He was to succeed Sherman, who, following Grant's inauguration, had been assigned to command the Army of the United States. Major General J. M. Schofield became the new commanding general of the Department of the Missouri.

Custer's men marched westward around the southern end of the Wichitas, across the North Fork and Salt Fork of Red River to Gypsum Creek. After encamping, he selected from both regiments some eight hundred of the most fit, to continue the campaign. The remainder, being footsore or otherwise disabled, along with most of the train, were sent under Colonel Myers to a point near the Washita battleground, there to await further orders.

On the morning of March 6, Custer left the camp on Gypsum Creek and marched due west. Near noon smoke was observed some miles ahead. There a small fire still smoldered, and the Osages found a trail leading westward. This was followed with all speed. On the afternoon of the eighth scouts reported nine Cheyennes only a short distance away busily engaged in erecting lodges for shelter from the drizzling rain.

The cavalry went forward at a gallop, but Custer's staghounds, Maida and Blucher, had launched a prior attack on the camp dogs, and needing no better warning, the warriors took to their heels at once, abandoning all their property even to their ponies. Custer and his troopers were much chagrined to find that their quarry had flown, and their feelings were scarcely eased by the sly kidding of the Kansans, one of whom described the "battle" as resulting "in no casualties and no captures except two tents, eleven ponies, some blankets and some buffalo meat."[11]

The movement westward continued without further incident

---

of the Arkansas, Brevet Major General George A. Custer, Commanding, from March 2, 1869, to March 21, 1869, S.-S. Papers (hereinafter cited as "Report of Operations"), 219.

[11] Spotts, *Campaigning with Custer,* 145.

until the afternoon of the eleventh, when scouts struck the trail of a single lodge leading to the southwest. It seemed to promise little, but Custer, desperate now to find the Cheyennes, decided to follow it, and the decision proved fortunate, for after a short distance the trail broadened to include eleven other lodges.

The command encamped that evening on the headwaters of Mulberry Creek and next morning resumed the pursuit though on drastically reduced rations, for supplies were very low. The trail soon turned northward skirting the Llano Estacado. It increased constantly in size and by evening could have been followed at a gallop had the condition of the animals permitted. But all of them were leg-weary, and many had died.

With mule meat the sole fare, the column marched for the next two days along a trail that hourly became fresher and larger. And as the evidence placed them ever closer to a large village, Custer ordered the utmost caution; no bugle calls should sound, and the discharge of firearms was forbidden.

Early on the morning of the fifteenth they reached the North Fork and there discovered an abandoned camp not more than two days old. Near noon, and some twenty miles farther on, Hardrope, the Osage trailer, reported a large herd of ponies, tended by two Indian boys, only a mile to the front.

Moments later the herders, sighting the advancing troops, drove the ponies rapidly toward the timbered banks of Sweetwater Creek about three miles away. While the command closed ranks and prepared for action, Custer, with a small escort, rode forward toward the herd. Some two miles on they saw Indians watching them from near-by sand hills. Custer advanced with his orderly signaling for a parley, and after a brief interval, a few warriors came forward to meet him.

At last the Cheyennes had been found: the Indians reported that the entire tribe was encamped along the Sweetwater for a distance of ten or fifteen miles. Two hundred lodges under Medicine Arrow were on the command's immediate front, while Little Robe with sixty more was farther downstream. Knowing that white captives were in the village, Custer decided against initiating hostilities immediately and asked that Medicine Arrow, the principal chief, be informed that he wished a conference. A short while later the chieftain appeared with forty of his warriors and agreed to a talk —in the village. To this proposal Custer agreed, and, after sending back orders that the Indians were not to be attacked, he left his command behind and rode to the chief's lodge completely surrounded by warriors.[12]

News of this decision produced a storm of indignation among ill-disciplined Kansas troops, many of whom had lost relatives in the raids of the previous summer. Colonel Moore pronounced it "a wet blanket, saturated with ice water."[13] Men in the ranks denounced Custer as a "coward and a traitor." The officers had great difficulty in keeping them from firing on the Indians—first begging, then arguing, and finally cursing them into obedience.

Meanwhile the conference in the village accomplished little, although Medicine Arrow seemed friendly and gave assurances of peaceable intentions. After the talk he conducted his guest to a suitable campsite only three-quarters of a mile away but out of sight of the village. Thither the command moved to pitch its tents, while several score Indians, young and old, looked on.

Late in the afternoon lookouts reported that the villagers were preparing for a hasty flight. Apparently to veil the true intentions of their people, several chiefs and some musicians now arrived to entertain the troops. Custer, fearing to attack because of the white captives, promptly seized four of the chiefs, among them Dull Knife and Big Head, prominent Dog Soldiers, proposing to hold them hostages pending further talks.

Re-establishing contact proved no easy matter, however, for the village stood deserted, its thoroughly frightened occupants having

[12] "Report of Operations," 219ff., 223; Custer, *Life on the Plains,* 306–309. Custer stated in his official report that all the while he was planning "to administer a well merited punishment."

[13] Moore, "Nineteenth Kansas Cavalry," *loc. cit.,* 45.

fled toward Little Robe's camp farther downstream. At length, late in the evening, Custer released one of the chiefs with a message demanding release of all white prisoners and an immediate march by the Cheyennes to Fort Sill. He asked too a further talk with Little Robe.

Not until the next afternoon did the chief put in his appearance, but he quickly gave assurances of his best efforts to persuade his people to accept Custer's demands. He could not promise, however, that they would listen to him. Moreover, while he readily admitted that they were holding two white women as captives, he feared that their release could not be had without payment of a large ransom.

In reply Custer declared that the women must be surrendered unconditionally and at once. The command would move closer to the Indian encampment—although not in its immediate vicinity—to facilitate negotiations. The chief, still doubtful of success, departed after promising to send reports of his progress.

Two days of procrastination followed, angering the troops and exhausting Custer's patience. On the evening of the eighteenth he sent an ultimatum demanding return of the captives by sunset the next day. Otherwise he threatened to hang the hostages and attack the camps.

When midafternoon of the nineteenth brought no indications of compliance, Custer ordered ropes prepared and a tree selected. Then the chiefs were brought to the site and shown the limb they would adorn. But even as the nooses were pulled over their heads, a small party were seen approaching, and eager eyes discerned among them the captive women.

The Indians, after a vain effort to bargain for the freedom of their chiefs, reluctantly freed their prisoners. One of them proved to be a Miss Sarah White, taken some seven months earlier on the Republican River, while to the great joy of young Brewster, the other was his long-sought sister.

The campaign now came to a swift conclusion, for Medicine

Arrow decided to come to terms. The Cheyennes would come in as soon as their ponies were strong enough for the journey, while the three captive chiefs would remain as hostages until their people had actually reached the reservation.

Believing the Indians sincere, Custer felt his mission accomplished and without delay marched for Colonel Myers' camp on the Washita, reaching it in two days. The united command then marched to Camp Supply and thence to Fort Hays, where the Nineteenth Kansas was mustered out of service, and the Seventh Cavalry was allowed to rest and refit.

The hostages were placed in the fort stockade, along with the women and children captured on the Washita. All were to be returned to their people when the main body reached the reservation. Unfortunately, the post commander decided to separate the chiefs and confine them in the guardhouse; and since no adequate explanation was made, the Indians supposed they were being led to the gallows. Pulling knives from under their blankets, they attacked the guards, while a few women rushed to their assistance. Two soldiers suffered stab wounds. But Big Head was shot and instantly killed, a bayonet thrust mortally wounded Dull Knife, and Fat Bear was clubbed unconscious with rifle butts.[14]

Their people, meanwhile, though delayed by bad weather and weak ponies, for the most part kept their promises and came in to the reservation. By early April, Colonel Grierson, now commanding at Fort Sill, could report that all the Arapahoes were in except one band under Spotted Wolf, known to be on the way. He expected no further trouble if they were properly fed.[15]

The Cheyennes came more slowly and with greater reluctance.

---

[14] Custer, *Life on the Plains*, 326. No interpreter was at the post, and explanations were made only by crude signs. See also "Report of Operations," 224ff., 231.

[15] Col. Grierson to the Asst. Adj. Gen., Department of the Missouri, Apr. 7, 1869, S.-S. Papers, 272; Capt. Alvord to Col. Grierson, Apr. 24, 1869, in *ibid.*, 262–63; *Annual Report of the Commissioner of Indian Affairs for the Year 1869*, 81. The Arapahoes totaled about 220 lodges or approximately 1,200–1,500 people.

Little Robe, Minimic, Red Moon, and Grey Eyes reached Fort Sill on April 8. They informed Grierson that the Cheyennes were actually on their way in when Custer had appeared. His seizure of three of their principal men had then frightened many of the bands and caused them to flee in all directions.[16] In May and June some of these straggled in, but it was July before Medicine Arrow with sixty-five lodges reached Camp Supply.

There yet remained one prominent absentee. Tall Bull had no faith in the white man's word and preferred to take his chances on the Plains. With over two hundred warriors and their families, he had moved northward to join some Sioux and Northern Cheyennes on the headwaters of the Republican. In these favored hunting grounds, as had his people before him, he now proposed to live, and to die.

But if Tall Bull had any illusions of remaining undisturbed, they were rudely interrupted. On May 1, General Carr was ordered to move the Fifth Cavalry from Fort Lyon to Fort McPherson, scouting meanwhile between the Arkansas and the Platte for signs of hostiles. Reaching Beaver Creek on May 15, he found tracks of Indian ponies.

He immediately encamped and ordered Lieutenant E. W. Ward with ten men to make a reconnaissance downstream. Five miles on the detachment saw smoke rising ahead and a few minutes later came upon a large Indian encampment. They succeeded in withdrawing unseen, but as they hurried back to report their find, they ran headlong into a returning hunting party of Cheyennes and Sioux.

In the wild melee that followed Ward found himself surrounded. Bill Cody dashed through the encircling lines back to the main camp. Carr, galloping to the rescue, met Ward, who had cut his

---

[16] Grierson to the Asst. Adj. Gen., Department of the Missouri, Apr. 10, 1869, S.-S. Papers, 278. These chiefs represented sixty-seven lodges. One hundred and twenty were out. See *Annual Report of the Commissioner of Indian Affairs for the Year 1869*, 82–83.

way clear, and the whole command now drove for the village. More than five hundred warriors resisted desperately to save their families.

At nightfall the Indians broke off and fled, leaving Carr in possession of the field. Four troopers had been killed and three wounded, while the warriors had lost twenty-five killed and an estimated fifty wounded. Next morning the village was destroyed, and pursuit was undertaken along a north-bound trail.

Near noon of the sixteenth Lieutenant J. B. Babcock and Troop M, acting as an advance guard, overtook the Indians on Spring Creek in Nebraska. There four hundred warriors suddenly turned and faced him. Showing great courage, he remained calm, and ordered his frightened troopers to use their horses as breastworks, and himself remained in the saddle to direct their fire. His horse had been shot from under him and annihilation seemed imminent when the main body arrived and drove off the attackers. As the Indians now scattered in small parties, making further pursuit futile, Carr turned his column toward Fort McPherson, where he arrived on May 20.[17]

Tall Bull's revenge was swift. On May 21 he came down the Republican and struck the settlements in Republic County, killing six men and one woman. On Sunday, May 30, his warriors swept like a hurricane through the Saline homesteaders, killing and wounding thirteen persons and carrying off two women, a Mrs. Weichel and a Mrs. Alderdice. Nor was the hated railroad neglected, for they tore up two miles of track on the Kansas Pacific near Fossil Creek, Kansas.

The task of running down Tall Bull fell to Carr and his regiment of Fifth Cavalry. While at Fort McPherson early in June, Carr received orders to clear the Republican country of Indians. Assembled and ready to move on June 9, the expedition consisted of eight

---

[17] Price, *Across the Continent with the Fifth Cavalry*, 134f.; *Record of Engagements*, 18; "Fifth Cavalry," 82. For his part in this action Lieutenant Babcock received the Medal of Honor. See also W. F. Beyer and J. Keydel, eds., *Deeds of Valor*, I, 148.

troops of regulars and the famed Pawnee scouts under Major Frank J. North. William F. Cody was again employed as guide.[18]

The command reached the Republican near the mouth of Dog Creek, and almost immediately discovered a week-old trail which led upstream. Pursuit proved difficult, for the Indians did not follow the course of the river directly. Rather they kept several miles from it, scattering by day and coming together again on the hard, dry prairie by night. Moreover they drove their animals in all directions and produced such a profusion of tracks that even the Pawnees were often befuddled.[19]

No Indians had yet been seen when the command encamped near 5:00 P.M. of June 15 on the banks of the Republican. But as the animals were being led to water a small party of Cheyennes charged the herd and attempted to stampede it, an effort which failed due to the alertness of the Pawnees. Major W. B. Royall took three companies and gave chase but was unable to overtake the marauders.

The march continued slowly westward with scouting parties searching vainly along tributaries of the river. On July 5, Royall, while scouting along Frenchman's Fork with three troops and fifty Pawnees, surprised twelve Cheyenne warriors and killed three of them. When Carr was informed, he decided to move the whole command up Frenchman's Fork and follow the warriors' trail, hoping it would eventually lead to the main camp.

By the morning of the tenth, as his column neared the South

18 "Fifth Cavalry," 82–83; Price, *Across the Continent with the Fifth Cavalry*, 135. Frank North, with his brothers James E. and Luther H., was raised on the Plains frontier and established a firm and friendly contact with the Pawnee Indians. During the outbreak of 1864, Pawnee scouts were used effectively in defense of the Union Pacific Railroad. Shortly thereafter Frank North was authorized to enroll a company of them, and to equip and uniform them like the regular cavalry. They rendered great service and in March, 1869, North, then a major, enlisted three companies of fifty men each, and was ordered early in the summer to report to Carr at Fort McPherson. See George B. Grinnell, *Two Great Scouts and Their Pawnee Battalion*, 18–180.

19 Report of Operations of the Republican River Expedition, Bvt. Maj. Gen. E. A. Carr, Commanding, from June 31 to July 30, 1869, S.-S. Papers (hereinafter cited as Carr, "Republican River Expedition"), 318.

Platte, the trail grew warm. Carr now left his train behind and with three days' rations pushed forward with all possible speed. So vigorously in fact did he pursue that he gained undetected, and unbeknown to himself, a position on the Indians' front. On the morning of the eleventh, with the Platte visible from bluffs on the south side, he ordered Royall to take two troops and one hundred Pawnees, scout along the riverbank, and determine if the hostiles had crossed, although he suspected that they were actually in his rear.

Shortly thereafter Cody proved his commander correct, for he came in to report that he had sighted a large pony herd some six miles away in a southwesterly direction. Eagerly the remaining troops and scouts advanced, taking cover by ravines and sand hills, until 1:30 P.M., when they halted about a mile north of Summit Springs in Colorado. There they expected to find the village.

While his Pawnees stripped for the fight, Carr formed the command into three columns. One company was placed on the left and another on the right, under Lieutenants George F. Price and John P. Walker respectively. These were to turn the flanks and drive on beyond to round up the pony herd now visible grazing two miles to the south. The center, under the immediate command of Major E. W. Crittenden, would make a frontal assault.

In a matter of minutes the columns were in position, and the advance began at a slow trot. At first a strong south wind kept the sound of drumming hooves from the unsuspecting village. Only a quarter of a mile had been covered, however, when a warrior on a fine white horse, riding near the pony herd, spied the troops and dashed at full cry to give the alarm.

Carr immediately ordered the trumpeters to sound a charge, and the whole command raced full tilt for the village now plainly in sight. The surprise was complete. Crittenden struck the encampment furiously, and the Cheyennes fled in all directions. Price turned the left flank, killing seven Indians, and went on to capture three hundred animals. The warrior and his white horse were cut down by a volley even as they reached the village.

Walker, however, found his progress barred by a large depression, and some of the villagers thus gained an avenue of escape. Tall Bull managed to find horses for his wife and little daughter but refused to run for it himself. With several others, he retreated to a deep ravine, killed his pony at the entrance, and there made his stand.

Surrounded by Major North and his Pawnees, the warriors in the ravine cut hand- and footholds up the sides in order to reach the rim and fire at their attackers. One by one they were picked off as they exposed themselves, and after twenty had been killed no more shots were heard. Among the bodies was that of Tall Bull.

Those Indians who managed to escape the village were pursued for several miles, and many were either killed or captured. Meanwhile, troopers searching the deserted lodges found the body of Mrs. Alderdice, her head horribly crushed, while from a tipi near the outskirts Mrs. Weichel crawled toward her rescuers, blood streaming from a bullet wound in her breast.[20]

As the afternoon waned, pursuit ended and the command encamped near the village. Carr, with but a single man wounded, could count fifty-two dead Indians. Seventeen women and children had been captured, among them Tall Bull's wife and child. Over four hundred animals had been taken with much other property including dried meat, buffalo robes, saddles, bows and arrows, and nearly one hundred rifles and revolvers. Next morning the village was destroyed, and the return to Fort McPherson began.[21]

[20] Grinnell, *Two Great Scouts,* 198; Carr, "Republican River Expedition," 318–19, 321–24. Mrs. Weichel recovered from her wounds. See also "Fifth Cavalry." 83.

[21] *Record of Engagements,* 22; Carr, "Republican River Expedition," 323–27; Grinnell, *Fighting Cheyennes,* 307; Proceedings of a Board Convened by Special Order No. 17, Headquarters, Republican River Expedition, Camp Cheyenne, July 11, 1869, S.-S. Papers, 329–30. A partial list of the property showed 274 horses, 144 mules, $1,500 in gold and currency, 9,300 pounds of dried meat, 100 pounds of tobacco, 361 saddles, 690 buffalo robes, 50

Carr's pursuit and defeat of Tall Bull broke the spirit of those Cheyennes remaining off the reservation, and now these bands too came in. In his report to Sherman, Sheridan indicated that all the tribes south of the Platte had been forced onto the reservations set aside for them. There they were available for "the good work of civilization, education, and religious instruction."[22] Time would prove the General's report overly optimistic.

Actually he had a good deal of unfinished business on his hands. His columns had not penetrated the Department of Texas, where recalcitrant bands of Kiowas and Comanches, still "out," were scarcely available for "the good work of civilization." Moreover, the bands of these tribes that had entered the reservation, unchastened by military defeat, contained many chiefs and subchiefs only too willing to lead raiders south of the Red. The year 1869 was a bloody one in the history of the Texas frontier.

pounds of powder, 20 pounds of bullets, 56 rifles, 22 revolvers, 200 lariats, 180 tin plates, 17 sabers, and an estimated 10 tons of flour, coffee, corn meal, articles of clothing, toys, and other equipment.

[22] *Annual Report of the Secretary of War for the Year 1869,* 43.

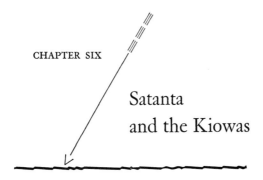

CHAPTER SIX

Satanta

and the Kiowas

THE WINTER CAMPAIGN OF 1868–
69 had driven the Southern Plains Indians in to their agencies at
Fort Sill and Camp Supply, and their control again reverted to the
Indian Bureau, charged with launching the "good work of civilization."[1] Severe criticism, however, even in the halls of a patronage-
conscious Congress, greeted the restoration of civil authority because of the Indian Service's notorious record of corruption and
inefficiency. Demands for its reform came from all sections of the

---

[1] The Cheyennes and Arapahoes refused to accept the reservation set aside for them at
Medicine Lodge and asked for another on the North Fork of the Canadian. This request
was approved by an executive order on August 10, 1869, which provided for a tract of
4,011,500 acres. It was May, 1870, however, before their agency was removed from Camp
Supply to the point at which the military road from Fort Harker to Fort Sill crossed the
North Fork of the Canadian. *Annual Report of the Commissioner of Indian Affairs for
the Year 1869*, 35; *Annual Report of the Commissioner of Indian Affairs for the Year 1870*,
265; *Annual Report of the Commissioner of Indian Affairs for the Year 1872*, 42; Hodge,
Handbook, II, 382; Bvt. Col. A. D. Nelson, Tenth Cavalry, Commanding at Camp Supply,
to the Asst. Adj. Gen., Department of the Missouri, June 22, 1869, S.-S. Papers, 313–14.

country, while a large body of public opinion favored continuance of military control.[2]

In its final report, made in October, 1868, the Indian Peace Commission had recommended that all superintendents and agents be removed and be replaced by competent appointees. The recently inaugurated Grant administration, sensitive to popular outcry, now acted on this recommendation. Moreover, in order to minimize political influence in the selection of new agents, their nomination was delegated to religious organizations interested in the work.

The most enthusiastic response came from the Society of Friends, old advocates of such a policy, and Quaker agents were soon assigned to both the central and the northern superintendencies. While other churches showed interest, they encountered such difficulty in finding suitable candidates that Grant had to give the remaining superintendencies, except that of Oregon, to army officers.[3]

Congress carried the reform still further. Under the fourth section of an appropriations act for the Indian Department, approved on April 10, 1869, the President was empowered to appoint nine prominent citizens to a Board of Indian Commissioners. These, with the Secretary of Interior, were to exercise joint control over disbursement of the appropriation. They were to have unlimited

---

[2] In the spring of 1869, Republican Representative James A. Garfield of Ohio had this to say of the Indian Bureau: "...after a considerable study of this subject, I am compelled to say that no branch of the national government is so spotted with fraud, so tainted with corruption, so utterly unworthy of a free and enlightened government, as this Indian department." Quoted in Schmeckebier, Office of Indian Affairs, 48–49. Loring B. Priest, *Uncle Sam's Stepchildren: The Reformation of United States Indian Policy, 1865–1887,* 29; *Annual Report of the Commissioner of Indian Affairs for the Year 1869,* 5. In a supplemental report the Indian Peace Commission recommended that control of Indian affairs be given to the War Department. *Annual Report of the Commissioner of Indian Affairs for the Year 1868,* 371.

[3] *Annual Report of the Commissioner of Indian Affairs for the Year 1869,* 5; Priest, *Uncle Sam's Stepchildren,* 29–30; Sherman, *Memoirs,* II, 437. Of 145 candidates the Methodists found all but one lacking in either ability or honesty or both. The army officers were soon compelled to surrender these posts, for on July 15, 1870, Congress passed an act providing that any officer on the active list accepting a civil appointment must vacate his commission. See Schmeckebier, *Office of Indian Affairs,* 54–55.

access to the records of the Indian office, and to inspect at will the various superintendencies and agencies.

Grant made the necessary appointments immediately, and within a month the commissioners were hard at work. Unfortunately, as their authority had been ill-defined, they soon found themselves involved with the Indian office, which sought to nullify their efforts. Furthermore, although they expended much energy in visiting the reservations and in interviewing the Indians, they found they could command little respect from the canny chiefs. These had quickly learned that the Board lacked authority to carry out their plans.[4]

Because the new policy emphasized peace, the Secretaries of War and Interior had to be called upon to redefine the role of the army. Henceforth, they agreed, Indians on the reservations would be under the exclusive control of their agents, who might, however, in extreme circumstances, call on the military for assistance. Those remaining off the reservations would be under jurisdiction of the army and would normally be regarded as hostile.[5]

This new policy, and a declining need for troops on occupation duty in the South, could only mean a drastic reduction in the size of the armed forces. By an act of March 3, 1869, Congress forbade all promotions, enlistments, and new commissions in the infantry until the number of regiments should be reduced from forty-five to twenty-five. The War Department complied by allowing enlistments to expire, and, at a high cost in morale, immediately discharged supernumerary officers.

These reductions brought the country's armed forces to a dangerously low level. Fewer than twelve thousand officers and men

---

[4] Priest, *Uncle Sam's Stepchildren*, 44–47; *Annual Report of the Board of Indian Commissioners for the Year 1869*, 3. The appointees were W. E. Dodge and Nathan Bishop of New York, William Welsh and George H. Stuart of Philadelphia, John V. Farwell of Chicago, Robert Campbell of St. Louis, E. S. Tobey of Boston, Felix R. Brunot of Pittsburgh, and Henry Lane of Indiana.

[5] Commissioner of Indian Affairs to All Superintendents and Agents, June 12, 1869, Kiowa Files, Military Relations, Indian Archives, Oklahoma Historical Society, Oklahoma City, Oklahoma (hereinafter cited as Kiowa Files, followed by folder designations).

occupied the garrisons and patrolled the vast hills and plains of the Departments of Texas and Missouri. Should the new peace policy fail of success and a major outbreak occur, the army would be hard-pressed to deal with it.[6]

While the army was assuming once more a secondary role, the Quaker agents were taking up their work with energy and enthusiasm. On July 1, 1869, Lawrie Tatum arrived at Fort Sill as agent for the Kiowas, Comanches, and Kiowa-Apaches, to relieve General Hazen, who returned to military duty.

Though without much knowledge of the manifold duties and responsibilities of an Indian agent, Tatum set to work at once, supported by a bountiful endowment of raw courage, rigid honesty, and native ability. He first moved the agency, which Hazen had located on Cache Creek across from the post office and commissary, on ground subject to flooding, to the higher side of the stream. Then he began erection of a schoolhouse and of dwellings for the agency employees. As autumn approached, he arranged for purchase of a steam engine, sawmill equipment, and a shingling machine.

Meanwhile, his courage and fair dealing had won him the respect of his charges, and he used this influence to urge upon them the planting and cultivation of corn, vegetables, and melons. Here, however, he got meager results, for although the men often promised to provide teams for plowing, they actually despised farming: they considered it woman's work and always found excuses to avoid the sowing. Otherwise their behavior was reasonably good— on the reservation.

Meanwhile Kiowa and Comanche bands—off the reservation— made the year 1869 one of the bloodiest in the history of the Texas frontier. Beginning in the spring, small parties slipped across Red

---

[6] Spaulding, *United States Army in War and Peace,* 341, 493. By November, 1870, when reorganization had been completed, the army comprised four military divisions and ten departments, with a total strength of 34,780 enlisted men and 2,488 officers. *Annual Report of the Secretary of War for the Year 1870,* 3.

River in ever-increasing numbers. They struck over a wide area, often penetrating far into the settlements. Equally active were the powerful Kwahadis, who, taking an occasional scalp, were chiefly bent on acquiring horses and cattle, which they stole "with impunity."[7]

As the raiding season advanced, the scale of operations increased, and the raiders grew bolder. Early in July a war party struck along Mary's Creek near Weatherford, ran off some stock, and remained in the vicinity for several days. They killed and scalped four persons before a posse of aroused citizens forced them to flee. In September a band of Comanches near Jacksboro rounded up more than one hundred horses and chased a former owner to within a mile of the town itself.[8]

The slender forces at the disposal of Major General J. J. Reynolds, commanding the Department of Texas, could not cope with the ever-elusive red men. In response to frantic calls for protection, coming from all quarters of the frontier, Reynolds authorized the formation of county militia to assist the regulars. Even the combined forces were, however, inadequate to plug the sievelike defenses. Indeed that stretch of Red River bordering the reservation became an "open hole" through which the raiding bands poured with little fear of interception.[9]

Reports of these depredations greatly distressed Lawrie Tatum. In interviews with Kiowa and Comanche chiefs he warned them

[7] Tabular Statement of Indian Depredations, Enclosure "A," Annual Report of the Department of Texas for the year 1869, Records of the War Department, Adjutant General's Office, File No. 1161–M–1869 (hereinafter cited as File No. 1161–M–1869), 3; Post Returns, Fort Griffin, June, 1869.

[8] *Annual Report of the Department of Texas for the Year 1869*, 2; H. Smythe, *Historical Sketch of Parker County and Weatherford, Texas*, 122–24; Tabular Statement of Indian Depredations, File No. 1161–M–1869, 5.

[9] *Annual Report of the Department of Texas for the Year 1869*, 2. The Indians did not always escape unscathed. A scouting party from Fort Griffin intercepted a band of Kiowa and Comanche raiders near the Double Mountain west of the fort and killed fourteen of them. Maj. Gen. J. J. Reynolds to the Adj. Gen., Washington, D.C., May 28, 1869, Records of the War Department, Adjutant General's Office, Letters Received, File No. 1166–M–1869.

repeatedly: the government was displeased, and they must stop their raiding. One chief merely replied that if Washington wanted his young men to cease their depredations, then Washington must move Texas far away where they could not find it.

The Indians also pointed out that only by such ill behavior could they get an increase in rations and annuities. If they should go on the warpath, kill some whites, and fight the soldiers, then the government would have to step in, make peace, and shower them with presents. They pointed, on the other hand, to the poverty-ridden Wichitas. These had long followed the white man's road, and they had been rewarded with the loss of all their lands.

Raiding declined in September as a major portion of all three tribes moved up the Washita for the annual fall hunt. Late in the month Mow-way and Ten Bears came in for rations, called on Colonel Grierson, and informed him that there was "no bad talk" among the Indians, that all would be back on Cache Creek before cold weather. Tatum's tribal roll, however, taken on November 30, showed many of the bands still off the reservation. Among these were the Kiowas of Satanta, Lone Wolf, Timbered Mountain, and Big Bow, and the Comanches of Iron Jacket and Parry-O-Corn. All of the Kwahadis, believed to number 1,950 souls, were of course still "out."[10]

In Washington an indignant General Sherman wrote William W. Belknap, secretary of war, that the Kiowas, Comanches, and Kiowa-Apaches had been leaving the reservation constantly to raid in Texas, and that he had no power to punish them. Their agent, who enjoyed sole jurisdiction, not only allowed them to come and go at will but furnished them food and clothing "while . . . on their predatory expeditions."[11] The General's criticism, although not entirely just, indicated how inauspicious had been the beginning of the peace policy.

---

[10] Col. Grierson to Agent Tatum, Sept. 30, 1869, Kiowa Files, Military Relations; Manuscript List of Indians, Kiowas, Comanches, and Apaches, Nov. 30, 1869, in *ibid.*
[11] Belknap to C. Delano, Secretary of Interior, Jan. 19, 1870, in *ibid.*

Rumors of fresh trouble came to Tatum early in 1870. As spring came on, the old restlessness stirred the Indian camps and reports reached the agent that his charges were getting guns, ammunition, and whisky from unscrupulous traders operating along the Canadian. Even those few who had earlier shown some interest in farming now refused to plant a crop. Disturbing reports came too from the Cheyenne-Arapaho reservation. There Quaker agent Brinton Darlington watched with growing concern the spread of disaffection among the Cheyennes. Medicine Arrow and Bull Bear were off the reservation with two hundred of their people, and Darlington was not sure of their whereabouts.

Harried troopers of the Tenth Cavalry at Camp Supply could have given the agent at least a partial answer. Bold Cheyenne warriors ran off stock within sight of the post and easily eluded pursuit. Strong escorts were necessary to insure the safety of supply trains on the Fort Dodge–Camp Supply road, and even these did not escape attack. Constant scouting produced little more than worn-out horses and men.[12]

Not until early June, however, did the significance of these portents begin to emerge. Then, at the great Kiowa Sun Dance, well attended by the Comanches, Kiowa-Apaches, and Cheyennes, many of the Indians decided to stay out on the Plains and take up the warpath.

Thus, when the dance ended, small parties fanned out in all directions to kill and plunder. On June 8, Cheyenne hostiles struck a train north of Camp Supply but were driven off by Troop F of the Tenth Cavalry escorting the train. Two troopers were wounded. Three days later Cheyenne warriors challenged the garrison at Camp Supply and withdrew only after an hour's skirmish with every available trooper at the post. On the same day three woodcutters were killed and scalped north of Supply on the Fort Dodge road. Throughout the rest of the month scouting detachments of

---

[12] Post Returns, Camp Supply, May, 1870; Organizational Returns, Tenth Cavalry, May, 1870.

the Tenth had almost daily brushes with small Cheyenne war parties.[13]

It was the Kiowas, however, who gave the most trouble. On June 12, White Horse, an inveterate Kiowa raider, led seven warriors to the quartermaster's corral at Fort Sill and made off with seventy-three mules. Captain J. W. Walsh, with two companies of Tenth Cavalry, took after the marauders but soon lost their trail in a maze of fresh buffalo tracks.

Ten days later the Kiowas struck again. Late that evening five warriors rode up to where some citizens employed by the quartermaster were encamped about two hundred yards from the agency. Without warning they opened fire, critically wounding one Levi Lucans. They then proceeded to the beef corral a mile away, killed a Mexican, and stole some horses. As a finishing touch they dashed among the agency buildings, yelling and shooting their guns. All of Tatum's employees, except the two schoolteachers, Joseph and Lizzie Butler, resigned forthwith.[14]

And once again the red raiders scourged the Texas frontier, killing fifteen persons in Jack County alone within the space of a month. In the Indian camps such chiefs as Ten Bears and Kicking Bird, those who had "taken the white man's hand" and held it firmly, found their counsel scorned. The latter, a warrior of real military ability, heard himself called a woman and a coward.[15]

Driven to desperation by these charges, and determined to restore his lost prestige, Kicking Bird gathered one hundred warriors and rode into Texas. On July 5 he hurled the gauntlet at Fort Richardson's Sixth Cavalry by capturing the mail stage at Rock

13 Post Returns, Camp Supply, June, 1870; Post Returns, Fort Dodge, July, 1870; Organizational Returns, Tenth Cavalry, June, 1870.

14 Tatum to Enoch Hoag, Supt. of the Central Superintendency, June 22, 1870, Kiowa Files, Depredations; Joseph Butler, "Pioneer School Teaching," *Chronicles of Oklahoma,* Vol. VI (Dec., 1928), 493; Tatum, *Our Red Brothers,* 33.

15 The Austin *Daily Journal* (May 14, 1871) contains a list of Indian depredations in Jack County from 1859 to May, 1871. See also Thomas C. Battey, *The Life and Adventures of a Quaker among the Indians,* 102–103. Battey, a teacher, lived with Kicking Bird's band for many months.

Station, sixteen miles west of the post. Captain C. B. McClellan with fifty-three troopers answered the challenge.[16]

Although a severe rainstorm slowed his pursuit, McClellan, on the morning of July 12, near the site of Henrietta, intercepted the Indians and prepared to charge. But he found quickly that he faced no ordinary antagonist. The chieftain coolly divided his force, and while skirmishing on the front, sent fleet detachments to strike the troopers on both flanks and threaten the pack train in their rear. Practically surrounded, McClellan dismounted his command and retreated, the men firing meanwhile from between the horses.

For the next eight hours, under a burning sun, the Indians drove the troopers from crest to crest on the rolling prairie until at last, with the approach of nightfall, Kicking Bird broke off the action. Next morning McClellan led his battered command back to Fort Richardson, reporting three men killed and twelve wounded. As for Kicking Bird, having proven his courage and ability, he now turned all his energy toward leading his people along the path of peace.[17]

So widespread had been the attacks that Tatum began to fear a major outbreak. However, in mid-July, Kiowa and Comanche runners brought word that the tribes desired to be friendly again, wishing to return and draw their rations. To this the agent could agree if they would assure him of their future good behavior and return the stolen stock.

On August 7 the principal Kiowa chiefs, along with several hundred of their people, reached the agency, returned a few of the stolen mules, and asked for rations. Meanwhile, however, Tatum had learned that White Horse had been to Texas, had killed a Mr. Koozer, and had taken captive Mrs. Koozer, her five

---

[16] Post Returns, Fort Richardson, July, 1870; Horace Jones, interpreter, to Tatum, Dec. 6, 1870, Office of Indian Affairs, Letters Received, Kiowa Agency. Jones told Tatum that Lone Wolf, Satank, Stumbling Bear, and White Horse accompanied Kicking Bird, as did thirty Cheyennes under White Beard.

[17] Nye, *Carbine and Lance,* 145; Post Returns, Fort Richardson, July 1870; Battey, *A Quaker among the Indians,* 103.

children, and a boy named Martin Kilgore. Determined to secure the release of these prisoners and to deliver a stern lecture to the Kiowas about their Texas raids, he arranged for a council and asked Colonel Grierson to attend.[18]

In one of the commissary buildings Tatum, Grierson, and their interpreters met with the chiefs and nearly one hundred of their warriors. There were no soldiers within a quarter of a mile. The agent warned his guests that their depredations were certain to incur the wrath of the government and loose the soldiers against them. Furthermore, he would pay no ransom nor would he issue any rations until their captives had been released. Grierson spoke in a similar vein, insisting that they must follow the white man's road.

Satanta replied by saying that he liked breech-loading guns and the scalping knife; that bad Indians got the most while those who submitted to the white man got nothing; and that since Grierson and Tatum were mad, "we might as well keep what we have and get all we can." As the chiefs concluded several warriors snapped cartridges into their guns, others strung their bows and drew arrows, while one pulled a knife from his belt and, standing in front of Tatum, began sharpening it on a whetstone. In imminent danger, Grierson went calmly to Satanta, took the chief's hand, and through the interpreter told him that he was not angry, that there was business to attend to, and that all must keep cool. Lone Wolf, with studied insolence, strolled over to Tatum, ran his hand under the agent's vest and placed it over his heart to see if he could "feel any scare." He found it beating normally.[19]

---

[18] Tatum, *Our Red Brothers*, 40–41; Austin *Daily Journal* (May 14, 1871). Grierson gave the peace policy his full support. In a letter to Tatum he wrote: ". . . it seems from recent events that in certain quarters I am considered rather too much of a Quaker myself for a soldier. . . . had I only launched out and killed a few Indians . . . I would no doubt have been considered by certain parties, successful. . . . I will not for the sake of material interests or for personal advancement seek to gain an opportunity to kill off some Indians and bring on a war." Sept. 30, 1869, Kiowa Files, Military Relations.

[19] G. W. Conover, *Sixty Years in Southwest Oklahoma*, 23–24; Tatum, *Our Red Brothers*, 42–44.

Thus the cold courage of two brave men calmed the excited Indians. Indeed when they departed, they assured Tatum that they desired peace and would comply with his terms. A few days later the whole tribe reached the agency and surrendered the captive Koozers. Tatum then issued the rations but refused a request for a more liberal supply of ammunition.

While the chiefs again promised to be good, the agent placed little faith in these assurances. The incessant raiding, and their bad behavior around the agency, were slowly undermining his confidence in the peace policy. In August he wrote the Executive Committee of Friends in Philadelphia that the depredations would not cease until the guilty were punished. If the Indians refused to surrender the raiders, then force must be used to take and punish the wrongdoers.[20] Such un-Quakerlike opinions were not for the Committee. While they were much grieved, they replied, to hear that the Kiowas were resisting the President's policy, the agent must stick to reporting facts and cease making suggestions: ". . . our appreciation of Christian truth would certainly forbid a recommendation that a squad of armed men should be sent in pursuit of the Indians."[21]

The Kiowa chiefs White Horse and Satank did much to confirm Tatum's opinion. During the fall and winter they constantly prowled the north Texas frontier, killing, scalping, and stealing. Shortly after the affair at the agency White Horse, with seven followers, left the reservation. Late on the afternoon of September 5 his band approached the double log house, on Denton Creek six miles southwest of Montague, which J. B. Maxey shared with T. W. Beall.

Maxey and Beall were away on business, but their wives were strolling in the yard, Mrs. Maxey carrying an infant in her arms. At the woodpile near the house Grandfather Maxey was gathering

20 Tatum to the Executive Committee of the Friends, Aug. 6, 1870, Kiowa Files, Depredations.
21 John Garrett to Tatum, Aug. 21, 1870, Kiowa Files, Foreign Relations.

wood, assisted by his grandchildren, Rhoda and Valentine, and the two Beall children, Annie and Hezekiah.

Using a ravine which intersected the creek some distance below the house, the savages, unobserved, could creep very close. Suddenly emerging, they opened fire, killing the Beall boy and mortally wounding the old man. Annie Beall, running toward her mother, was overtaken and slain while both the Maxey children were captured. The two women escaped to the house and slammed the door, but not before a bullet had pierced Mrs. Maxey's arm, killing her babe, and another had plowed a furrow along Mrs. Beall's head.[22]

Three weeks later the heartbroken Maxey reached the agency, reported the tragedy, and begged Tatum to recover his children. With the aid of an Apache chief, Pacer, Tatum did eventually rescue Valentine. Rhoda, it seems, had been murdered because she cried too much.[23]

In December, Satank, the worst Indian on the reservation in Tatum's opinion, led a raid into Parker County, Texas, killed three men, and stole some horses and mules. After his return he had the gall to boast of his exploit to the post interpreter at Fort Sill.

Late in the winter these forays declined somewhat, but neither Tatum nor Grierson dared entertain a hope that the new year would bring any change for the better. Kicking Bird reported that few of the Kiowa bands were reliable. Lone Wolf said that the Kwahadis were determined to drive back the Texas settlements two or three days' journey. Moreover, small parties of Cheyennes had been active south of the Red and would surely act in concert with the Kiowas and Comanches.[24]

[22] J. M. Franks, *Seventy Years in Texas*, 61ff.; Tatum to Enoch Hoag, Sept. 26 and Nov. 4, 1870, Kiowa Files, Depredations.

[23] Tatum, *Our Red Brothers*, 50–51. Recovery of the boy took nearly three years, for he had been traded to the Kwahadis with whom communication was difficult.

[24] Tatum to Enoch Hoag, Nov. 15 and Dec. 9, 1870, Kiowa Files, Depredations; Capt. J. P. Schindel, Sixth Infantry, Camp Supply, to the Asst. Adj. Gen., Department of the Missouri, Feb. 16, 1871, Cheyenne-Arapaho Files, Military Relations, Indian Archives,

Early in 1871, Satanta and Satank were again at work brewing trouble for the Texans, and by March, Tatum was convinced that they intended to provoke a general war. The usual spring restlessness was aggravated by a delay in the annuities and by the appearance of surveying parties on the reservation. Would there now soon be a railroad to frighten off the game?

Reconciled at last to calling on the military, Tatum formally requested Colonel Grierson to conduct patrols along Red River. These should endeavor to control those points where hostiles from the reservation usually crossed into Texas. Grierson immediately placed two companies of the Tenth Cavalry at the mouth of Cache Creek to scout for southbound war parties and if possible to turn them back. These hundred men were all the commander at Fort Sill could spare, but ten times their number could not have done the job.[25]

Fears of an outbreak were not confined to the Texas frontier. Reports of Indian discontent had also disturbed Major General John Pope, who had replaced Schofield as commanding general of the Department of the Missouri. Gravely concerned for the safety of western Kansas, Pope early disposed his troops to drive off raiding bands should they appear. At the same time he urged Enoch Hoag, superintendent of the central superintendency, to use every available means to quiet the rising unrest.[26]

Meantime the expressed fears of Indian agents and army officers had led the Department of Interior to invite the southwestern tribes to send delegations to Washington. There, it was hoped, kind treatment and a personal experience of the power and resources of

Oklahoma Historical Society, Oklahoma City, Oklahoma (hereinafter cited as Cheyenne-Arapaho Files, followed by folder designations).

[25] Tatum to Grierson, March 25, 1871, Kiowa Files, Depredations; Annual Report of the Military Division of the Missouri, Records of the War Department, Adjutant General's Office, Letters received, File No. 1305–1871 (hereinafter cited as File No. 1305–1871).

[26] Maj. Gen. John Pope to the Adj. Gen., Military Division of the Missouri, Feb. 1, 1871, Kiowa Files, Depredations; Maj. Gen. John Pope to the Adj. Gen., Military Division of the Missouri, Feb. 8, 1871, Cheyenne-Arapaho Files, Depredations.

the government might dispose the delegates to urge caution upon their tribal brothers.[27]

The plan was only partially successful, for the Kiowas and Comanches refused to send anyone. However, chiefs from the Cheyennes and Arapahoes, among them Little Robe, Stone Calf, and Little Raven, were brought to the capital and other Eastern cities and there royally entertained. When they returned home, both Darlington and Lieutenant Colonel J. W. Davidson, new commanding officer at Camp Supply, reported them so impressed that there could be little to fear from their people, at least for the rest of 1871.

The Civilized Tribes of Indian Territory also made an effort to promote peace. At their annual council, held in Okmulgee, they passed a resolution declaring their willingness to meet and "talk" with their unruly neighbors. The result was a council held at the Wichita Agency early in May. Little was accomplished, however: many prominent men of the civilized tribes spoke eloquently of the white man's road, but few of the Kiowas and Comanches attended, and those who did were in no mood to listen. Even Kicking Bird rose to speak bitterly of the lands taken away from his people.

Meanwhile Texan demands for more protection were reaching Washington in an ever-increasing volume. By a formal resolution the state legislature pointed out that in the preceding five years the Indians had "murdered several hundreds of the citizens of Texas, have stolen and destroyed property to the amount of millions of dollars in value, have not only retarded the settlement of the frontier counties of the State, but have almost depopulated several counties thereof."[28] General Sherman and the Commissioner of Indian Affairs were deluged with letters. Typical was one from I. P. Vollintine of Weatherford, who declared that with-

[27] *Annual Report of the Board of Indian Commissioners for the Year 1871,* 4. The visits were conducted under the auspices of the Board of Indian Commissioners.

[28] U.S. Congress, *Sen. Misc. Doc. No. 37,* 42 Cong., 1 sess., 1–2.

in the three weeks prior to his writings, nine persons had been killed and scalped in his vicinity. "For God's sake," he wrote, "see if anything can be done for us."[29]

Sherman, disinclined to accept these reports at face value, felt that he could not ignore them either. He decided on a personal inspection to get a firsthand view of conditions. Accompanied by Inspector General Randolph B. Marcy, he reached San Antonio on April 28. A few days later the two officers, escorted by seventeen troopers of the Tenth Cavalry, started for the frontier outposts.

Fair weather attended their journey, and the party arrived at Fort Richardson on May 17, after traveling a vast semicircle via Forts McKavett, Concho, and Griffin. Not an Indian had been seen, but there had been constant reports of depredations. Moreover, Marcy, who long before had surveyed much of the region traversed, noted that in the area just west of Fort Richardson many ranches had been abandoned because of Indian raids. ". . . indeed this rich and beautiful section does not contain today so many white people as it did when I visited it eighteen years ago."[30]

That evening Sherman conferred with the post commander, Colonel Ranald S. Mackenzie, Fourth Cavalry, a brilliant young officer whom he trusted. Next day a delegation of Jacksboro citizens, citing a long list of outrages, told him that raids by reservation Indians had been almost continuous. Sherman listened politely, but his own trip along the frontier had been so uneventful that he was inclined to believe his informants exaggerated.[31]

---

[29] I. P. Vollentine to E. S. Parker, Jan. 19, 1871, Kiowa Files, Depredations.

[30] Extracts from Inspector General R. B. Marcy's Journal of an Inspection Tour while Accompanying the General in Chief during the Months of April, May, and June, 1871 Phillips Collection, University of Oklahoma, Norman (hereinafter cited as Marcy's Journal), 187, 191.

[31] Post Returns, Fort Richardson, May, 1871; Robert G. Carter, *On the Border with Mackenzie*, 76–80. After graduation at the head of the West Point class of 1862, Mackenzie's rise had been spectacular. Three times wounded and three times brevetted for gallantry in action, he was a brevet brigadier general at the close of the Civil War. In the reorganization following the war he was appointed colonel of the Forty-first Infantry and served for nearly three years along the Río Grande. In 1870 he became colonel of the Fourth Cavalry. See George W. Cullum, *Biographical Register of Officers and Graduates*

Late that night, however, a lone man, wounded and near exhaustion, staggered into the post hospital. He identified himself as Thomas Brazeale, a teamster, and as his wounds were attended, he told a frightful story. With eleven other employees of freighter Henry Warren, he had been engaged in driving a ten-wagon train, loaded with corn, from Weatherford to Fort Griffin. On the afternoon of May 18, while on the open prairie about ten miles east of Salt Creek and some twenty miles west of Fort Richardson, they had sighted a large war party rapidly approaching.

Hurriedly corralling their train, the teamsters had crawled beneath their wagons, hoping to fight off the hundred or more warriors who swarmed about them. With five of their number killed and all their mules run off, Brazeale and the other survivors had fled on foot, seeking some heavy timber a few hundred yards away. He did not know the fate of his companions.[32]

Hearing the news early next morning, May 19, Sherman ordered Mackenzie to take up the pursuit at once. If necessary he might follow the raiders right into the reservation to attack them. At the same time Sherman sent a courier to Colonel William Wood, commanding at Fort Griffin. Wood was ordered to move immediately with a strong force to search the headwaters of the Little Wichita for signs of the hostiles. The General himself would meanwhile proceed to Fort Sill and await results.[33]

Mackenzie, with four troops of the Fourth Cavalry, left Fort Richardson at noon and early in the evening, under a driving rain, reached the scene of the attack. Seven bloated and horribly mutilated bodies lay there, among them that of the trainmaster, Samuel

---

of the United States Military Academy at West Point, New York, 1802–1867, II, 570–71; Captain Joseph H. Dorst, "Ranald Slidell Mackenzie," Cavalry Journal, Vol. X (Dec., 1897), 371–73.

[32] Carter, On the Border with Mackenzie, 80; Maj. J. K. Mizener, Fourth Cavalry, to the Asst. Adj. Gen., Department of Texas, May 20, 1871, File No. 1305–1871.

[33] Post Returns, Fort Richardson, May, 1871; Sherman to Mackenzie, May 19, 1871, File No. 1305–1871; Sherman to Wood, May 19, 1871, in ibid.; Post Returns, Fort Griffin, May, 1871. Wood received these orders at two o'clock in the morning and sent out a troop under Lieutenant Henry Sweeney immediately. See Marcy's Journal, 192.

Elliott, who had been chained face down to a wagon pole and burned to death. Corn and the camping equipment littered the area, while all the stock, consisting of forty-one mules, were missing.[34]

The trail of the raiders proved difficult to follow in the heavy rain, but next day Lieutenant Peter Boehm, with a detachment of twenty-five men, struck a party of four warriors near the Big Wichita and killed one of them. Boehm believed they were a hunting party from the main band. Thus encouraged, Mackenzie pushed on toward Red River.[35]

Sherman, meantime, had reached Fort Sill on May 23, sought out Tatum, and informed him of the attack on Warren's train. Asked if he knew of any Indians presently raiding in Texas, the agent, who impressed Sherman as "a good and honest man," could not answer at once but agreed to co-operate in every way to apprehend the guilty parties. Within a few days the Indians would all be in to draw rations, and he would then make his inquiries.[36]

On Saturday morning, May 27, Satanta, Satank, and several other chiefs and young men, along with their women and children, came in for their rations. When the chiefs came to see Tatum in the agency office, Satanta began a long tirade, accusing him of stealing goods and withholding arms and ammunition. In view of these grievances he, with one hundred warriors and several other chiefs, had lately gone to Texas, captured a train, and killed seven men. "If any other Indian comes here and claims the honor of leading the party he will be lying to you, for I did it myself."[37]

---

[34] Carter, *On the Border with Mackenzie,* 81–82; Mackenzie to the Asst. Adj. Gen., Department of Texas, June 17, 1871, File No. 1305–1871.

[35] Maj. J. K. Mizener to the Asst. Adj. Gen., Department of Texas, June 11, 1871, File No. 1305–1871.

[36] Sherman to Gen. E. D. Townsend, the Adj. Gen., Washington, D.C., May 24, 1871, in *ibid.;* Tatum, *Our Red Brothers,* 116.

[37] Tatum to Jona Richards, Wichita Indian Agent, May 30, 1871, Kiowa Files, Trial of Satanta and Big Tree. The Indian loss in the attack was three killed and four seriously wounded.

Telling his employees to go ahead with the issue, Tatum excused himself and quickly penned the following note:

Col. Grierson
Post Comd.

Satanta, in the presence of Satank, Eagle Heart, Big Tree and Woman's Heart, in a defiant manner, has informed me that he led a party of about 100 Indians into Texas, and killed 7 men and captured a train of mules. He further states that the chiefs Satank, Eagle Heart, Big Tree, and Big Bow were associated with him in the raid. Please arrest all of them.

LAWRIE TATUM
Ind. Agent.[38]

He then went in person to see Sherman and Grierson, whom he found along with Inspector Marcy, on the front porch of the latter's quarters.

A few minutes later Satanta arrived, accompanied by interpreter Horace P. Jones. The chief had learned that a "big white chief" from Washington was there and wished to talk with him. Under questioning from Sherman, he readily admitted the attack on the train, but as he saw the General's temper rising he revised his story, giving himself a minor role. Then realizing that all was not well, he started for his pony, but Grierson's orderly, confronting him with drawn pistol, forced him to sit down.[39]

Satank, Eagle Heart, and Big Tree were now summoned to Grierson's quarters. Satank alone obeyed and was at once arrested. A detachment of the Tenth Cavalry found Big Tree in the trader's store. He plunged through a window and dashed for the timber but was quickly surrounded and taken. Eagle Heart, on his way to answer the summons, saw Big Tree's arrest, took to his heels, and made good his escape.[40]

---

[38] Tatum to Col. Grierson, May 27, 1871, in *ibid.*

[39] Tatum, *Our Red Brothers,* 118; Sherman to Townsend, May 27, 1871, File No. 1305–1871; Sherman to Sheridan, May 29, 1871, in *ibid.*

[40] Tatum, *Our Red Brothers,* 118; Tatum to Richards, May 30, 1871, Kiowa Files, Trial of Satanta and Big Tree; Sherman to Sheridan, May 29, 1871, File No. 1305–1871;

Sherman told the other Kiowas that he intended taking their three chiefs to Texas for trial. Meanwhile the stolen mules must be returned. Kicking Bird declared that Grierson and Tatum well knew he had tried constantly to keep his people on the right path, and he begged that, in view of the good he had done, the prisoners be set free. He, himself, would then see to it that the mules were returned. Sherman acknowledged his efforts but declined the request.[41]

As a guard of twenty soldiers placed themselves before the porch, the Indians grew excited. At this point Lone Wolf galloped up armed with two Spencer carbines and carrying a bow and quiver slung across his back. Dismounting, he tied his pony to the fence and, with great deliberation, laid the guns on the ground. Then he carefully arranged his blanket and tightened his belt. This done, he picked up his weapons and strode to the porch, tossing one of the carbines to an unarmed Indian and the bow and arrows to another. Seating himself, he coolly cocked his carbine and gazed steadily at Sherman.

As the guards brought up their weapons, triggers at full-cock, a bloody fight seemed imminent. Suddenly Satanta threw up his hands and shouted, "No, no, no."[42] Other unarmed Indians echoed the cry, and Sherman ordered the soldiers not to fire.

Unfortunately, many of the Indians had edged away, and just outside the fort were sentries under orders to allow none to leave. These sought to stop them. One young warrior discharged two arrows, wounding one of the sentinels, and on turning to run was shot and killed. Sounds of the firing alarmed the Kiowas and Co-

Richard H. Pratt, "Some Indian Experiences," *Cavalry Journal,* Vol. XVI (Dec., 1906), 210. Pratt was one of the arresting officers.

41 Sherman to Sheridan, May 29, 1871, File No. 1305–1871; Tatum, *Our Red Brothers,* 118.

42 MS in Papers of Lt. J. W. Myers, Panhandle-Plains Historical Society, Canyon, Texas (hereinafter cited as Myers' MS); Sherman to Townsend, May 28, 1871, File No. 1305–1871; Marcy's Journal, 196f.

manches encamped near the commissary, and, fearing that their chiefs were being slaughtered, they stampeded. Within minutes the camps stood deserted.

About a dozen chiefs were detained while Sherman carefully explained his plans for Satanta, Satank, and Big Tree, and once more demanded return of the mules. This Kicking Bird promised to do. The remaining chiefs were then allowed to leave although Tatum had urged that Lone Wolf also be arrested: the agent regarded him as an inveterate troublemaker. The prisoners were placed in irons to await the arrival of Mackenzie, who would take them to Texas for trial by civil authorities.[43]

The heavy rains had thwarted Mackenzie's search for Satanta's party, and he turned toward Fort Sill, where he arrived on June 4. Four days later he was ready to return to Texas with his prisoners. Two wagons were driven to the guardhouse, and a fractious Satank was shoved into the first with a corporal and two privates on either side of him. Satanta and Big Tree, with two guards, climbed meekly into the second vehicle, and the column moved off.[44]

George Washington, a Caddo, rode a piece beside the wagons to receive any messages the chiefs might wish to send their people. Satanta told him to tell the Kiowas that he might never see them again, that he wished them to cease their raiding and return the stolen mules. Satank shouted that he would die the first day out and to tell his people that they would find his bones beside the road. The old warrior then drew his blanket over his head and began chanting the death song of the Koitsenko society, of which he was chief:

[43] Tatum to Jona Richards, May 30, 1871, Kiowa Files, Trial of Satanta and Big Tree; Marcy's Journal, 197; Butler, "Pioneer School Teaching," *loc. cit.*, 504; Sherman to Sheridan, May 30, 1871, File No. 1305–1871.

[44] Ranald S. Mackenzie to the Asst. Adj. Gen., Department of Texas, June 5, 1871, File No. 1305–1871; Grierson to the Asst. Adj. Gen., Department of the Missouri, June 9, 1871, in *ibid*. Big Tree, fearful of being shot, helped force Satank into the wagon. See Tatum to Enoch Hoag, June 10, 1871, Office of Indian Affairs, Letters Received, Kiowa Agency.

O sun, you remain forever, but we Koitsenko must die.
O earth, you remain forever, but we Koitsenko must die.[45]

Under his blanket the crafty Satank was struggling quietly to free his manacled hands. Some three-quarters of a mile from the post he succeeded, although his hands got badly skinned in the process. Then, pulling a butcher knife he had managed to conceal, he threw aside his blanket, gave a piercing yell, and lunged for the corporal, wounding him slightly.[46]

His three guards, taken completely by surprise, leaped from the wagon and in their haste forgot their carbines. Satank snatched one of these, working fiercely at the lever to chamber a cartridge. Guards riding in the second wagon fired a volley at the old Kiowa. The impact of several bullets knocked him to the bed of the wagon, but he regained his footing, still clawing at the carbine's lever, and was shot again. Mortally wounded, Satank died in a few minutes, a Koitsenko to the end. His body, thrown beside the road, was promptly scalped by Mackenzie's Tonkawa scouts.[47]

On June 14, Mackenzie, reaching the raw little frontier town of Jacksboro, allowed a swarm of the curious to view the chiefs. They had been removed from the wagon, lashed securely to horses, and surrounded by a strong guard to prevent any attempt at a lynching. After the crowd had satisfied its curiosity the prisoners were taken to near-by Fort Richardson and confined in the guard-house there.[48]

---

[45] Mooney, "Calendar History," *loc. cit.*, 329; Grierson to the Asst. Adj. Gen., Department of the Missouri, June 9, 1871, File No. 1305–1871; Tatum, *Our Red Brothers*, 118; Butler, "Pioneer School Teaching," *loc. cit.*, 506.

[46] Robert G. Carter, *The Old Sergeant's Story*, 79; Tatum to Enoch Hoag, June 10, 1871, Office of Indian Affairs, Letters Recieved, Kiowa Agency.

[47] Grierson to the Asst. Adj. Gen., Department of the Missouri, June 9, 1871, File No. 1305–1871; Carter, *On the Border with Mackenzie*, 91–95. Satank jammed the carbine because a shell was already in the chamber. Several shots went wild and the teamster, Antonio Borell, was wounded. The chief was buried at Fort Sill. See Tatum to Enoch Hoag, June 10, 1871, Office of Indian Affairs, Letters Received, Kiowa Agency; Tatum, *Our Red Brothers*, 121.

[48] Carter, *On the Border with Mackenzie*, 97–98; Post Returns, Fort Richardson, June 1871.

Both Big Tree and Satanta were indicted for murder, and their trials were set to begin on July 5. On the appointed day they were transferred from military prison to the county courthouse while throngs of people packed the courtroom, milled about in the streets, and filled the town's many saloons and gambling houses. Tension ran high, for rumors were circulating that the Kiowas might attack in an effort to free their chiefs.

The trials opened with Judge Charles Soward presiding and with District Attorney S. W. T. Lanham heading the prosecution. Two Weatherford lawyers, Thomas Ball and J. A. Woolford, conducted the defense on a plea of not guilty. A "cowboy" jury, pistols in their belts, heard the testimony of Colonel Mackenzie, Agent Tatum, and Thomas Brazeale.

High point of the proceedings came with Lanham's summations to the jury. A colorful and effective speaker, his impassioned oratory thrilled the crowd and raised emotions to a fever pitch. Big Tree he thunderously denounced as a "tiger-demon who has tasted blood and loves it as his food." But he fired most of his salvos at Satanta, "the arch fiend of treachery and blood—the cunning Cataline . . . the inciter of his fellows to rapine and murder . . . abject coward . . . canting and double-tongued hypocrite."[49]

When the lawyers finished their arguments the jury, in each instance, returned a verdict of guilty. On July 8, Judge Soward, calling the Indians before him to pronounce sentence, offered them the opportunity to make a statement. Standing in his chains and speaking in bad Spanish, Satanta tried to appease the court by declaring that Lone Wolf, Kicking Bird, Satank, and other bad Indians had led him astray. If allowed to return to his people, he would never again make war on the Texans; if he were killed, the frontier would run with blood. Unimpressed, Soward sentenced both chiefs to die by hanging on September 1.

The trials had, however, attracted national attention, and both Soward and Tatum now received many letters, chiefly from Quaker

[49] J. W. Wilbarger, *Indian Depredations in Texas*, 563.

circles, interceding for the Indians. Wrote John B. Garrett of Philadelphia: ". . . how earnestly do I desire that their lives be spared and Christian influences brought to bear for their conversion and Salvation." "I believe," wrote another Friend, "that if by any means their punishment should be imprisonment for life, it would be more consonant with Christianity and vastly more effective in deterring their people from a repetition of crimes." Other letters expressed a fear that the affair might bring utter ruin to the peace policy.[50]

Tatum too concluded that life imprisonment would provide a more effective deterrent to the Kiowas and urged Soward to use his influence with Governor Davis of Texas. The judge complied, and on August 2, Davis issued a proclamation commuting the sentences to life imprisonment. The prisoners, held in military custody pending the Governor's decision, were then transferred to the penitentiary at Huntsville.[51]

Thus had arisen a new departure in the treatment of Indians guilty of crime, but Davis' action was severely criticized throughout his state. Many believed that commutation would mean the eventual release of the chiefs and that the frontier would then suffer as never before. From General Sherman came a grim warning that, if the Indians went free, "no life from Kansas to the Rio Grande will be safe, and no soldier will ever again take a live prisoner."[52]

[50] John B. Garrett to Tatum, July 14, 1871, Kiowa Files, Trial of Satanta and Big Tree; James E. Rhoads to Tatum, July 7, 1871, in *ibid.;* William Nicholson to Tatum, June 30, 1871, in *ibid.*

[51] Special Order No. 185, Sept. 12, 1871, Headquarters, Department of Texas, File No. 1305–1871; Kiowa Files, Trial of Satanta and Big Tree; Tatum, *Our Red Brothers,* 122; Wilbarger, *Indian Depredations in Texas,* 571.

[52] Soward to Tatum, Sept. 19, 1871, Kiowa Files, Trial of Satanta and Big Tree; Sherman to Townsend, May 28, 1871, File No. 1305–1871.

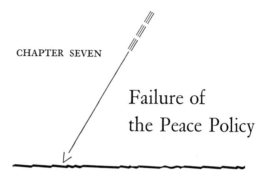

CHAPTER SEVEN

Failure of
the Peace Policy

E NRAGED BY THE RESTRAINT OF
Satanta and Big Tree and the killing of Satank, the Kiowas made
ready for war and sought help of the Comanches and Cheyennes.
But their emissaries to the Cheyenne camps near the Antelope Hills
failed to arouse any enthusiasm, and the Comanches too proved
reluctant. Kicking Bird worked tirelessly for peace. Aided by Satanta's message, he succeeded in holding the Kiowas in check,
although they refused for a time even to consider returning the
stolen mules.[1]

Meanwhile the Indian Department had adopted a new policy
toward reservation Indians. Shortly after the attack on Warren's
train, Sherman, in a letter to Secretary Belknap, had suggested that
rations be denied the families of those absent on raids, and that the

[1] Grierson to the Asst. Adj. Gen., Department of the Missouri, June 19, 1871, File No.
1305–1871; Col. J. W. Davidson to the Asst. Adj. Gen., Department of the Missouri, July
10, 1871, in *ibid.; Annual Report of the Commissioner of Indian Affairs for the Year 1871,*
471.

military be permitted to enter Indian Territory at any time to pursue raiders and to recover stolen property. Correspondence between Belknap and C. Delano, secretary of interior, led to the approval of Sherman's suggestions, modified only by a proviso that, when possible, the Indian agent should accompany such military expeditions.[2]

Agent Tatum, as well as Grierson and Mackenzie, had urged that the Kiowas be punished unless they returned the mules, and that a strong force be sent against the Kwahadis who had never been on the reservation. Grierson and Tatum felt that if the latter band were once soundly beaten there would be little future trouble in controlling the Indians.[3]

As the change in policy now made such a campaign possible, Grierson and Mackenzie quickly agreed on a plan of operations. They proposed a co-ordinated movement of cavalry regiments from Forts Sill and Richardson against any Kiowas or Comanches who might be found along the main Red River and its tributaries. As the point of rendezvous for their forces they selected a site on Otter Creek near old Camp Radziminski.[4]

Mackenzie concentrated ten companies of the Fourth Cavalry at Gilbert's Creek, a small tributary of Red River. He then moved to the camp on Otter Creek, where he conferred with Grierson on August 10.[5] A few days later the two commands separated and moved northwestward, scouting along the Salt and North forks of Red River. The weather was so hot that merely grasping a rifle barrel would blister a trooper's hand.[6]

And while the columns of Mackenzie and Grierson toiled in the

[2] Sherman to Townsend, May 24, 1871, File No. 1305–1871; Delano to E. S. Parker, Commissioner of Indian Affairs, June 20, 1871, in *ibid.;* Parker to Belknap, June 21, 1871, Kiowa Files, Military Relations.

[3] Grierson to the Asst. Adj. Gen., Department of the Missouri, Sept. 21, 1871, File No. 1305–1871; *Annual Report of the Commissioner of Indian Affairs for the Year 1871,* 503.

[4] Mackenzie to Tatum, July 31, 1871, Kiowa Files, Military Relations.

[5] Carter, *On the Border with Mackenzie,* 105; Grierson to Mrs. Grierson, Aug. 11, 1871, Grierson Letters; Post Returns, Fort Richardson, Aug., 1871.

[6] Carter, *On the Border with Mackenzie,* 126; Post Returns, Fort Sill, Aug., 1871.

summer heat over broken terrain and across gypsum-impregnated streams—which took their toll of both horses and men—Kicking Bird at last prevailed upon the Kiowas to return the stolen stock. By August 11 forty-one horses and mules had been turned over to Tatum. The Agent then told them that nothing more would be required but that Eagle Heart, Fast Bear, and Big Bow, all of whom had accompanied Satanta, would no longer be recognized as chiefs. Kicking Bird assured the agent that his people wanted peace. All of them, he said, were back on the reservation and en-camped on Buffalo Creek near its junction with the North Fork of Red River.[7]

Tatum immediately forwarded this intelligence to Grierson, who returned to the camp on Otter Creek. Leaving Captain L. H. Carpenter and a detachment to await Mackenzie, he then moved on to Fort Sill with the remainder of his regiment. Mackenzie, after a long and fruitless march to the vicinity of the Antelope Hills, came in on September 1.[8] When he learned that the Kiowas had complied with Sherman's terms and were back on the reserva-tion, he saw no alternative but to return disconsolate to Fort Rich-ardson. His adjutant remarked that the only reward Mackenzie had for his efforts was a full-course dinner, complete with prune pie, which the enterprising Carpenter served up shortly after the regi-ment had reached their Otter Creek camp.[9]

Mackenzie, still mindful of the Kwahadis, was determined to strike them before winter should curtail his movements. Late in September he concentrated eight troops of cavalry and two of in-fantry at old Camp Cooper on Ketumshe's Creek, a tributary of the Clear Fork of the Brazos. With Lieutenant Boehm and a few

[7] Tatum to Enoch Hoag, Aug. 12, 1871, File No. 1305–1871; Maj. G. W. Schofield, Temporary Commander at Fort Sill, to the Asst. Adj. Gen., Department of the Missouri, Aug. 11, 1871, File No. 1305–1871.

[8] Grierson to Tatum, Aug. 14, 1871, Kiowa Files, Military Relations; Carter, *On the Border with Mackenzie,* 142.

[9] Carter, *On the Border with Mackenzie,* 142–43. Carter quotes Mackenzie as amazed at Carpenter's resourcefulness in providing such a meal. He especially liked the prune pie, about which he commented, "Prune pie! Prune pie! Well I'll be damned."

Tonkawa scouts leading the way, the command moved out on October 3 and three days later reached Catfish Creek near the mouth of Blanco Canyon. There a supply camp was established and the infantry was assigned to guard the stores.[10]

Mackenzie now moved northwestward along the Freshwater Fork of the Brazos and on the evening of October 9 encamped at the mouth of Blanco Canyon. The men had a warm meal and, after the animals had been staked out with picket pins well driven in, crawled under their blankets to sleep. But they had not been unobserved, and at midnight their slumber was rudely interrupted. A large party of warriors rode full tilt by the camp, shrieking wildly, dragging buffalo hides, and ringing cowbells.

For a short time confusion reigned supreme. Terror-stricken horses and mules reared and plunged at the restraining ropes and picket pins. Bleary-eyed troopers sought frantically to prevent a stampede. Although largely successful, they lost nearly seventy animals, including one of Mackenzie's best horses.

Early next morning Captain Heyl and Lieutenant Carter, leading a small pursuit party, advanced too far from the main body and were suddenly confronted by an overwhelming force of Kwahadis under Chief Quanah. Only the timely arrival of Lieutenant Boehm and his scouts saved the little group from annihilation. One trooper was killed and two wounded.

Mackenzie, with the rest of the regiment, soon reached the scene, and the Comanches were followed up the rough floor of Blanco Canyon. All that day and into the next Mackenzie pursued the elusive foe, who twisted, turned, and backtracked to throw him off. Finally, still following the trail, the cavalry climbed the steep canyon wall and toiled wearily to the rim. There they found themselves on a seemingly limitless prairie: ". . . as far as the eye could

10 Post Returns, Fort Richardson, Sept., 1871; Carter, *On the Border with Mackenzie*, 159–62. The exact location of this camp is in dispute but appears to have been on Catfish Creek. *Army and Navy Journal*, Vol. X (Nov. 16, 1872), 213. See also Carl Coke Rister, "Harmful Practices of Indian Traders of the Southwest, 1865–1876," *New Mexico Historical Review*, Vol. VI (July, 1931), 231–48.

reach, not a bush, or tree, a twig or stone, not an object of any kind or a living thing was in sight."[11] They had emerged upon the vast Llano Estacado.

Now the trail, leading to the northwest, became warm, and soon far in the distance the Comanches were sighted. Their women and children were with them, and it appeared that at long last the Kwahadis' day of retribution was at hand. But as Mackenzie closed upon his quarry, a howling norther struck, chilling the column to the marrow. Black storm clouds followed, dropping a curtain of darkness behind the fleeing Indians, buffeting the troopers with rain and snow.

Ill prepared for such conditions and fearful that the men might become separated in the darkness, Mackenzie called off the pursuit and encamped his miserable command. October 12 dawned clear and calm, but the Indians had disappeared, and the chase had to be abandoned. The disappointed troopers retraced their steps, entered Blanco Canyon, and followed their old route down its course.

Suddenly the Tonkawas spotted two Comanches following the same trail up the canyon. Mackenzie detailed Boehm and his scouts to handle the startled Indians, who scurried into a ravine and opened fire with bow and gun. Then, growing impatient, he got behind the Lieutenant to direct the fight and was wounded in the thigh by an arrow. While he hurried to the rear to have it removed the Tonkawas closed in on the Comanches, killed them, and then scalped them—even to the ears.

Mackenzie now determined on a search along the headwaters of the Pease River, but his wound so weakened him that he had to return to the camp on Catfish Creek. Dr. Gregory, the surgeon, trying to get the fretting commander to rest, decided to tell him that if his leg got any worse amputation would be necessary. He had got as far as the word "amputate" when Mackenzie seized a cane and made for him. A flying departure through the tent flap saved the good doctor from a thrashing.

[11] Carter, *On the Border with Mackenzie,* 162–67, 179, 188.

Yet despite his iron will and a rugged constitution Mackenzie found himself unable to remain in the field. Dispatching a column under Major Clarence Mauch to continue search for the Indians, he moved with the remaining troops to Cottonwood Springs on the Double Mountain Fork of the Brazos, there to await results. Mauch's scouting proved futile, and he rejoined the command on November 6. A few days later the regiment returned to Fort Richardson, their fruitless compaign at an end. But the Kwahadis, although still unpunished, had not seen the last of Mackenzie.[12]

Tatum's Indians remained comparatively peaceful during the winter of 1871–72, but early in the spring the Comanches renewed their depredations in Texas.[13] The Kiowas refrained at first through fear of the possible consequences to their imprisoned chiefs, but the lure of the war trail proved too great. In April, White Horse and Big Bow led a strong force of warriors across the Red and rode rapidly southwestward.[14]

On the afternoon of April 20 they reached the San Antonio–El Paso road at Howard's Wells in Crockett County. There they found encamped an unescorted government contractor's train and immediately swarmed upon the unwary teamsters. All members of the train were either killed or wounded except Marcella Sera. This poor woman was witness to the death of her husband and her infant son, and to the agonies of eight teamsters who were tied to the wheels of their flaming wagons and "burned to a cinder."[15]

Scarcely had the raiders departed when Lieutenant Colonel Wes-

---

[12] *Ibid.*, 193, 197–99, 202–205; Post Returns, Fort Richardson, Nov., 1871.

[13] Two agency herders and a bugler of Company B, Tenth Cavalry, were killed in the late fall by Kiowas under Big Bow. See Grierson to the Asst. Adj. Gen., Department of the Missouri, Sept. 25, 1871, Annual Report of the Military Division of the Missouri, 1871.

[14] Maj. G. W. Schofield to the Acting Asst. Adj. Gen., Department of Texas, June 30, 1872, Records of the War Department, Adjutant General's Office, Letters Received.

[15] Capt. Michael Cooney to the Post Adj., Fort Clark, Texas, May 9, 1872. Baby Sera was scalped along with his grandmother. According to Marcella Sera, some Mexicans and two Negroes were in the attacking party. See Affidavit, Marcella Sera to Lt. Patrick Cusack, Ninth Cavalry, June 20, 1872, Records of the War Department, Adjutant General's Office, Letters Received.

ley Merritt, Ninth Cavalry, en route from Fort Stockton to Fort Clark with the regimental band and Troops A and H, reached the scene. While Merritt and the band pitched camp, Captain Michael Cooney and the troopers raced to overtake the Indians. The trail proved easy to follow and led Cooney into a narrow valley some eight miles from the site of the massacre. Hardly had he entered it when he was met with a withering fire from warriors entrenched behind large rocks and scrub brush.

In the first volley Lieutenant F. R. Vincent, leading Troop H, was shot through both legs, and seven horses were either killed or wounded. The troopers were, for the most part, raw recruits, and their return fire was wild and ineffective. With dusk approaching, Cooney ordered a retreat and returned to Howard's Wells, where Lieutenant Vincent died from loss of blood. Next morning the Indians had vanished.[16]

Other Kiowa bands struck heavily in north Texas. On May 19 a war party attacked a group of citizens near Old Fort Belknap. Although losing one of their number the whites fought back, killed two of the attackers, and wounded two others. One of the slain was Kompaite, brother of White Horse.

This chief was swift to take revenge. With a woman and six warriors he left the reservation and crossed into Texas. Late in the afternoon of June 9 they cautiously approached the home of Abel Lee, who lived on the Clear Fork of the Brazos a few miles below Fort Griffin. As Lee was sitting near the door reading, while his wife and four children were in the house preparing supper, the Indians opened fire and killed him instantly.

The family started to his side but, seeing the Kiowas running toward them, sought to escape by fleeing through the house. Mrs. Lee had reached the back door when an arrow struck her and inflicted a mortal wound. One of her arms was then severed and her body was mutilated. The children managed to reach the yard,

---

[16] Cooney to the Post Adj., Fort Clark, Texas, May 9, 1872, Records of the War Department, Adjutant General's Office, Letters Received.

but there fourteen-year-old Rebecca was slain, while Susanna, six-teen, Millie, nine, and John, six, were captured.[17]

Nor did the Kiowas and Comanches limit their operations to the Texas frontier. In small parties they constantly prowled near the agency, struck at the Camp Supply mule herd, and relieved the Five Civilized Tribes of hundreds of horses. They killed a courier, Private Alexander Christopher of the Sixth Cavalry, en route from Fort Dodge to Supply. South of Fort Dodge a strong party ran off 125 horses and mules of the Sixth Cavalry and made good their escape.[18] They were even accused of murdering one Richard Jordan, his wife, his brother George Jordan, and their hired man Frederick Norman far to the north on Pawnee Creek in Kansas.[19] Little wonder that Grierson could write that this summer's depredations were worse than ever before. Thoroughly disillusioned, Lawrie Tatum suspended the usual issue of rations and demanded the return of the Lee children.[20]

This critical state of affairs led the Civilized Tribes to make another effort at promoting peace. At their Okmulgee council they appointed a delegation to meet with representatives of the wild tribes at Old Fort Cobb in an attempt to persuade the latter to mend their ways. They selected July 22 as the date for the meeting.

Tatum opposed the council. Having withheld rations from the

[17] *Army and Navy Journal,* Vol. X (Sept. 7, 1872), 52; Post Returns, Fort Griffin, June, 1872; Battey, *A Quaker among the Indians,* 150. Battey said that Big Bow accompanied White Horse on this raid.

[18] Post Returns, Fort Dodge, May, 1872; Capt. Orlando Moors to the Asst. Adj. Gen., Department of the Missouri, Kiowa Files, Depredations.

[19] Maj. Schofield, Commanding at Fort Sill, to Tatum, July 25, 1872, Kiowa Files, Depredations; Tatum, *Our Red Brothers,* 132; Tatum to Agent Richards, June 5, 1872, Kiowa Files, Depredations; Lt. Col. Thomas H. Neill, Commanding at Fort Hays, Kansas, to the Asst. Adj. Gen., Department of the Missouri, Oct. 6, 1872, Cheyenne-Arapaho Files, Depredations. Neill believed that the Cheyennes were also involved.

[20] *Annual Report of the Commissioner of Indian Affairs for the Year 1872,* 247; Tatum to Wichita Agent Jonathan A. Richards, June 7, 1872, Kiowa Files, Depredations; Grierson to Gen. C. C. Augur, Commanding the Department of Texas, Nov. 10, 1872, Grierson Letters.

Kiowas since the Lee tragedy, he now believed that they were ready to restore their captives. A council might delay such action. But Cyrus Beede, chief clerk to Superintendent Hoag, was at the agency and favored such a meeting. Under his urging Tatum yielded and agreed to attend, along with Beede and George Conover, an agency employee.

Delegations from the Caddo, Wichita, and affiliated tribes, together with representatives from the Cheyennes and Arapahoes, arrived at the appointed time, but the principal objects of the conference, the Kiowas and Comanches, failed to put in their appearance. This delayed proceedings, and after a week of waiting Tatum returned to the agency to be with his wife, who had taken ill. Kiowa warriors had, meanwhile, fired into the camp of Captain Nicholas Nolan and Troop A, Tenth Cavalry, guarding the line of Red River. Such behavior did not augur well for their conduct should they attend the council.

Finally, ten days after the scheduled opening of the council, the Kiowas and most of the Comanches arrived. A belligerent White Horse strode to Horace Jones, the interpreter, and told him that he had come to Fort Cobb for the sole purpose of killing Tatum, "but now Tatum is gone and you are not worth killing, and I will let you off, you are not of sufficient importance."[21]

Speaking for the Kiowas, Lone Wolf declared that Fort Sill and all the troops must be removed and the reservation extended to the Río Grande on the south and the Missouri on the north. He would not talk of peace until Satanta had been returned unharmed to his people, and even then he would make no promises about raids in Texas—this was the Kiowas' legitimate occupation! White Horse added that he and his young men would raid when it pleased them and that he had no intention of returning the Lee children. Exposing an arm wound, he boasted that he was the leader of the party that had slain the teamsters at Howard's Wells. Spokesmen for the

---

[21] Conover, *Sixty Years in Southwest Oklahoma*, 37, 39; Tatum, *Our Red Brothers*, 125; Post Returns, Fort Sill, July, 1872.

Civilized Tribes warned the bellicose chiefs that the government would punish them, but such words had scant effect.[22]

After the conference Kicking Kird, who had remained silent, came to Horace Jones and told him to tell Tatum that he did not agree with Lone Wolf and White Horse, that he desired peace, and that he would do all in his power to recover the children. This he succeeded in doing, for late in August, Susanna and Milly were brought to the Wichita agency and turned over to Agent Richards, and on September 30 little John Lee was delivered to Tatum at Fort Sill.

Meanwhile the Indian Department had decided to send a commission to visit the Kiowas, Comanches, Cheyennes, Arapahoes, and the Caddoes, Wichitas, and affiliated tribes for the purpose of securing representative delegations to visit Washington. Captain Henry Alvord and Professor Edward Parrish of Philadelphia received the appointment, and were authorized to promise the release of Satanta and Big Tree, provided the Kiowas promised to observe their treaty obligations in the future.

The commissioners reached Fort Sill on August 25 and set to work at once to arrange for a meeting with the tribes concerned. All the work soon fell on Alvord, for Professor Parrish became ill and died at Tatum's agency on September 9. Alvord, however, proved equal to the task and held the first council on September 6. He impressed the Indians with the necessity for sending delegations to the capital. There all their problems could be discussed and satisfactory solutions reached. Unless this were done the Great Father must surely punish them.

Most of the tribes agreed at once to send delegates, but it took all of Alvord's persuasive powers—and they were considerable—to prevail upon the Kiowas and Comanches. The sullen attitude of

---

[22] Tatum, *Our Red Brothers,* 126. On this same day a band of Kiowas again fired into Nolan's camp. Schofield attended the conference, and his letter to the Adjutant General contains a full account of the proceedings. See Post Returns, Fort Sill, July, 1872; Maj. G. W. Schofield to the Acting Asst. Gen., Department of Texas, Aug. 5, 1872, Select Documents, War Department, Adjutant General's Office, Letters Received.

the former caused Alvord to promise only that they might see Satanta and Big Tree: he said nothing of their outright release. After many weary hours of negotiations they finally agreed to send Lone Wolf, Sun Boy, Wolf-Lying-Down, and one other. All the Comanche bands eventually complied except the Kwahadis.

Alvord's next and perhaps more difficult task was to induce Governor Davis to release Satanta and Big Tree into the custody of military authorities who would escort them to Fort Sill. In this too he succeeded, and he then set the date of departure for the delegations to Washington at September 20.

Lieutenant Robert G. Carter, Fourth Cavalry, stationed at Fort Richardson, received orders to proceed to Dallas with one troop of cavalry. There Satanta and Big Tree would be turned over to him, and he would take them to Fort Sill. Returning with the chiefs, Carter was met at Denton Creek by the noted scout Jack Stilwell with a message from Major G. W. Schofield, Tenth Cavalry, commanding at Fort Sill in the absence of Colonel Grierson.[23]

Schofield declared that, as several thousand Indians were gathered right around Fort Sill, he feared that the arrival of the chiefs in irons might precipitate a bloody fight. With only five troops of cavalry on hand—far too few in such a situation—he urged Carter to veer eastward to the railhead at Atoka. There Alvord would meet him with the Washington delegations.[24]

Carter complied at once, marching for Gainesville, where he telegraphed his change of plan and received the approval of General C. C. Augur, commanding the Department of Texas. Moving northward, he crossed Red River at Preston and on September 26 went into camp a short distance from the railhead. Jack Stilwell rode ahead to inform Alvord that the chiefs were near at hand.

The commissioner, meanwhile, his wary delegates riding wagons

[23] Carter, *On the Border with Mackenzie,* 354–55; Post Returns, Fort Sill, Apr., 1872. Schofield replaced Grierson on April 23, 1872. Grierson was placed on detached service as superintendent of recruiting service at St. Louis.

[24] Organizational Returns, Tenth Cavalry, Sept., 1872; Carter, *On the Border with Mackenzie,* 356.

which Schofield had obligingly provided, had managed to reach Atoka without undue difficulty. Carter's note caused him some uneasiness, for he feared his Indians might stampede if they learned their chiefs were near by. He therefore requested Carter to keep away from the station until the delegations were safely on their way. The chiefs could then follow by a later train. This procedure was adopted, and both parties arrived in St. Louis on September 28. Next day Satanta and Big Tree were allowed a joyful reunion with their people at Everett House. Then, following a tour of the city, the prisoners were returned to Texas while Alvord went on to Washington with his Indians.

Through most of October the delegations talked with the Commissioner of Indian Affairs and other prominent officials. In return for a promise of future good behavior the Kiowas received assurances that, if Governor Davis should consent, Satanta and Big Tree would be released at the end of six months. With the conclusion of official conferences the Indians toured several Eastern cities and points of interest before returning home in November. They had seemed to enjoy the trip, and the Indian Department hoped that their behavior would now rapidly improve.[25]

If Indian officials, however, were content to rely upon peaceful persuasion to stop the raids and depredations of the wild tribes, the army was not. In the previous March a minor skirmish on the Texas frontier had thrown new light on at least one source whence marauding bands got guns and ammunition. On March 28, 1872, Sergeant Wilson, Troop I, Fourth Cavalry, with a small detachment from Fort Concho overtook and engaged a party of raiders. He killed two, wounded three, and captured a Mexican boy.

Under questioning the prisoner stated that he was in the employ

[25] *Army and Navy Journal*, Vol. X (October 26, 1872), 165; Tatum, *Our Red Brothers*, 128; Philip McCusker, Interpreter, to Agent Jonathan Richards, Oct. 21, 1872, Cheyenne-Arapaho Files, Foreign Relations; *Annual Report of the Commissioner of Indian Affairs for the Year 1872*, 250. The long trip exhausted old Ten Bears, however, and he died shortly after his return. Only his son attended his death, for his earnest efforts to follow the white man's road had alienated his people. See Battey, *A Quaker among the Indians*, 90.

of New Mexican traders who supplied the Indians with guns, ammunition, and whisky in return for stolen cattle and horses. Thoroughly frightened, the Mexican also revealed the name of his employer, the location of various trading stations, and the general method of operation. Finally, to the astonishment of his questioners, he stated that there was a good wagon road across the Llano Estacado, with plenty of grass and water, over which the stolen cattle were driven into New Mexico.[26]

In the course of many years this illicit trade had inflicted staggering losses on Texas cattlemen, reaped handsome profits for its promoters, and produced a bountiful harvest of scalps for the Indians.[27] Long the object of vociferous complaint from frontier ranchers, the trade had been largely ignored by military authorities, who seemed to believe the losses greatly exaggerated. Confronted now with direct evidence of large-scale operations, they took steps to end the illegal and dangerous barter.

Late in May, General Augur ordered Mackenzie into the field for the dual purpose of breaking up the trade and striking a blow at the Kwahadis, who had yet to feel the weight of the government's armed might.

Eager to resume operations, Mackenzie moved from Fort Richardson on June 14, with three troops of the Fourth Cavalry and one company of the Twenty-fourth Infantry. The captive Mexican went along to help find the road which he insisted led across the Staked Plain. The column marched by its route of the previous year to the old supply camp on Catfish Creek. There Mackenzie halted while Captain N. B. McLaughlen with two troops rode

[26] *Annual Report of the Secretary of War for the Year 1872,* 55f. Post Returns for this period from Forts Sill, Dodge, Richardson, and Griffin and Camp Supply reveal constant efforts to apprehend whisky dealers on the reservations.

[27] In 1867, Superintendent of Indian Affairs for New Mexico, A. B. Norton, reported that a vast trade was being conducted between Mexicans and Comanches in Texas cattle. He wrote: ". . . in fact the territory is filled with Texas cattle." *Annual Report of the Commissioner of Indian Affairs for the Year 1867,* 194–95. For a good description of the development of this trade, see J. Evetts Haley, "The Comanchero Trade," *Southwestern Historical Quarterly,* Vol. XXXVIII (Jan., 1935), 157–76.

some ninety miles southward to Mucha Que in search of traders or stolen herds of cattle. Other scouting parties ranged to the north and west.[28]

These efforts went unrewarded, even though McLaughlen found plenty of "signs," and Mackenzie decided to move at once across the Plains. The command marched a short distance up the Fresh Fork of the Brazos and then out upon the Llano Estacado. With the aid of the Mexican they soon struck a well-traveled road, paralleled by many cattle trails, running westward toward New Mexico.

Twelve days of steady marching, with sufficient water and plenty of good grass, brought the command to the little New Mexican town of Puerto del Luna some thirty miles south of Las Vegas. There the trails scattered. Since no information could be had from the close-mouthed citizens, Mackenzie turned northward to the Canadian and down that stream to Fort Bascom.

After obtaining forage and rations he marched southeastward, struck another broad cattle trail, and followed it across the head of Tule Canyon to the vicinity of Quitaque Creek, but encountered no herds. The weary column then moved on to their old supply camp, "having marched nearly six hundred and forty miles in thirty marching days, and which wore the shoes off three quarters of the horses in the command."[29]

While a delighted Augur wrote Sheridan that Mackenzie had dispelled the myth that troops could not successfully operate on the Llano Estacado, the latter was preparing to move against the Kwahadis. On September 21 he completed preparations and moved northward toward the headwaters of Red River with Lieutenant Boehm and his Tonkawa scouts, five troops of the Fourth Cavalry, and one company of the Twenty-fourth Infantry. Eight days later

[28] Post Returns, Fort Richardson, June, 1872; Carter, *On the Border with Mackenzie*, 376; *Army and Navy Journal*, Vol. X (Nov. 16, 1872), 213. Captain McLaughlen joined Mackenzie from Fort Concho with Troops I and D. Post Returns, Fort Concho, June, 1872.

[29] Carter, *On the Border with Mackenzie*, 376; *Army and Navy Journal*, Vol. X (Nov. 15, 1872), 213; Records of the War Department, Adjutant General's Office. Copies of Records Relating to the Mackenzie Trail, File No. 2236858 (hereinafter cited as File 2236858).

they reached McClellan's Creek, a tributary of the North Fork of the Red. There the scouts discovered a fresh trail leading downstream.[30]

This was followed with all possible speed until near midafternoon, when the column came upon a large Comanche village. The inhabitants, unaware of the troopers' approach, were busily engaged in drying meat and making pemmican. Mackenzie, charging at a gallop, reached the camp's outskirts before its startled warriors snatched up their weapons and opened fire. For forty minutes a wild melee raged among the lodges and around a near-by ravine where many defenders had entrenched themselves. Then the Indians broke and fled for their lives.

Most of the warriors effected their escape, but the women and children were not so fortunate, for the troopers cut off and captured 120 of them. In addition over 1,200 ponies—nearly the entire herd—were taken. The troops counted 23 dead Indians, and it was believed that many more had been thrown into the creek by their people. Mackenzie's loss was 2 men killed and 2 wounded, one mortally.[31]

Once the fighting ceased the troops set to work and destroyed the 262 lodges which comprised the village, along with a great deal of other property and camp equipment. This done, the return march began, with a large detachment bringing along the immense pony herd. At nightfall they encamped with the prisoners in a corral formed by the wagons. Boehm and his Tonkawas were assigned to guard the captured animals.

The command had hardly settled in its blankets when enraged Comanche warriors swarmed around the camp firing at the hud-

[30] File No. 2236858; Tabular Statement, Annual Report of the Department of Texas, 1873, Records of the War Department, Adjutant General's Office, Letters Received. Carter, *On the Border with Mackenzie*, 377.

[31] Major W. A. Thompson, "Scouting with Mackenzie," *Cavalry Journal*, Vol. X (Dec., 1897), 431; *Record of Engagements*, 33; File No. 2236858; Tabular Statement, Annual Report of the Department of Texas, 1873.

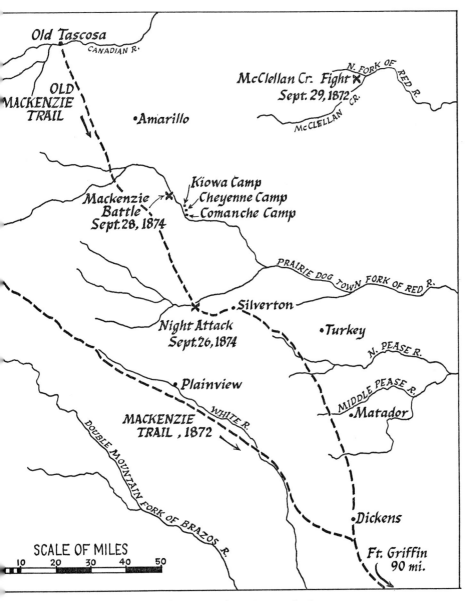

The Mackenzie Campaign Area of 1872–75

dled troopers, filling the air with war whoops, clanging cowbells, and raising such a din that the pony herd stampeded, as did the mounts of the Tonkawas. In the confusion a few of the prisoners crawled through the spokes of the wagon wheels and made their escape. Next morning, according to Lieutenant Carter, the Tonkawas came in leading one small, forlorn-looking burro loaded with their saddles and "everyone afoot, looking sheepish and woefully dejected, the butt and ridicule of the entire command."[32] Loss of the pony herd was a bitter lesson for Mackenzie, but he had learned much and would not lose another.

No further incident marked the return to the supply camp, which was reached on October 8. After resting a week, Mackenzie proceeded by way of Fort Griffin to Fort Concho, where the captive Comanches were interned in a corral. There they were to await the outcome of negotiations with their people for the release of all white prisoners.[33] Meanwhile they received kind treatment and were the object of friendly visits by the ladies and children of the garrison. These visits, however, stopped abruptly when the good women discovered that both their hair and that of their offspring was "plum full of 'em."

Mackenzie's destruction of their lodges and property and his capture of many of their women and children brought the Kwahadis into the reservation for the first time. They came to the agency and admitted their defeat. They told Tatum that they were ready to give up their old ways and would do as he wished if their women and children were returned. The agent reminded them that they had held some white captives for several years. Let them bring to him those unfortunates, and he would do all in his power to secure the release of their own people.

[32] *Army and Navy Journal*, Vol. X (Nov. 16, 1872), 213; Carter, *On the Border with Mackenzie*, 379; Clinton L. Smith and Jeff D. Smith, *The Boy Captives*, 127–31.

[33] Carter, *The Old Sergeant's Story*, 85; *Army and Navy Journal*, Vol. X (Nov. 16, 1872), 213; Maj. Gen. C. C. Augur, Commanding the Department of Texas, to Lawrie Tatum, Nov. 22, 1872, Kiowa Files, Captives.

Within a few days, largely because of the persistent efforts of Horseback, an old Nokoni chief, four white boys were brought to the agency.[34] Tatum then wrote Mackenzie, asking that the Comanche captives be given their freedom a few at a time. His request was approved and forwarded to General Augur, who at once ordered the release of five of Horseback's relatives. However only four of them reached the reservation, for one died on the way.[35]

With Satanta and Big Tree still in the penitentiary and with over one hundred women and children remaining behind the corral walls at Fort Concho, the Kiowas and Comanches stayed quietly in their camps near the agency. The Texas frontier enjoyed an unprecedented period of peace during the winter of 1872–73. Kicking Bird managed to recover seventeen stolen mules while Horseback, continuing his work among the Comanches, ultimately obtained the release of twelve captive Mexicans.

But Lawrie Tatum had little hope that such behavior would last for long. He was certain that, once their people were freed, the war parties would again harass the frontier. He had steadfastly opposed the plan to free the chiefs, and he had urged the Executive Committee of the Friends to support him in advocating prompt punishment for every crime. The Committee's reply had been a reprimand, and now that the Kiowas had obtained a promise for the release of Satanta and Big Tree, Tatum felt his position untenable. With the return of all captives known to be in the hands of the Kwahadis, he resigned, effective March 31, 1873.[36]

His successor, James Haworth, was thoroughly in accord with the views of the Executive Committee and was suspicious of the military. Faith and kind treatment, he thought, would suffice to

[34] The boys, all Texans, were John Maxie taken in 1869, Adolph Kohn and Temple Friend captured in 1867, and Clinton Smith taken in 1869. Conover, *Sixty Years in Southwest Oklahoma,* 40; Battey, *A Quaker among the Indians,* 83–89.

[35] Gen. C. C. Augur to Maj. John Hatch, Commanding at Fort Concho, Dec. 5, 1872, Kiowa Files, Captives; Tatum, *Our Red Brothers,* 142; Post Returns, Fort Concho, Dec., 1872.

[36] *Annual Report of the Commissioner of Indian Affairs for the Year 1872,* 219; Tatum, *Our Red Brothers,* 132; Enoch Hoag to Tatum, Mar. 31, 1873, Kiowa Files, Agents.

lead the Indians along the road to civilization; and he himself needed no assistance from the army. To make this clear to Lieutenant Colonel John W. Davidson, Tenth Cavalry, who took command at Fort Sill on May 4, and to impress the tribesmen with his confidence in them, he dismissed the small detachment which guarded his agency.[37]

His conciliatory efforts coincided with General Augur's decision to release the Fort Concho prisoners. Feeling that the Comanches had complied with his demands, he issued orders on May 24 for the return of their women and children. These were placed in wagons and started for Fort Sill under escort by Captain Robert MacClermont and twenty-one troopers. MacClermont brought them safely through but only by means of a wide detour around Jacksboro, where several hundred citizens had gathered to stage a mass lynching.[38]

A few Comanches lolling around the agency spotted the train when it was still some distance away and rode at full speed to meet it, while others dashed for the Comanche camps to spread the glad tidings. Next day, June 11, the prisoners were formally returned to their people, and MacClermont received the warm thanks of the chiefs along with their promises to remain always on the path of peace. Echoes of the promises had scarcely died away, however, when a few Comanche raiders struck in Texas. Others would have done so had they not been turned back by the Kiowas. These feared the government might use such raids as an excuse to break their promise concerning Satanta and Big Tree.

The Kiowas were, meanwhile, beginning to give up hope, for the release of the chiefs had been long delayed. True to the promise made their delegation in Washington, the government, acting through Secretary Delano, had opened negotiations with Governor

[37] *Annual Report of the Commissioner of Indian Affairs for the Year 1873*, 219; Battey, *A Quaker among the Indians*, 141; Post Returns, Fort Sill, May 4, 1873.

[38] *Annual Report of the Department of Texas for the Year 1873*, 1; Post Returns, Fort Concho, May, 1873; *Annual Report of the Commissioner of Indian Affairs for the Year 1873*, 219; Battey, *A Quaker among the Indians*, 163; Tatum, *Our Red Brothers*, 168.

Davis for the release of Satanta and Big Tree and had secured his promise to free the chiefs in April. But neither the government nor Davis had reckoned on the public resentment which such a move would create in Texas. The legislature had voted unanimously against a pardon, and the press had poured criticism upon the Governor's head.[39] The San Antonio *Daily Herald* had editorialized:

> Our sentiments have been so explicitly and pointedly stated, that we will only add that the Governor, if he does pardon these brutes, should be held to the most rigid personal accountability for the wanton abuse of the pardoning power.[40]

Feelings of the Texans in the matter might possibly have been ignored. But the wave of national indignation which had accompanied the outbreak of the Modoc War and the murder of General E. S. Canby, coupled with stern opposition to the plan from General Sherman, had caused Delano, with Grant's consent, to revoke the request made to Davis.[41]

There had been talk of war when this news reached the Kiowa camps, but Kicking Bird had managed to restrain the angry chiefs and had persuaded them to await further developments.[42] Delano, meanwhile, had been deluged with letters, principally from Quaker sources, urging that the government keep its promise, and the Civilized Tribes of Indian Territory had forwarded a memorial to the same effect. This pressure was too much for the Secretary, and on May 27 he again asked Davis to release the prisoners.[43]

---

[39] Delano, Secretary of Interior, to Edmund J. Davis, Mar. 22, 1873, Kiowa Files, Satanta and Big Tree.

[40] San Antonio *Daily Herald* (Apr. 3, 1873).

[41] Mooney, "Calendar History," *loc. cit.*, 197; C. Delano to E. J. Davis, Apr. 18, 1873, Kiowa Files, Satanta and Big Tree. In 1872–73 efforts to drive a small band of Modocs to a reservation led to war. In April, 1873, these Indians treacherously murdered General Canby, who was acting as a peace commissioner. See Hodge, *Handbook*, I, 918.

[42] Battey, *A Quaker among the Indians*, 250–53; Lt. S. L. Woodward to Col. Grierson, July 19, 1873, Grierson Letters. Woodward wrote constantly to Grierson and described affairs at Fort Sill in minute detail.

[43] C. Delano to E. J. Davis, May 27, 1873, Kiowa Files, Satanta and Big Tree.

The Governor wished to honor the request. Before doing so, however, he visited Washington and made arrangements for a council with the Kiowas at Fort Sill on October 1. There the chiefs would be released subject to certain conditions which he proposed to announce in person. He agreed, meantime, to turn Satanta and Big Tree over to the army immediately for delivery to Fort Sill, where they must be kept in military prison until time for the council. Until then, Davis wanted it distinctly understood, no promises whatsoever were to be given the Kiowas regarding his possible course of action.[44]

On August 19, Lieutenant Hoffman, with Troop E, Sixth Cavalry, took charge of Satanta and Big Tree and that evening left Huntsville for Fort Sill. The party arrived without incident on September 4, and the chiefs were placed in the post guardhouse.[45] Governor Davis arrived on Friday, October 3, accompanied by his secretary, several state officials, and a group of private citizens interested in recovering stolen stock. Also on hand for the occasion were E. P. Smith, commissioner of Indian affairs, Enoch Hoag, superintendent of the Central Superintendency, and agents Haworth, Richards, and John D. Miles, the latter having been assigned to the Cheyenne-Arapaho reservation upon the death of Brinton Darlington in 1872.[46]

Next morning preliminary talks were held with a few chiefs to decide upon a time and place for the "grand council." The Indians objected strongly to holding it inside the post: it was a bad place, some of their people had been killed there, and their thoughts would be bad if they went there. Davis, however, refused to con-

---

[44] Edmund J. Davis to Lt. Col. John W. Davidson, Aug. 14, 1873, in *ibid.;* Cyrus Beede to J. M. Haworth, Aug. 5, 1873, in *ibid.;* Telegram, Edmund J. Davis to Enoch Hoag, Aug. 11, 1873, in *ibid.*

[45] *Army and Navy Journal*, Vol. XI (Aug. 30, 1873), 36; Chauncey McKeever, Asst. Adj. Gen., Department of Texas, to Lt. Col. Davidson, Aug. 23, 1873, Kiowa Files, Satanta and Big Tree.

[46] J. M. Haworth to Jonathan Richards, Sept. 4, 1873, Kiowa Files, Trial of Satanta and Big Tree; Woodward to Grierson, Oct. 10, 1873, Grierson Letters.

sider any other place, and the Indians finally agreed to assemble on the post parade ground on Monday, October 6.[47]

At the appointed time the Indians gathered before a tent pitched in front of Colonel Davidson's headquarters on the south side of the parade ground. Facing them from behind a long table were Governor Davis, Commissioner Smith, and the other officials. Near by Satanta and Big Tree sat on a bench under close guard. Few troops were in evidence, but most of the garrison were on the alert in their quarters with weapons near at hand and their stabled horses saddled and ready for action.[48]

Commissioner Smith introduced the Governor. Davis began by saying that Texas desired peace with the Kiowas and Comanches and that the two chiefs had been well cared for while in prison. Then, without more ado, he explained the conditions under which he would be willing to free them. Recently Comanche war parties had struck again in Texas: he now called upon them to deliver up at least five of these raiders. They must return all stock which could be identified as having come from Texas. They must encamp near Fort Sill, draw their rations individually, and answer to a roll call; and finally, an agent must live among them to report frequently on their behavior. In conclusion he indicated his belief that these conditions could be satisfied within thirty days. Meanwhile Satanta and Big Tree would remain in custody until such time as Colonel Davidson felt that terms had been complied with.[49]

Several prominent chiefs, including Lone Wolf, replied to the Governor. All professed a strong desire for peace, and agreed to

[47] Woodward to Grierson, Oct. 10, 1873, Grierson Letters; Battey, *A Quaker among the Indians*, 199–200.

[48] Records of the War Department, Adjutant General's Office, Letters Received, File No. 4447–1873 (hereinafter cited as File No. 4447–1873); C. E. Campbell, "Down among the Red Men," *Collections of the Kansas State Historical Society*, Vol. XVII (1928), 637; *Army and Navy Journal*, Vol. XI (Nov. 8, 1873), 197.

[49] File No. 4447–1873; Battey, *A Quaker among the Indians*, 201; Post Returns from Forts Sill, Griffin, Richardson, McKavett, and Concho for May-October, 1873, indicate that detachments of cavalry were in constant pursuit of Indian raiding parties.

the terms as stated, but asked for an immediate release of the prisoners. Davis refused and thereby aroused the ire of Superintendent Hoag. "Your refusal to release them," he charged, "at once blocks the way at the outset, as, if Satanta and Big Tree are not released, it would be impossible to put agents among them, but if they were released the agent could go among them."[50] Angrily the Governor replied, "If they are so warlike as that, we had as well fight them at once."

Commissioner Smith now intervened to ask Davis if he would consider the Indians as acting in good faith, and release the chiefs, when the five raiders were brought in. Receiving an affirmative answer, he turned to the now sullen crowd and told them that the five warriors must be brought in within twenty-four hours; they must go home and talk about this and nothing else. So the council ended, and Satanta and Big Tree were returned to the guardhouse.

Matters did not rest there however, for Agent Haworth prevailed upon Smith to put pressure on the Governor for the immediate release of the chiefs. In a long letter the Commissioner pointed out that, since the government had made a definite promise to the Kiowas, it now, as a result of the council, stood in a very questionable light. If the Governor would free the prisoners, he could rest assured that all the conditions laid down at the council would be faithfully observed. This approach softened Davis' attitude, and he agreed to meet once more with the Indians.[51]

Meanwhile, in the Kiowa camps there was bitter disappointment. Kicking Bird believed that his people had been betrayed. Lone Wolf, although realizing that such a course would cost his people dearly, talked gloomily of war. At length, late that night, in a joint council with the Comanches, it was decided to rescue the chiefs by force unless they were released voluntarily.

When the second council was held, on the morning of October

---

[50] Woodward to Grierson, Oct. 10, 1873, Grierson Letters. Lieutenant Woodward attended the council and wrote Grierson a detailed account of the proceedings.

[51] *Ibid.;* File No. 4447–1873; Battey, *A Quaker among the Indians,* 202f.

8, the Indians left nothing to chance. When they arrived at the meeting place many of the warriors, with bows strung and carbines and revolvers fully loaded, stationed themselves so as to have a clear line of fire at the Governor and the other officials. Swift horses were ready for Satanta and Big Tree, while to avoid arousing suspicion a few mounted women dallied in the background. But their efforts were unnecessary, for Davis, to the great joy of the Kiowas, released the chiefs without further ceremony. In so doing he unwittingly saved many of those present from death or injury.

In order to remind the Indians of the conditions previously imposed by the Governor and to warn them that the more warlike spirits must be restrained, Commissioner Smith called for a council to meet that afternoon at the agency. Nearly all of the prominent chiefs of the Kiowas and Comanches, as well as many of the young men, dutifully gathered at one of the agency commissaries; there were so many, in fact, that they overtaxed the facilities of the council room, and a large number had to remain on the front porch.

Flanked by Superintendent Hoag and Agent Haworth, the Commissioner wasted no time in getting to the business at hand. He opened the proceedings with a peremptory demand that the Comanches surrender within twenty-four hours five of their number who had recently raided in Texas. An angry murmur ran through the assembled Indians and there was the ominous click of cartridges being thrust into rifle magazines. Lone Wolf gained the floor and launched a tirade against Smith's ultimatum, whereupon the Commissioner incautiously branded the chief as a liar and a crybaby.

This was too much for the warriors crowded on the porch. They pushed furiously into the room, demanding that they be allowed "to kill the old fool who wants to kill our young men." Some of the older chiefs and Phil McCusker, the post interpreter, in whom the Indians had great confidence, managed to quiet them and told them that their time to speak had not yet come.

Then Cheevers, a young Comanche chief, spoke:

179

Tell that Washington chief that I am a Comanche and that my people have been doing no wrong and should not be asked to pay for any wrong done by the young men of other tribes, but that I know there are bad men among all people, among white men as well as among red men, but among us those who persist in doing these bad actions against the wishes and contrary to the orders of the chiefs are renegades whom we have cast out and those are they who are bringing all this trouble on the Indians. You will find them west of the Antelope Hills and you should round them up and you may keep them as long as you choose, but do not ask these good young men of either tribe to sacrifice themselves for the evil done by others.[52]

At this point Black Horse, a Comanche war chief, made a violent demonstration, pounding his breast with one hand and shaking his rifle with the other, but the more peacefully disposed chiefs succeeded in getting him to withdraw from the room.

All danger of bloodshed passed when Kicking Bird and then Woman's Heart rose to make short talks and to second what Cheevers had said. The latter now offered to lead a few warriors along with a detachment of troops in search of the raiders. Somewhat mollified, Smith gave the Indians thirty days to get results. If, at the end of that period, nothing had been done, rations and annuities would be withheld. Upon this note the council ended, and the Indians went to their camps.

As good as his word, Cheevers soon came to Fort Sill accompanied by Quirts Quip, a Yamparika chief, and eighteen warriors. They were enlisted as scouts, given uniforms, and placed on the payroll. On October 12 they received orders to guide Captain Phillip Lee, Lieutenant Silas Pepoon, Lieutenant J. Will Myers, and fifty picked troopers to a point on the Double Mountain Fork of the Brazos where it was thought a raiding party was encamped.

Cheevers seemed eager enough to locate the renegades. He led the troops hither and yon over a wide area scouting likely hiding places, always with the same result: no Indians could be found. He

---

[52] Campbell, "Down among the Red Men," *loc. cit.,* 638f.

Brevet Major General George Armstrong Custer
U.S. Signal Corps Photo (Brady Collection)
National Archives

Brevet Brigadier General Alfred Sully
U.S. Signal Corps Photo (Brady Collection)
National Archives

Colonel Ranald S. Mackenzie
U.S. Signal Corps Photo (Brady Collection)
National Archives

Colonel B. H. Grierson

War Department

National Archives

Colonel George A. Forsyth

U.S. Signal Corps Photo

National Archives

Ten Bears (Comanche)
Bureau of Indian Affairs
National Archives

Big Tree (Kiowa)
U.S. Signal Corps Photo
National Archives

Satank (Kiowa)
U.S. Signal Corps Photo
National Archives

Kicking Bird (Kiowa)
U.S. Signal Corps Photo
National Archives

Lone Wolf (Kiowa)
U.S. Signal Corps Photo
National Archives

Satanta (Kiowa)
U.S. Signal Corps Photo
National Archives

White Horse (Kiowa)
U.S. Signal Corps Photo
National Archives

Quanah Parker (Comanche)
U.S. Signal Corps Photo
National Archives

then concluded that the birds had flown, probably to Mexico, and the travel-worn little column returned empty-handed to Fort Sill.

On the surface at least the Comanches had now carried out their part of the bargain. But if they congratulated themselves on evading the surrender of any of their young men, they were due for a shock. On November 30, Agent Haworth received a telegram from Commissioner Smith telling him to inform the Comanches that the five raiders must be turned in within ten days. If not, rations and annuities would cease.[53] Next day the agent made known these terms to the Indians. Cheevers, Horseback, Quirts Quip, Iron Mountain, and other well-disposed chiefs expressed their willingness to camp near the agency and assist in rounding up raiding bands; but many others viewed the demand as a declaration of war and at once formed hostile parties to strike the Texas frontier.[54]

Haworth, now fearful of a major Comanche outbreak, dispatched Thomas Battey to the camps of Kicking Bird and Lone Wolf to urge them to come in to the agency. They would thus prevent the Kiowas from becoming involved with the Comanches. Battey found both chiefs anxious to avoid trouble but angry at the government for making a road that the Comanches could not travel. Any effort to bring in five of their number would result in a fight in which many of them would be killed. Both, however, agreed to do as the agent requested, although Lone Wolf indicated that he would be slow to do so as his people had just completed a successful hunt, were heavily loaded with buffalo hides and meat, and could not move quickly.

By the time Battey returned from his trip Haworth had received new instructions from Washington. The government had changed its mind: rations and annuities would be issued after all. Both Haworth and Battey were greatly relieved, but the vacillation of the government had done much harm. To many of the Indians

[53] E. P. Smith to Haworth, Nov. 30, 1873, Office of Indian Affairs, Letters Sent, Kiowa Agency.

[54] Battey, *A Quaker among the Indians,* 229; Woodward to Grierson, Dec. 5, 1873, Grierson Letters.

it offered an excuse and a stimulus to take up the lance and the scalping knife.

As the turn of the year approached, the incidence of raids and depredations increased. Nor did they involve only the Comanches, for young Kiowa warriors as well succumbed to the attraction of the old trails south of the Red River. General Augur reported that most of the war parties came from the reservation. Only on rare occasions, he said, were they intercepted, for the Indian was ever alert, was always well mounted, and had an unsurpassed knowledge of the area in which he operated.

Shortly after this report some of Augur's cavalry made one of those rare interceptions which had far-reaching consequences. On December 4, word reached Fort Clark that a strong war party had swept along the lower Nueces River and had killed several ranchers. Lieutenant Charles L. Hudson, Fourth Cavalry, with forty-one men and six Seminole scouts, left at once to search for the raiders.

Three days later, near South Kickapoo Springs, Hudson found thirty-one ponies which the Indians had left to await their return. An intensive scout brought results, for near noon on December 9 a party of thirty-nine Indians were sighted resting their horses on high, rising ground some two and one-half miles away. As the cavalry advanced, the warriors dismounted, led their horses to the rear, and took up positions behind a rocky ridge.

At four hundred yards they opened an ineffective fire with their carbines. This Hudson ignored. Pressing forward, he urged his troopers up the rock-strewn slope, even though recent rains had made the going treacherous. Upon reaching the top the command dismounted, took cover, and opened fire at seventy-five yards. A hot ten-minute duel at such close quarters was enough for the Indians, who sought safety in wild flight. They left nine dead upon the ridge and lost fifty of their horses. Hudson's loss was but one man wounded, three horses killed, and two wounded.[55]

---

[55] File No. 4447–1873; Lt. Charles L. Hudson to the Post Adj., Fort Clark, Dec. 15, 1873, Office of Indian Affairs, Letters Received, Kiowa Agency.

The survivors of this disastrous raid made straight for the reservation and the camps of the Kiowas and Comanches. These they reached on January 13, 1874. Their report brought grief to both camps and especially to the Kiowas, for among the dead were Tauankia, son of Lone Wolf, and Gui-Tain, a nephew of the chief and the son of Red Otter.[56] Lone Wolf was inconsolable. According to Lieutenant Woodward, adjutant at Fort Sill, the chief had, in deep mourning, "burned everything he has, killed his ponies and slashed himself all up."[57] Henceforth the chief's only thought was that of revenge, and Kicking Bird would find the "peace road" a lonely one.

The Kiowas and Comanches now struck the Texas frontier with a vengeance, and their war parties were augmented by recruits from the Cheyennes. During the year previous the latter tribe had evinced increasing restlessness. They were upset by the appearance of surveyors on their reservation and by the doings of a swarm of unprincipled traders who had plied them liberally with whisky. Agent Miles, with the help of a force from Camp Supply, had arrested many of the traders and had destroyed over four hundred gallons of their whisky, but he had been unable to stop completely the illicit traffic.[58]

On March 19, 1873, a drunken band of warriors had struck a crew of surveyors on the Cimarron, killed four of them, and mutilated the body of crew boss E. W. Deming. Indian informants told Miles that the war party had come from Grey Beard's band. A demand had been made for the surrender of the killers, but the Cheyennes had not complied, and the government, fearful of provoking war, had not pressed the issue.

[56] Battey, *A Quaker among the Indians,* 245; Nye, *Carbine and Lance,* 183; Phillip McCusker to E. P. Smith, Jan. 19, 1874, Office of Indian Affairs, Letters Received, Kiowa Agency. McCusker was in the Kiowa camp at the time. He told Smith that Lone Wolf wanted to get his son's remains and bury them at Fort Sill with a cross on the grave.

[57] Lt. S. L. Woodward to Col. Grierson, Feb. 24, 1874, Grierson Letters.

[58] *Annual Report of the Commissioner of Indian Affairs for the Year 1873,* 220–23; Agent John D. Miles to Supt. Hoag, Dec. 26, 1873, Cheyenne-Arapaho Files, Depredations.

This affair had left the Cheyennes restless and uneasy. However, they had behaved fairly well until late in the year, when reports reached Miles that their war parties were participating with the Kiowas and Comanches in raids on the Texas frontier. This had led the agent to visit their camps, then in the vicinity of Antelope Hills. He had found them peaceful, at least on the surface, but he had also discovered whisky "in considerable quantities."[59]

Little Robe had added to the agent's worries by telling him that Satanta was stirring up trouble. The latter was instructing the Kiowas not to murder on a big scale during the winter but to launch a full-scale war in the spring, presumably with the help of the Comanches and the Cheyennes.[60]

And as the spring of 1874 approached, General Pope wrote Sheridan that the Department of the Missouri was experiencing increased Indian activity. He was making troop dispositions designed to prevent their penetrating into the settlements. In receipt of similar reports from General Augur, the military looked with grim foreboding toward a time when the grass would be green and the war ponies fat.

[59] T. H. Barrett, U. S. Surveyor, to Agent Miles, Mar. 25, 1873, Cheyenne-Arapaho Files, Depredations; Agent Miles to Jonathan R. Richards, Apr. 16, 1873, in *ibid.; Annual Report of the Commissioner of Indian Affairs for the Year 1873,* 223.

[60] Agent Miles to Supt. Hoag, Dec. 25, 1873, Kiowa Files, Depredations.

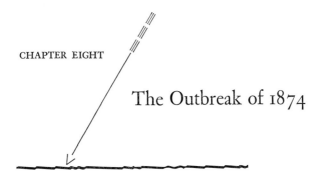

CHAPTER EIGHT

The Outbreak of 1874

SPRING CAME EARLY IN 1874 AND with it a seething restlessness in the camps of the Comanches, Kiowas, and Cheyennes. Talk of war was common, and reports reached Fort Sill that the Indians were acquiring guns and ammunition far in excess of ordinary hunting needs. George Fox, a licensed trader in Kicking Bird's camp, wrote Colonel Davidson about this lively arms trade, observing that the Comanches were "well armed and better prepared for hostilities than ever before."[1] Agent Haworth was told that the Cheyennes were also acquiring large quantities of arms, including the latest model Colt revolvers.[2]

In part the widespread disaffection stemmed from a desire to avenge the loss of relatives killed in raids on Texas. Augur's hard-riding cavalry had made frequent interceptions during the late

[1] Apr. 2, 1874, Kiowa Files, Depredations; *Annual Report of the Commissioner of Indian Affairs for the Year 1874*, 129; Battey, *A Quaker among the Indians*, 261.

[2] J. S. Evans to Haworth, Apr. 17, 1874, Office of Indian Affairs, Letters Received, Kiowa Agency.

winter. On February 5, Lieutenant Colonel George Buell, scouting out of Fort Griffin with a detachment of the Tenth Cavalry and some Tonkawa scouts, killed eleven Comanches in a single strike near the Double Mountains, Texas.[3] Lone Wolf, brooding over the death of his son and burning with a desire for vengeance, had infected many of the Kiowas with his bitterness.

The temper of all three tribes was inflamed over the wanton slaughter of the buffalo—cornerstone of the nomadic red man's way of life. Prior to 1869 white hunters had sought these lumbering animals primarily as a source of meat. With the building of the transcontinental railroads, and the growth of a hide market in the New England leather industry, the work of complete extermination began. With the problem of transportation and marketing solved, an immense business developed.

Merchants at Dodge City, Wichita, Leavenworth, and other conveniently located towns, sensing quick profits, organized small armies of hunters and sent them forth with guns, ammunition, and supplies. One authority describes what followed in these words:

> No sooner do they [buffalo] stop to feed than the sharp crack of a rifle warns them to change position. Every drink of water, every mouthful of grass, is at the expense of life and the miserable animals, continually harassed, are driven into localities far from their natural haunts—anywhere to avoid the unceasing pursuit.[4]

The slaughter on the Southern Plains reached its peak in 1873 when the Atchison, Topeka, and Santa Fe Railway alone transported 251,433 robes, 1,617,600 pounds of meat, and 2,743,100 pounds of bones. During the three years 1872–74 an estimated 3,698,730 buffalo were killed, with the Indians contributing only 150,000 of this total. No official efforts were made to curb or regulate the slaughter although the Texas legislature discussed the

---

[3] Post Returns, Fort Griffin, Feb., 1874; U.S. Congress, *H.R. Exec. Doc. No. 1*, 43 Cong., 2 sess., 40.

[4] J. A. Allen, *History of the American Bison*, 179.

problem in 1875. The discussion ended abruptly when General Sheridan, addressing a joint session, declared, "Let them kill, skin and sell until the buffalo is exterminated, as it is the only way to bring lasting peace and allow civilization to advance."[5] By the end of that year the Southern herd had ceased to exist.

Small wonder then that the Indian hated the buffalo hunter and longed for his scalp. His only avenue of escape from the confinement of the hated reservation and the handouts at the agency was being closed forever. But the hunter was not the only white man who stimulated wrath and encouraged discontent among the tribes. In ever-increasing numbers white horse thieves and whisky peddlers entered the reservation to engage in their illegal and dangerous traffic. Agent Haworth believed that Texans stole at least as many horses from his Indians as they did from the Texans, and in letters to his superiors he complained that his agency was overrun with whisky peddlers and that widespread drunkenness was the result. These activities served to demoralize his charges and led to depredations.[6]

The activities of buffalo hunters, horse thieves, and whisky peddlers, when combined with a resentment over loss of their lands and age-old raiding proclivities, and stimulated by desires to avenge the death of kinsmen, formed a combination of such explosive potential that major trouble was inevitable.

About May 1, Lone Wolf left the reservation with a large party of warriors bent on recovering the body of Tau-ankia and wreaking vengeance on the Texans.[7] Davidson learned of the mission and issued warnings to post commanders in Texas to be on the lookout. Colonel H. B. Clitz, commanding at Fort McKavett, sent out

---

[5] Garretson, *American Bison,* 128; Hornaday, "Extermination of the American Bison," *loc. cit.,* 496–501.

[6] Battey, *A Quaker among the Indians,* 238–89; *Annual Report of the Commissioner of Indian Affairs for the Year 1874,* 214; Haworth to Enoch Hoag, Feb. 23, 1874, Office of Indian Affairs, Letters Received, Kiowa Agency.

[7] Mooney, "Calendar History," *loc. cit.,* 199; Lt. Orleman, Tenth Cavalry, Fort Sill, to the Post Adj., May 1, 1874, Fort Richardson, Texas, Kiowa Files, Military Relations.

Captain Eugene B. Beaumont with seventy-two troopers of the Fourth Cavalry to fend off the raiders. Beaumont scouted thoroughly over the area between McKavett and Fort Clark as well as in the vicinity of old Fort Terrett but failed to find any trace of the Indians.[8]

Meanwhile, Major William Bankhead, with Troops F and L, Fourth Cavalry, had left Fort Clark to join in the hunt. Proceeding directly to the battlefield where Tau-ankia had been killed, Bankhead picked up the fresh trail of a war party and pursued it at once. For 240 miles he stayed close on the heels of the Indians, fleeing north across the country west of old Fort Terrett. In that barren and drought-stricken region the troopers, finding water only twice in five days, suffered extreme discomfort from the heat and dust.

At length the column emerged on the main El Paso road some twenty-eight miles above Fort Concho. There they found that the Indians had stolen twenty-five horses and three mules belonging to Company D, Ninth Infantry. The hostiles having obtained fresh mounts, Bankhead gave up the now unequal chase and returned to Fort Clark. Captain C. A. Wickoff, in temporary command at Fort Concho, who wrote Davidson concerning the loss of the horses and mules, believed that the Indians had returned to the reservation.[9]

The Comanche camps, meantime, buzzed with fresh excitement. Among the Kwahadis a new medicine man, Isatai, had risen. Several visits with the Great Spirit had endowed him with "supernatural" powers: he could control the elements, cure the sick and raise the dead; his stomach could produce cartridges in great quan-

---

[8] Haworth to Davidson, Feb. 17, 1874, Adjutant General's Office, Letters Received, 1874; Haworth to Enoch Hoag, May 9, 1874, Office of Indian Affairs, Letters Received, Kiowa Agency; Post Returns, Fort McKavett, June, 1874; *Army and Navy Journal,* Vol. XI (June 20, 1874), 708.

[9] *Ibid.;* Capt. C. A. Wickoff, Eleventh Infantry, Commanding at Fort Concho, to the Commanding Officer, Fort Sill, Indian Territory, May 22, 1874, Kiowa Files, Military Relations.

tity; he could influence the guns of the whites so that they could do no harm to the Indians.[10]

Isatai's fame spread so rapidly that Agent Haworth feared the worst and sent a conciliatory message to the Kwahadi camp. Their reply was prompt and pointed. No depredations would be committed around the agency unless the soldiers bothered their camps; in that event warriors would descend on the agency and kill everyone they could find.

Friendly Penatekas told Colonel Davidson that Isatai was urging a general war on the whites. The Great Spirit had told him that the white man's way had caused the Caddoes, Wichitas, and others who had adopted it to go rapidly downhill and that the same thing would happen to the Comanches unless they went to war. This, said the Penatekas, was just the message that the ill-disposed bands wanted to hear.[11]

While Isatai was stirring the war spirits of the Comanches, a band of white horse thieves threw the Cheyennes into a frenzy. Early in May, 1874, a party of whites raided the herd of Little Robe and stole forty-three ponies. The chief's young son, assisted by a small party of warriors, tried but failed to recover the stolen animals. The Indians then ran off the first cattle they encountered on the Kansas border, were pursued by federal cavalry, and in the fight which followed Little Robe's son was badly wounded.

Cheyenne retaliation was swift. War parties killed three men near Medicine Lodge, Kansas, and another on the road between Fort Dodge and Camp Supply. They struck several small parties of buffalo hunters along the Canadian River in Texas. Nor were detachments of troops immune. Major C. E. Compton and fifteen men of the Sixth Cavalry from Fort Dodge were hit both going to

---

[10] Haworth to Enoch Hoag, May 5, 1874, Office of Indian Affairs, Letters Received, Kiowa Agency; Davidson to the Asst. Adj. Gen., Department of Texas, July 20, 1874, War Department, Adjutant General's Office, Letters Received, File No. 3144–1874 (hereinafter cited as File No. 3144–1874).

[11] Davidson to the Asst. Adj. Gen., Department of Texas, July 20, 1874, File No. 3144–1874; Dallas *Daily Herald* (Aug. 13, 1874).

and returning from Camp Supply. A mail party from Supply to Dodge was also attacked.[12] Agent Miles wrote a hurried note to Haworth: "There is no use talking, some of our Indians are on the warpath."[13]

Late in May, 1874, Isatai ordered the Comanches to assemble for a medicine dance at the junction of Elk Creek with the North Fork of Red River. This was something new for the Comanches, who had never before made medicine as a tribe, although many had attended the annual Kiowa Sun Dance. So great was the prophet's prestige that even the friendly chiefs like Horseback and Quirts Quip were on hand. Also present was a strong delegation of the now thoroughly aroused Cheyennes.

Whisky flowed freely as Isatai harangued the assembled Indians, boasted of his powers, and told them that their god bade them avenge the death of their kinsmen. Most of the Comanches and Cheyennes smoked the war pipe and decided to attack the hated Tonkawas encamped near Fort Griffin. Although the hostiles threatened to slaughter their animals, Horseback, Quirts Quip, and the Penatekas refused to take any part in the venture and moved in near the agency.[14]

The planned attack on the Tonkawas went awry, however, for Agent Haworth got wind of it and warned the commanding officer at Fort Griffin, who promptly moved the imperiled tribe into the fort. When Comanche spies brought this news to the hostile camps a substitute target was selected: they would wipe out a party of buffalo hunters at Adobe Walls.[15]

[12] Agent Miles to Agent Haworth, June 17, 1874, Kiowa Files, Depredations; Mr. E. C. Lefebere to Agent Miles, June 14, 1874, Cheyenne-Arapaho Files, Depredations; Post Returns, Fort Dodge, June, 1874; Post Returns, Camp Supply, June, 1874.

[13] June 17, 1874, Cheyenne-Arapaho Files, Depredations.

[14] Battey, *A Quaker among the Indians,* 305–30; Haworth to Enoch Hoag, June 3, 1874, Office of Indian Affairs, Letters Received, Kiowa Agency. The Comanches believed that the Tonkawas had eaten their dead relatives. See also Rupert N. Richardson, "The Comanche Indians and the Adobe Walls Fight," *Panhandle-Plains Historical Review,* Vol. IV (1931), 30.

[15] *Annual Report of the Commissioner of Indian Affairs for the Year 1874,* 220;

In the spring of 1874 a group of Dodge City merchants had established a trading post at Adobe Walls on the Main Canadian in the Panhandle of Texas. Interested in the buffalo-hide business as well as in general merchandising, they designed the place to serve as a headquarters for a large number of hunters whom the merchants equipped and supplied.

Adobe Walls had shortly assumed most of the aspects of a small town with two stores, a saloon, and a blacksmith shop. Forming a rough south-to-north line and facing east was Rath and Wright's store, James Hanrahan's saloon, Thomas O'Keefe's blacksmith shop, and Charley Myers' and Fred Leonard's store. The latter building formed the northeast corner of a big picket enclosure, which contained a mess-house in the southwest corner and a well near its center.

A thriving business in arms, ammunition, sundry supplies, hides, and whisky had soon developed, not only with the buffalo hunters but also with many Indians and especially the Cheyennes and Arapahoes. Freight trains made regular trips to and from Dodge City, 150 miles away. Lucrative though the business was, it was both illegal and dangerous for it had been established in the heart of the Indian buffalo range and without license from either the army or the Indian bureau.

Seven hundred warriors, mostly Comanches and Cheyennes but with a sprinkling of Kiowas, Arapahoes, and Apaches, gathered for the attack. After marching for three days, they encamped on June 26 some six miles from their objective. They now made their final preparations. The warriors painted themselves, prepared their weapons, and made their war medicine. The early morning of June 27 found them ready.[16]

The buffalo harvest was at its height in June, 1874, and most of

Mooney, "Calendar History," *loc. cit.,* 202. Cerán St. Vrain and William Bent had established a trading post in 1837 near this site in order to trade with the Cheyennes, Comanches, and Kiowas. See also Grinnell, *Fighting Cheyennes,* 308.

16 Mooney, "Calendar History," *loc. cit.,* 203; Grinnell, *Fighting Cheyennes,* 312; Wilbur Sturtevant Nye, *Bad Medicine & Good: Tales of the Kiowas,* 182. Nye's book

the hunters were in outlying camps. On the evening of June 26 only twenty-eight men and one woman remained at Adobe Walls. Most of the men went to sleep that night in beds made on the ground outside; all had retired early for a hard day's work lay ahead.

About 2:00 A.M. the cottonwood ridgepole of Hanrahan's saloon suddenly cracked with a sound like a rifle shot. The noise awakened two men sleeping in the saloon, who aroused several others to aid them in making repairs. They grumbled as they worked, little realizing that fate in the form of a broken ridgepole would save most of their lives. Dawn was breaking in the east when the task was completed, and many of the men decided to stay up and make an early start on the day's hunt.

At the moment, a few hundred yards away, Isatai gave the order for his long line of Cheyennes, Comanches, and Kiowas to charge. At a dead run they bore in toward Adobe Walls while its inhabitants, awake and instantly alert, ran for the shelter of the buildings. All but two, the Shadler brothers asleep in their wagon, won this mad race, and none too soon. They had scarcely slammed the doors before the Indians swarmed around the buildings firing into the windows and hammering on the doors with their gun butts.

Some of the finest marksmen in the West defended Adobe Walls that day, and their accurate fire soon drove off the attackers. The respite was brief, however, for again the warriors charged, were driven off, and charged again and once more were repulsed. These assaults having failed, the Indians adopted siege tactics by taking cover and conducting a sharp rifle duel with the hunters.

Miraculously, since the initial charge none of the whites had been hurt. Now Billy Tyler and Fred Leonard dashed into the picket enclosure from Myers' and Leonard's store and attempted to reach a bastion in the northwest corner, but many of the warriors had taken cover behind the fence, and they laid down such a curtain of

---

contains the account of Quanah Parker, one of the Comanche leaders in this fight, as told to General Hugh Scott in 1890.

fire that both men were forced to beat a hasty retreat for the store. Leonard got inside unharmed, but Tyler was shot through the lungs just as he entered the door and died a short time later.

Noon came and still the fight raged. In the saloon, which housed nine grim defenders, supplies of ammunition ran dangerously low. The noted scout Billy Dixon and saloonkeeper James Hanrahan crawled through a window and raced for Rath's, where thousands of rounds were stored. A shower of bullets accompanied them but they reached their goal unscathed. Hanrahan gathered up a sack of ammunition and made a safe if flying return to his beleagured establishment. Dixon, entreated by the people in Rath's to remain with them, did so.

By midafternoon the Indians, discouraged at their lack of success, finally retired, leaving thirteen of their dead on the field and allowing their weary antagonists to emerge from their makeshift fortresses. In addition to the Indian dead the hunters counted fifty-six dead horses, forty-six of which were Indian ponies, and the bodies of twenty-eight oxen belonging to the unfortunate Shadler brothers.[17]

At dark on the second day after the battle one Henry Lease volunteered to go to Dodge City for aid. He reached there without difficulty, but General Pope refused to send relief to Adobe Walls. The illegal entry of the hunters into the area had greatly angered Pope, who declared that if he sent troops it would be to "break up the grogshops and trading establishments rather than protect them."[18]

The immediate danger to the hunters had passed, however, for

---

[17] The number of Indian dead is open to dispute. Agent Haworth placed their loss at six Comanches and five Cheyennes, with one Comanche dying afterward from wounds. Grinnell said that six Cheyennes and only three Comanches were killed. Dixon, however, stated that immediately after the fight he and his companions counted thirteen dead warriors in the vicinity of the buildings. See *Annual Report of the Commissioner of Indian Affairs for the Year 1874*, 220; Grinnell, *Fighting Cheyennes*, 313; Olive K. Dixon, *Life of "Billy" Dixon*, 170–77.

[18] Dixon, *"Billy" Dixon*, 180; New York *Tribune* (July 14, 1874). General Pope in his annual report blamed the Cheyenne unrest squarely on the activities of the buffalo hunters. See U.S. Congress, *H.R. Exec. Doc. No. 1* 43 Cong., 2 sess., 30.

the outcome of the battle ruined Isatai's influence. One Cheyenne wanted to quirt him but the others intervened—his disgrace was already complete for he had made "polecat medicine."[19] The affair at Adobe Walls only heightened the desire of the Indians for revenge. There were other and more vulnerable targets—and the main body of the Kiowas must be prevailed upon to join in an all-out war.

By the end of June the Cheyennes, with few exceptions, were hostile. From the camps of Grey Beard, Stone Calf, Heap of Birds, Medicine Water, and others, war parties poured forth in a constant stream.[20] They placed the Fort Dodge–Camp Supply and the Darlington-Wichita roads under a state of virtual siege; they struck along the southern Kansas frontier, in eastern Colorado, and in New Mexico. Vigorous defensive action by federal cavalry prevented their penetrating far into the settlements, but isolated ranches, unwary hunters and freighters, and small detachments of troops were in constant danger of attack.[21]

On July 2, 1874, Cheyenne warriors killed and scalped William Watkins thirty miles north of their agency. Next day on the Darlington-Wichita road at the site of present Hennessey, Oklahoma, they struck the three-wagon train of Patrick Hennessey, which was carrying supplies to Anadarko. Hennessey's three companions were killed. He himself was chained to the rear wheels of one of the wagons, covered with corn and oats, and burned to death.[22]

---

[19] Grinnell, *Fighting Cheyennes*, 313; Nye, *Bad Medicine & Good*, 182.

[20] Philip McCusker to Agent Richards, July 4, 1874, Kiowa Files, Depredations; U.S. Congress, *H.R. Exec. Doc. No. 1*, 43 Cong., 2 sess., 29; *Annual Report of the Commissioner of Indian Affairs for the Year 1874*, 233.

[21] Post Returns, Fort Hays, Fort Dodge, Camp Supply, June, 1874; *Annual Report of the Secretary of War for the Year 1874*, 26; B. K. Wetherell at Lee and Reynolds Ranch near Red Fork, Indian Territory, to Enoch Hoag, July 4, 1874, Kowa Files, Depredations. Wetherell informed Hoag that he expected all the ranches to be "cleaned out" and that it was unsafe for anyone to come along "the trail."

[22] Wetherell to Hoag, July 4, 1874, Kiowa Files, Depredations; *Annual Report of the Commissioner of Indian Affairs for the Year 1874*, 233–34; New York *Tribune* (July 8, 1874). The *Tribune* carried a full report of the affair as telegraphed by Agent Miles to the Commissioner of Indian Affairs.

These atrocities, coupled with the knowledge that the agency was surrounded by hostiles, caused Agent Miles at Darlington to fear that his employees would be massacred and government property destroyed. On the night of July 3, therefore, he sent young Johnny Murphy to Fort Sill, seventy-five miles to the south, with an appeal for troops. On a spirited little sorrel Murphy reached the post at sunrise the following morning. After delivering his message, he waited until nightfall and then made the return trip, arriving at Darlington near 9:00 A.M. next day.

Colonel Davidson started Troop M, Tenth Cavalry, to aid Miles, but shortly thereafter he received an urgent request for protection from the Wichita Agency at Anadarko, where an attack by Kiowas and Comanches appeared imminent. Since Darlington was outside Davidson's department this new threat had priority, and a courier was dispatched with orders which diverted the troops to Anadarko.[23]

Agent Miles, meanwhile, had gathered a small force from among his employees and, on the night of July 4, had left for Caldwell, Kansas, to seek additional military support. Next day the party reached the scene of the Hennessey massacre and gave the still-smoldering remains of the trainmaster a hasty burial. They then hurried on to Caldwell, where Miles telegraphed Commissioner Smith as well as military authorities.[24]

This appeal evoked a quick response, and soon a strong force of cavalry and infantry marched from Fort Dodge for the threatened agency. In addition, General Pope placed three mounted troops on patrol duty along the Wichita-Darlington road, strengthened his forces in the Medicine Lodge area, and reinforced the garrison at

[23] *Annual Report of the Commissioner of Indian Affairs for the Year 1874*, 234; Organizational Returns, Tenth Cavalry, July, 1874.

[24] *Annual report of the Commissioner of Indian Affairs for the Year 1874*, 234; Interpreter Phil McCusker to Wichita Agent Jonathan Richards, July 2, 1874, Kiowa Files, Depredations. McCusker said that the vicinity of the Cheyenne-Arapaho Agency was alive with hostiles. A near-by rancher, Ed Mosier, had buried the other bodies but became frightened and did not touch Hennessey. See the New York *Tribune* (July 8, 1874); Battey, *A Quaker among the Indians*, 310; U.S. Congress, *H.R. Exec. Doc. No. 1*, 43 Cong., 2 sess., 30–31.

Camp Supply. As the war clouds gathered the friendly chiefs Whirlwind, White Shield, and Little Robe came into the agency for safety. The lines were clearly drawn—three hundred lodges of Cheyennes, totaling 1,800 persons, were absent from the reservation and presumed to be hostile.[25]

But if the Comanches and Cheyennes believed that the main body of the Kiowas would join them, they were doomed to disappointment. The Kiowas held their annual medicine dance in July on the North Fork of Red River some fifty-five miles northwest of their agency. Large Comanche and Cheyenne delegations attended and did their utmost to persuade them to declare for war. They succeeded, however, only in bringing the Kiowa chiefs Swan and Lone Wolf, still thirsting for revenge, into their camps. More than three-fourths of the tribe followed the peaceful Kicking Bird into camps near Fort Sill.[26]

After the dance the hostile Comanches and Kiowas struck the Texas frontier with unprecedented violence. From the ranks of the former, Mow-way, Tabananica, Black Duck, Big Red Food, Little Crow, and White Wolf each recruited raiding parties. Among the Kiowa hostiles were Big Bow, who gathered in two hundred horses and mules on a single sweep, and the implacable White Horse, who was equally successful; but it remained for the brooding Lone Wolf to mount the most spectacular attack.[27]

With the aid of Maman-ti, a popular medicine man and war chief, he raised a force of fifty warriors and pushed into Texas. Noon of July 12 found them searching for prey in rocky, timbered Lost Valley a few miles northwest of Jacksboro. They found it in the form of Major John B. Jones and twenty-six Texas Rangers,

[25] Post Returns, Camp Supply, July, 1874; *Annual Report of the Commissioner of Indian Affairs for the Year 1874*, 233–34; Mooney, "Calendar History," *loc. cit.*, 204.

[26] Haworth to Hoag, July 11, 1874, Office of Indian Affairs, Letters Received, Kiowa Agency.

[27] Interpreter Phil McCusker to Lt. M. M. Maxon, July 30, 1874, Records of the War Department, Adjutant General's Office, Letters Received, File No. 3300–1874 (hereinafter cited as File No. 3300–1874); Records of the War Department, Adjutant General's Office, Letters Received, File No. 2815–1874 (hereinafter cited as File No. 2815–1874).

who entered the valley in search of Comanches who had stolen some horses from the near-by Loving Ranch.

Relying on the old strategem of using a few decoys, the Indians lured the Rangers into a headlong charge—straight into an ambush. A wild melee followed that ended with the Rangers' finally taking refuge in a narrow, dry ravine which skirted a line of timber. Three of them were wounded, one mortally.

The warriors took cover behind a near-by ridge and poured a heavy fire into the depression. Major Jones, a man of iron nerve, frequently exposed himself in order to observe his foe's movements and on one such occasion leaned nonchalantly against a post oak while bullets threshed its branches. The afternoon was very hot, and after several hours in the ravine the men began to suffer greatly from thirst. Cameron Creek trickled less than a mile away to the north, but Jones felt the risk too great to allow anyone to go for water.

At length, with evening approaching and with movements on the ridge indicating a retirement, Rangers Mel Porter and David Bailey decided to make a dash for the creek and fill the empty canteens. Mounting their horses, the pair rode to the little stream, and while Porter went down for the water Bailey sat his horse on the bank and watched for Indians.

Just when success seemed a matter of moments, a large party of warriors came sweeping in from the west. Bailey, shouting a warning to his companion, put spurs to his horse and made for the ravine. He never reached it, however, for his mount suddenly shuddered and stopped. In an instant the red pursuers engulfed him. Porter had better luck by plunging into the creek. He waded several miles before emerging and made his way to Loving's Ranch some twelve miles away. Just before dusk Ranger John Holmes volunteered to go to Fort Richardson for help and succeeded in getting through.[28]

[28] Ed Carnal, "Reminiscences of a Texas Ranger," *Frontier Times*, Vol. I (Dec., 1924), 20–22; Walter Prescott Webb, *The Texas Rangers*, 312f.; Post Returns, Fort Richardson, July, 1874; A. J. Sowell, *Early Settlers and Indian Fighters*, 799, 801f.; Nye, *Carbine and Lance*, 197f.

When night fell Jones placed the wounded on the remaining horses and painfully made his way to Loving's without further mishap. Before daylight Captain Baldwin with a detachment of Troop I, Tenth Cavalry, arrived from Richardson to assist the battered Rangers, but the Indians had left the vicinity. The Texans had suffered a loss of two killed and two wounded and had lost most of their horses as well. Jones placed the Indian losses at three killed and three wounded.[29]

Emboldened by these successes, hostile Kiowa and Comanche bands ventured close to Fort Sill to commit depredations. On June 13 they attacked Evans' wood camp eleven miles from the post, killed a man, and ran off a large herd of cattle. At about the same time two men were killed near Elm Spring Station. With these roving war parties striking in all directions, freighters bound for Fort Sill abandoned their trains on the road while farmers in the Washita Valley left their homes and came in for safety.[30]

The long-feared outbreak had come, and Davidson took precautionary measures designed to protect his post and to draw a line between the friendly and the hostile Indians. His post order of July 17 required all the former to encamp on the east side of Cache Creek at points designated by their agent. No Indian could approach nearer to the post than the agency unless accompanied by a messenger from the agent.[31]

On the same day General Sheridan telegraphed Sherman outlining the situation. He then got orders to concentrate the Sixth and Tenth Cavalry regiments at Fort Sill, to send word to the friendly Indians to get out of the way, and to launch a vigorous campaign against the hostiles. Once defeated they were to be stripped of all their arms, horses, and mules.[32]

[29] Carnal, "Reminiscences," *loc. cit.,* 22; New York *Tribune* (July 18, 1874). The *Tribune* quoted a dispatch from Fort Richardson.

[30] Davidson to the Asst. Adj. Gen., Department of Texas, July 20, 1874, File No. 3144–1874; New York *Tribune* (July 31, 1874).

[31] General Order No. 36, Fort Sill, July 17, 1874, Kiowa Files, Military Relations.

[32] File No. 2815–1874; Post Returns, Fort Sill, July, 1874.

Meanwhile, for more than two months, discussions had been going forward between the War and Interior Departments concerning measures to be taken in the event of a general war. On July 20 they reached agreement: the army would pursue and punish hostile Indians wherever they could be found; reservation lines would be ignored in the conduct of operations; great care would be taken to protect the innocent, a sufficient time being allowed for them to come in to their agencies. Agents were to co-operate with the military in enrolling all the loyal Indians, and every man among them capable of bearing arms must answer a roll call. Those who might venture in after the deadline must be examined: the innocent would be enrolled and the guilty would be held by the military as prisoners of war.[33]

These instructions were forwarded immediately to General Sherman and to Commissioner Smith, who, in turn, sent them to their subordinates. On July 26, Colonel Davidson received orders to enroll the friendly Comanches, Kiowas, and Kiowa-Apaches. Next day he informed the Indians that the enrollment would begin on July 31 under the supervision of Captain G. K. Sanderson and Agent Haworth.[34]

Sanderson first visited the Comanche camps, where he had no difficulty in enrolling the bands of Horseback, Quirts Quip, and Cheevers. It was a different matter, however, with the Kiowas, for word of the enrollment and especially the roll call occasioned great excitement among them. Haworth feared that if they were forced to submit many of them would flee to the Plains, and Sanderson decided to delay registration until August 3 and to dispense with the daily roll call in favor of one each Thursday just prior to the

---

[33] E. P. Smith, Commissioner of Indian Affairs, to the Secretary of Interior, May 14, 1874, Kiowa Files, Depredations; U.S. Congress, *H.R. Exec. Doc. No. 1,* 43 Cong., 2 sess., 26; *Annual Report of the Secretary of War for the Year 1874,* 4.

[34] Sherman to Sheridan, July 20, 1874, File No. 2815–1874; Enoch Hoag to Jonathan Richards, July 21, 1874, Kiowa Files, Depredations; New York *Tribune* (July 22, 1874); Col. Davidson to the Asst. Adj. Gen., Department of Texas, Aug. 10, 1874, File No. 3300–1874; *Annual Report of the Secretary of War for the Year 1874,* 41.

issue of rations. This concession molified them somewhat, but so reluctant were some of the chiefs that the last of them were not enrolled until August 6, three days beyond the initial deadline. The Apaches had registered the previous day without protest, and on August 8, with the expected arrival of Iron Mountain and his Yamparikas, Davidson closed the enrollment.[35]

At Darlington virtually all the Arapahoes quietly submitted to the registration, which was conducted by Agent Miles and Lieutenant Colonel Thomas H. Neill. Only 280 of nearly 2,000 Cheyennes were on the reservation. Agent Richards at Anadarko carried out his assignment among the Wichitas and affiliated tribes without difficulty.

Some days after the close of enrollment a few Comanche chiefs, among them Big Red Food, Little Crow, and Assanonica, sent word to Davidson that they wished to come in. Assanonica received permission provided he surrendered his arms, but the others, all of whom had fought at Adobe Walls, were refused. Big Red Food then moved his Nokonis, some sixty lodges in all, to the Wichita Agency at Anadarko, where he demanded subsistence from Acting Agent J. Connell. Connell feared trouble was brewing, for Lone Wolf and his band were in the vicinity, and in his camp were many Kiowas who had recently enrolled at Fort Sill. Captain Gaines Lawson, Eleventh Infantry, commanding the lone company guarding the agency, agreed with Connell and he sent for Colonel Davidson. The latter received Lawson's message at 6:00 P.M. on August 21, 1874. Four hours later he left for Anadarko at the head of four companies of the Tenth Cavalry, and near noon next day he crossed the Washita and entered the agency grounds.[36]

[35] Davidson to the Asst. Adj. Gen., Department of Texas, Aug. 10, 1874, File No. 3300–1874; Capt. G. K. Sanderson to Col. Davidson, Aug. 5, 1874, in *ibid.*; Capt. Sanderson to Agent Haworth, Aug. 5, 1874, Kiowa Files, Military Relations; Agent Haworth to Agent Richards, Aug. 4, 1874, in *ibid.* Prominent Kiowa absentees were Lone Wolf, Big Bow, and Red Otter. According to Sanderson, all of the Kwahadis and Kotsotekas, most of the Nokonis, and many of the Yamparikas were hostiles. He placed the number of Kiowa hostiles at seventy to one hundred. See Sanderson to the Post Adj., Fort Sill, Aug. 8, 1874, File No. 3300–1874.

The agency was badly located and ill arranged. At this point the river bent to the south, forming an arc which was closed on the north by a bluff. The agent's residence, the school, shops, and stables were all under the bluff and a mile from the river upon which they depended for water. The commissary was on the river, while on the bluff to the northeast was Shirley's store and to the northwest was the agency sawmill.[37]

It was Saturday and issue day at the agency. Nearly all the Caddoes, Wichitas, Pawnees, Delawares, and Penateka Comanches were in and out of the commissary. Big Red Food had made his camp close to that of the Penatekas and some two hundred yards from the commissary. Davidson sent immediately for the chief, told him that enrollment had been completed, that he had been given an opportunity to come in, and that he had not done so—now he must surrender his arms and move his people to Fort Sill.[38]

After some urging by Tosh-a-way, a friendly Penateka, Big Red Food agreed to Davidson's terms and under escort by Lieutenant Woodward and forty troopers he went to his camp to gather up the weapons. There, however, an argument developed over the surrender of bows and arrows which Big Red Food wished to retain for hunting. While a courier went to Davidson for an answer, some of Lone Wolf's Kiowas who were near by began to taunt the Nokonis, calling them women and asking if they intended to allow a few "buffalo soldiers" to disarm them.

This proved too much for Big Red Food. He suddenly gave a loud whoop, leaped from his pony, and escaped into the brush un-

[36] *Annual Report of the Secretary of War for the Year 1874*, 41; *Annual Report of the Commissioner of Indian Affairs for the Year 1874*, 238; U.S. Congress, *H.R. Exec. Doc. No. 1*, 43 Cong., 2 sess., 41; J. Connell to Agent Miles, Aug. 25, 1874, Cheyenne-Arapaho Files, Depredations; Col. Davidson to the Asst. Adj. Gen., Department of Texas, Aug. 27, 1874, Records of the War Department, Adjutant General's Office, Letters Received, File No. 3490–1874 (hereinafter cited as File No. 3490–1874).

[37] Gen. C. C. Augur to Gen. Sheridan, Sept. 13, 1874, File No. 3490–1874.

[38] *Annual Report of the Commissioner of Indian Affairs for the Year 1874*, 220–21; Connell to Miles, Aug. 25, 1874, Cheyenne-Arapaho Files, Depredations; Davidson to the Asst. Adj. Gen., Department of Texas, File No. 3490–1874.

harmed by a volley which the troopers fired at him. His Nokonis and the Kiowas returned the fire, and there began a hot skirmish, which served chiefly to riddle the tents of the friendly Penatekas. Ignoring the flying bullets, Tosh-a-way risked his life to ride toward the troops and shout in broken English, "No shoot there; him Penateka house, him mighty good friend!"[39]

Meanwhile, Davidson had instructed Lawson that in the event he heard firing from the Nokoni camp he was to deploy his infantry at once toward the sawmill in order to prevent the Indians from escaping up the Washita. This Lawson did, and he succeeded in driving the retreating hostiles up over the bluffs bordering the river.

As the shots crackled, Davidson faced his troopers toward the Nokoni camp and began to advance. As they moved forward, however, they were fired on by Kiowa warriors who were lurking behind the commissary and its corral. Two soldiers were wounded and a number of horses were hit. Davidson's position was awkward in the extreme. The area swarmed with friendly Indians, who were fleeing in all directions; if he fired on his attackers, many of the innocent might be hurt.[40]

Some time was required to get these people out of the way and Davidson, being uncertain where to strike or whence he might be attacked, ordered his command into the thick timber along the river, where they dismounted to fight on foot. One troop advanced on the commissary and the corrals, and at the cost of one man wounded, cleared them in time to prevent the hostiles from setting the commissary afire.

This failed to discourage the Kiowas, who proceeded to cross the river and move downstream about four hundred yards to the house and outbuildings of the Delaware chief Black Beaver. Davidson followed close on their heels, charged and scattered them with

[39] Campbell, "Down among the Red Men," *loc. cit.,* 648.

[40] Davidson to the Asst. Adj. Gen., Department of Texas, Aug. 27, 1874, File No. 3490–1874. Davidson reported that among his attackers were members of the bands of Woman's Heart, Poor Buffalo, Double Vision, Satanta, and Red Otter.

one man and one horse wounded. This done, he had to wheel and move swiftly back to protect the agency. It was now threatened by a swarm of Indians who, having gained the bluffs, swept like a hurricane through Shirley's store.[41]

Fearing for the safety of several parties who were out cutting hay and herding cattle, Black Beaver's son-in-law E. B. Osborne and two other men staying with him, Barrett and Lawson, decided to go out and warn them. They failed to find the parties they sought and were returning when they were attacked. Osborne and Barrett were armed with the latest type repeating rifles but hastily and ineffectually emptied these guns at their assailants. Rendered defenseless, they were easy prey. Lawson, however, was armed with a double-barreled shotgun, a fearsome weapon at close range, and by alternately threatening to fire and then retreating he reached Black Beaver's house in safety. The Indians had, meanwhile, killed four of the men whom the three had sought to warn.[42]

Davidson managed to reach the agency in time to forestall an attack there, and as nightfall approached he succeeded in clearing the bluff of hostiles. The fighting now ceased and the troops turned to the destruction of the lodges and other property of the Nokonis. When this had been accomplished they occupied Shirley's, the commissary, and the agency cornfield.

During the night nearly three hundred warriors gathered to recapture the bluff, and early Sunday morning they began the ascent. Davidson sent Lawson with some of his infantry to reinforce the men at Shirley's, while Captain Louis H. Carpenter took three troops, moved up the west slope, and drove off the Indians, some of whom had managed to reach the top. Since a strong north wind was blowing, the Indians started grass fires in an effort to burn the

---

41 *Ibid.;* Connell to Miles, Aug. 25, 1874, Cheyenne-Arapaho Files, Depredations.

42 Campbell, "Down among the Red Men," *loc. cit.,* 648. A few Caddoes participated in these killings, with evidence pointing to one, Hu-wah-nee, as Osborne's slayer. See Lt. R. H. Pratt to Black Beaver, June 7, 1875, Kiowa Files, Depredations; Connell to Miles, Aug. 25, 1874, Cheyenne-Arapaho Files, Depredations.

agency. Counterfires offset this threat but then got out of control. Indeed, for a time it appeared that the buildings would be destroyed, but this danger soon disappeared.

Although parties of Kiowas and Comanches were seen at a distance throughout the day, no further fighting occurred. Davidson placed his loss at four men and six horses wounded and that of the Indians at fourteen "shot off their horses."[43]

All the tribes of the Wichita Agency had fled when the fighting broke out, but on Monday morning their representatives came in, had the situation fully explained to them, and went out to bring back their people. Meanwhile, runners had gone to the friendly camps at Fort Sill with word that all the Indians were being killed. In the panic that followed all but forty-four of the Kiowas, many Comanches, and thirty of the Kiowa-Apaches had run off.[44]

The latter did not stop until they reached Mexico, but the Kiowas and Comanches sent in couriers saying that they had no intention of joining the hostiles and wished to return. This request was granted provided they returned before September 10. However, because of heavy rains and swollen streams many of them did not reach Fort Sill until September 23.[45]

After the Anadarko fight the hostile Kiowas and Comanches fled into the western reaches of Indian Territory; there some of them remained, while others went on to join the Kwahadis on the Staked Plain. Their confederates, the Cheyennes, concentrated on the edge of the Plains some 225 miles southwest of the Darlington Agency. It was now the task of Augur and Pope to throw strong columns

[43] Davidson to the Asst. Adj. Gen., Department of Texas, Aug. 27, 1874, File No. 3300–1874; Post Returns, Fort Sill, Aug., 1874.

[44] Campbell, "Down among the Red Men," loc. cit., 649; Connell to Miles, Aug. 25, 1874, Cheyenne-Arapaho Files, Depredations; Annual Report of the Secretary of War for the Year 1874, 42; U.S. Congress, H.R. Exec. Doc. No. 1, 43 Cong., 2 sess., 41.

[45] Annual Report of the Secretary of War for the Year 1874, 42; Haworth to Gen. Augur, Sept. 26, 1874, Kiowa Files, Military Relations. Haworth reported that encamped near the agency on the date of writing were 585 Kiowas, 479 Comanches, and 306 Kiowa-Apaches.

of troops into this rough and broken country, find the Indians, defeat them, and drive them into the reservations.[46]

Plans for the campaign were completed late in July. On his part General Pope ordered three commands into the field. The principal one, under Colonel Nelson A. Miles, consisting of eight troops of the Sixth Cavalry and four companies of the Fifth Infantry, would march south from Fort Dodge. Another, under Major William R. Price, comprising four troops of the Eighth Cavalry, was to operate east from Fort Union, New Mexico; a third, commanded by Lieutenant Colonel Thomas H. Neill, would base on the Darlington Agency and strike any hostiles found in that vicinity.[47]

Augur also sent out three columns. The strongest, under Colonel Mackenzie, consisted of eight troops of the Fourth Cavalry, four companies of the Tenth Infantry, one of the Eleventh Infantry, and about thirty scouts. It would march north from Fort Concho, establish a base of supply at the old camp on Catfish Creek, and search along the headwaters of Red River. Lieutenant Colonel Davidson with six troops of the Tenth Cavalry, three companies of the Eleventh Infantry, and forty-four scouts would operate west from Fort Sill. Lieutenant Colonel George P. Buell would range in the area between Mackenzie and Davidson with a force comprised of four troops of the Ninth Cavalry, two of the Tenth Cavalry, two companies of the Eleventh Infantry, and thirty scouts.[48]

For the purposes of the campaign Augur and Pope were authorized to disregard the lines separating their respective departments and, if necessary, to invade the reservations. The columns, converg-

---

[46] Mooney, "Calendar History," *loc. cit.,* 205; Campbell, "Down among the Red Men," *loc. cit.,* 649; File No. 2815–1874; Interpreter Phil McCusker to Lt. M. M. Maxon, July 30, 1874, File No. 3300–1874; *Annual Report of the Commissioner of Indian Affairs for the Year 1874,* 234. Agent Miles reported all the Cheyennes hostile except the bands of Whirlwind, White Shield, Little Robe, and Pawnee.

[47] U.S. Congress, *H.R. Exec. Doc. No. 1, 43* Cong., 2 sess., 26; Post Returns, Fort Dodge, July-August, 1874.

[48] Sheridan to Sherman, Sept. 5, 1874, File No. 2815–1874; Woodward to Grierson, Aug. 8, 1874, Grierson Letters; *Annual Report of the Secretary of War for the Year 1874,* 40.

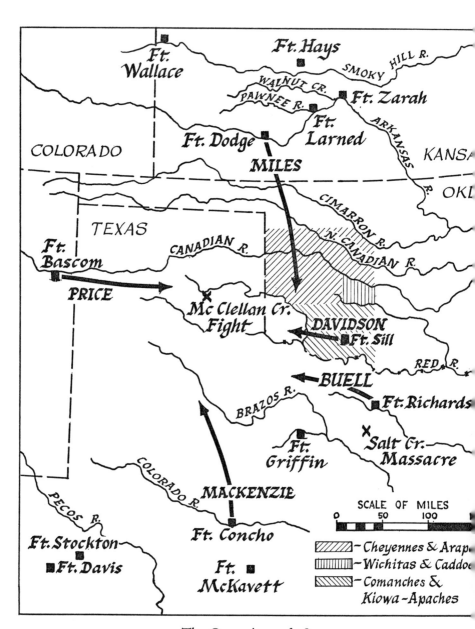

The Campaigns of 1874–75

ing from the north, south, east, and west, would maintain, if possible, a continuous offensive until a decisive defeat had been inflicted on the hostile bands. Their arms and animals should be taken from them and their leaders punished. If this were done another major outbreak would be impossible, and a great stride would have been made down the road toward civilization.

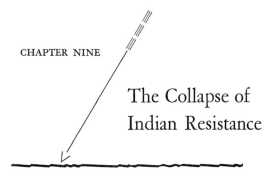

CHAPTER NINE

The Collapse of
Indian Resistance

O N JULY 27, 1874, COLONEL MILES received orders to organize an expedition at Fort Dodge and move south of the Arkansas to campaign against the hostile Indians. Fifteen days later he was ready to march. He had formed eight troops of cavalry into two battalions under Major C. E. Compton and Major James Biddle; Captain H. B. Bristol commanded four companies of infantry, and Lieutenant James W. Pope a detachment of artillery. Lieutenant Frank D. Baldwin led a force of about fifty scouts, composed of a few Delaware Indians under Chief Fall Leaf, some Army sharpshooters, and veteran plainsmen.[1]

Miles proposed to march southward on a broad front in order to

---

[1] Pope to Miles, File No. 2815–1874; Miles, *Personal Recollections*, 164. Specifically, the regular units in Miles's force consisted of Troops A, D, F, G, H, I, L, M, Sixth Cavalry, and Companies C, D, E, I, Fifth Infantry, numbering about 744 effectives. See U.S. Congress, *H.R. Exec. Doc. No. 1, 43* Cong., 2 sess., 31.

prevent, if possible, any Indians from slipping to his rear and escaping northward. To accomplish this purpose he sent out Major Compton and his battalion on August 11 to make a wide southwestward sweep. Three days later he himself advanced with the main command toward Camp Supply, which was to serve as his base of operations.[2]

The march was made in stifling heat, for the summer of 1874 was one of the hottest on record. Many of the streams and water holes had dried up while swarms of locusts had invaded the countryside, eaten off much of the grass, and stripped the wilted foliage from the trees. The scarcity of water brought intense suffering to the men, and of a large number of dogs that accompanied the command only two survived to reach Camp Supply.[3]

When Miles reached Beaver Creek he sent Baldwin and his scouts forward toward Adobe Walls, where they arrived on August 18. The gateposts of the hunters' corral offered them a grisly welcome for they were decorated with the decaying heads of the Indians slain six weeks before. The scouts' arrival proved timely, for hardly had they made camp when they had their first brush with the hostiles.

Two hunters, Tobe Robinson and George Huffman, had gone into the valley of the Canadian to hunt for wild plums. A small party of Indians pursued them and they made a run for it. Robinson got safely back to Adobe Walls but Huffman was cut off, lanced, and killed within plain sight of the scouts' camp. Baldwin mounted his little command and gave chase but was soon outdistanced and returned to camp.

On August 20, after accepting the services of Billy Dixon and several other hunters as volunteers, Baldwin moved down the Canadian and at the mouth of Chicken Creek surprised a small group

[2] Miles, *Personal Recollections,* 164; Post Returns, Fort Dodge, Aug., 1874.

[3] Miles, *Personal Recollections,* 164; Agent Haworth to E. P. Smith, Commissioner of Indian Affairs, Aug. 17, 1874, Office of Indian Affairs, Letters Received, Kiowa Agency. Haworth said that temperatures were 111–12° "in the shade."

of Indians, killed one, and wounded another. He then marched to rejoin Miles, whom he reached on August 24 some twelve miles west of the Antelope Hills. Miles had come by way of Camp Supply, where he had replenished his store of goods.

Since Baldwin's report indicated a general Indian retirement toward the southwest, Miles took up the pursuit with vigor. Under a broiling sun which sent daily temperatures soaring to above one hundred degrees, and over exceedingly rough and broken terrain, the long column managed to average twenty-five miles a day—no mean achievement. Added to the other rigors of the march was a scarcity of water, which, when found, was more often than not so impregnated with gypsum as to be unfit even for coffee.

At the Sweetwater, reached on August 26, the scouts discovered a large trail leading southwestward. The trail grew larger as the command pushed on to the North Fork of Red River. With the chase growing warm, Miles detached his train so as to drive forward with greater speed. On the evening of August 29 he reached the Salt Fork of Red River. He was in motion again by 4:00 A.M. next morning, with Baldwin's scouts two miles in the advance.

A march of eight miles brought the toiling troopers to a level plain which ended on the south in a line of low hills that bordered the Staked Plain. The trail, now very large and fresh, led into a narrow defile between two hills. The scouts were just entering it when a swarm of Cheyenne warriors suddenly charged. Baldwin coolly dismounted his men and repulsed the attack on foot while Miles deployed and came forward at a gallop.

The hostiles fell back through the defile to the line of hills and then, as the main body of troops came up, retreated to a range of high ravine-cut bluffs. Sending a few skirmishers to keep them busy, Miles formed his line with Compton's battalion on the right, Biddle's on the left, and Pope's artillery in the center, and then ordered a general advance. The Indians retreated but for the next five hours fought a strong rear-guard action among the ravines and bluffs. At length, hotly pressed, they broke and fled in small parties out on the Staked Plain.[4]

Miles now called a halt to rest his exhausted troops. Next day, August 31, he resumed the pursuit, but after a march of twenty miles he gave it up. His men had reached the limit of their endurance, his train was far in the rear, and supplies were running low. He decided to turn back to a point near the Antelope Hills, replenish his stores, and then renew the campaign.

If the weather had made the advance difficult, it rendered retirement even more so, for the fickle Plains now suddenly unleashed torrential rains along with a howling norther. A few minutes before, the command had been sweating and steaming; now it was sodden and shivering as it plodded slowly northeastward through deep mud and across swollen streams which before had offered only stagnant pools.

Miles, sorely in need of supplies, sent his train of thirty-six wagons under Captain Wyllys Lyman, Fifth Infantry, and a small escort ahead to secure fresh stores thought to have been transported from Camp Supply to Oasis Creek on the Canadian. Lyman reached the rendezvous on September 5, but when he found no train awaiting him, he sent Lieutenant Frank West, with five troopers, on to Camp Supply.[5] West hurried the departure of a train, which reached Lyman on September 7 at Commission Creek where the supplies were transferred. As yet no Indians had been seen, but on the previous day one of the teamsters, a man named Moore, had gone hunting and had been killed and scalped.[6]

A few red horsemen were seen in the distance as Lyman began

---

[4] Miles to the Asst. Adj. Gen., Department of the Missouri, File No. 2815–1874; Miles, *Personal Recollections,* 163, 167–70; Post Returns, Camp Supply, Aug., 1874.

[5] Miles to Pope, Sept. 14, 1874, File No. 2815–1874; *Army and Navy Journal,* Vol. XII (Oct. 31, 1874), 186.

[6] *Army and Navy Journal,* Vol. XII (Oct. 31, 1874), 186; Lyman to the Adj. Gen., U.S.A., Sept. 25, 1874, File No. 2815–1874; Miles to the Asst. Adj. Gen., Department of the Missouri, Mar. 4, 1875, File No. 3490–1874.

his return trip, but they soon disappeared. Although the apparent absence of hostiles was reassuring, he took every precaution to protect his train. The escort, Company I, Fifth Infantry, marched in two files to the right and left of the wagons, while Lieutenant West with thirteen troopers of the Sixth Cavalry screened the advance.

The train made steady progress. On the morning of September 9, however, as it was approaching a ridge on the divide between the Canadian and the Washita, a large body of hostiles suddenly appeared on the front and on both flanks. Skirmishing began at long range, but yeoman service by West and his detachment permitted the train to crawl slowly on southward. This continued until 2:00 P.M., when Lyman reached a deep ravine about a mile from the Washita.

Just as the train emerged from the ravine, the Indians abandoned their previous tactics and swarmed about the hastily corralled wagons. With a superb exhibition of horsemanship they circled close to pour in a heavy fire, nearly overwhelming the defenders in their first rush. In the small rear guard Sergeant DeArmond, a veteran soldier, was hit and instantly killed, while the commander, Lieutenant Granville Lewis, was disabled by a bullet through his left knee. On the hard-pressed front Wagonmaster Sandford suffered a mortal wound while bringing up ammunition.[7]

The troopers remained steady, however, and accurate marksmanship soon blunted the fury of the attack. The Kiowas and Comanches—they were now so identified—drew off and opened a harassing fire at long range.[8]

The fighting stopped at sunset when the Indians settled down for a siege. Lyman put his men to work digging rifle pits around and

---

[7] Lyman to the Adj. Gen., Sept. 25, 1874, File No. 2815–1874. Sergeant DeArmond was posthumously awarded the Medal of Honor for his part in the fight. See File No. 3490–1874.

[8] *Ibid.* The Kiowas and Comanches were those who had fought Davidson at Anadarko, moved westward, discovered and attacked the train. According to an Indian participant, Maman-ti, Lone Wolf, Big Bow, and Satanta were in this fight. See Nye, *Bad Medicine & Good,* 190–94.

close beside the wagons. At nightfall a few men, venturing out to a stagnant pool some four hundred yards away, came back with a little water to augment the scanty supply.

Sporadic firing began at dawn, and continued all day and into the night. Lyman's position was now critical. Lieutenant Lewis and Wagonmaster Sandford, and now Sergeant Singleton, had been severely wounded. All were in pain and needed medical attention. There was no surgeon with the train. The water supply was near exhaustion, the men were suffering from thirst, and their efforts to reach the waterhole had been frustrated by Indian riflemen.

In this extremity Scout William F. Schmalsle volunteered to go to Camp Supply for aid. After Lyman had penned a hasty note, the scout mounted and dashed from the wagon corral. Sounds of pursuit reached the anxious ears in the train, and the men could only pray that Schmalsle had outdistanced his pursuers.

Marked by intermittent firing and occasional dashes by individual warriors who rode close to the wagons, September 11 came and passed.[9] Sandford was now dying, and the command was suffering intensely from thirst. About eight o'clock next morning, however, the Indians were observed to be withdrawing, although small parties continued to fire at the train. Gathering a few men, West marched out, skirmished with these warriors, reached the water hole, and returned with enough water to relieve immediate needs. A short time later all had more than enough, for a violent rainstorm developed, drenched the miserable troopers, and made a lake of the wagon corral.

That morning Schmalsle reached Camp Supply. Lieutenant Colonel W. H. Lewis, commanding the post, quickly gathered every available man. By noon Lieutenant Henry Kingsbury, forty-five troopers, seven scouts, and the post surgeon were moving rapidly to Lyman's assistance. This relief, with Schmalsle in the van, reached the train at 2:00 A.M. the morning of September 14 after

---

[9] One Young Kiowa, Botalye, made four dashes past the wagons to prove his courage. See Nye, *Bad Medicine & Good*, 192–94.

a march of eighty-eight miles. Later the same day Lyman was able to rejoin Miles near the Washita crossing. His loss was two killed and three wounded. He believed that at least thirteen warriors had been slain.[10]

Some of the Indians who withdrew from the Lyman fight had found another target a few miles away. On the night of September 10, Miles, from his camp on McClellan Creek, sent Sergeant Woodhall, Privates Rath, Harrington, and Smith, and two noted scouts, Billy Dixon and Amos Chapman, to Camp Supply with dispatches. At six o'clock on the morning of September 12, as they approached the Washita, they were suddenly surrounded by over one hundred Kiowa and Comanche warriors.[11]

In the first rapid exchange of shots Smith was mortally wounded, Dixon got a slight leg wound, and Chapman's leg was broken by a bullet. Fortunately the warriors made no attempt to ride them down but were content to circle and fire, though at close range. Chapman, who had lived among these Indians for years, heard them frequently calling out, "Amos, Amos, we got you now."

When attacked the men were in the open on a little hillock but not far from a shallow buffalo wallow about ten feet across. This would afford some cover, and with Dixon carrying Chapman, all except Smith, who was left for dead, reached the wallow. Woodhall and Harrington were, however, badly wounded in the process. For the next several hours they alternately dug and shot while the warriors continually dashed and circled about to fire at them.

By midafternoon the wounded men, who had maintained sitting positions so as better to fire their weapons, were so weak from loss of blood that they could scarcely move. All were suffering from thirst until that same rainstorm which had drenched Lyman's battlefield now swept over this one. Water collected in the wallow

---

[10] Lewis to the Asst. Adj. Gen., Department of the Missouri, Sept. 12, 1874, File No. 2815–1874; Lyman to the Adj. Gen., Sept. 25, 1874, in *ibid.;* Post Returns, Camp Supply, Sept., 1874.

[11] Dixon, *"Billy" Dixon,* 199; Miles to the Adj. Gen., U.S.A., Sept. 24, 1874, File No. 2815–1874.

to form a muddy and blood-tinged well whence they now slaked their thirst.

After a time the wind shifted to the north and became very cold. This discouraged the Indians, who retreated out of range, drew their blankets tightly around them, and sat huddled on their ponies. Private Rath took advantage of the lull and ran to Smith's side to salvage his rifle and revolver. To his surprise he found him still alive, and with Dixon's aid he managed to bring the dying man into the wallow. A few hours later Smith expired.[12]

When night came, the Indians had disappeared. Rath started to Camp Supply for aid but, unable to find the trail, he soon returned. At daylight Dixon started out but had gone only a mile when he encountered Major Price's command, whom he led back to his companions. For reasons best known to himself Price did little to relieve the miserable men. His surgeon made a perfunctory examination, some of his soldiers tossed them a bit of hardtack, and he sent a courier to Miles with the news. Then he moved on. Not until midnight of September 13, when aid came from Miles, did the wounded men receive proper medical attention.[13]

Price had left Fort Bascom on August 28 with four troops of the Eighth Cavalry, a few guides including five Navaho Indians, and two mountain howitzers. He had marched down the south side of the Canadian for some 150 miles. There on September 4 he had found an Indian trail bearing off to the southeast. Sending Lieutenant Henry J. Farnsworth with Troop H, one howitzer, and the whole train on toward the Antelope Hills, Price with the rest of the command had followed the trail out on the Staked Plain.

Two days later he had found signs of Indians retreating, and at

---

[12] Campbell, "Down among the Red Men," *loc. cit.*, 654; Dixon, *"Billy" Dixon*, 201f., 205f.; Miles to Pope, Sept. 24, 1874, File No. 2815–1874. Smith died early on September 13.

[13] Dixon, *"Billy" Dixon*, 209–14; Price to the Asst. Adj. Gen., Department of the Missouri, Sept. 23, 1874, File No. 2815–1874; Miles to the Adj. Gen., Sept. 24, 1874, in *ibid.* Miles recommended the Medal of Honor for all six men. Chapman's leg was later amputated, but he recovered as did all the wounded.

3:00 P.M., a short distance north of the Salt Fork of Red River, he had struck the trail of Miles's wagons. Late on the afternoon of September 7 he had reached Miles, who was falling back toward the Washita. After conferring with the latter he had turned north to find his train, and near noon on September 12, while moving between the Sweetwater and the Dry Fork of the Washita, he had observed a long line of objects moving across his front.

Price had at first thought them to be a column of troops but had soon discovered his error, for they were actually some of the Indians who had withdrawn from the Lyman fight. He had pushed out skirmishers but the hostiles, in no mood to dally, had determinedly charged his flanks and rear. For the next two and one-half hours Price had been hard put to do more than hold his own. At one moment he had very nearly suffered the capture of his howitzer. When, as the afternoon waned, the Indians finally drew off, he had been content to let them go. His rations were low and fourteen of his horses had been wounded.

He had moved on to find Farnsworth and early next morning, signaled by Dixon, had accompanied him to the wallow. He then wandered close by the scene of Lyman's fight, heard the sound of firing, but made no move to investigate, and finally made connections with his train on September 14 on the Canadian. His independent command ended three days later when General Pope merged his force with that of Miles.[14]

For the time being, because of delays in securing supplies, Miles was forced to limit his operations. He established camps on the Canadian, Washita, and Sweetwater whence small detachments were kept on constant reconnaissance. He also eased Pope's fears—that large bodies of hostiles might escape to the north and depredate on the Kansas and Colorado frontiers—by sending Biddle's bat-

[14] Price to the Asst. Adj. Gen., Department of the Missouri, Sept. 23, 1874, File No. 2815–1874; Miles to the Asst. Adj. Gen., Department of the Missouri, Mar. 4, 1875, File No. 3490–1874; Miles to Price, Sept. 17, 1874, File No. 2815–1874.

talion to base on Camp Supply and to range westward from that point.[15]

Meanwhile Colonel Davidson's column, which was scheduled to take the field late in August, had been delayed by the affair at Anadarko. Not until September 10 was it ready to move. After providing adequate protection for the Wichita Agency and a sufficient garrison for Fort Sill, Davidson's remaining field force consisted of six troops of the Tenth Cavalry, three companies of the Eleventh Infantry, a section of mountain howitzers, and forty-four Indian scouts under Lieutenant R. H. Pratt. His plan of operations was first to march up the Washita to catch any Indians between himself and Miles, if not successful "to drop down on the North Fork and McClellan Creek, and, failing in finding Indian camps there, to move along the eastern base of the Staked Plains, and on them, to meet Colonel Mackenzie."

Davidson reached the Washita at Fort Cobb on September 12. He then turned up the divide between that stream and the North Fork of Red River, since high water forced him well off the watercourses. The march proved uneventful until September 17, when he captured a Mexican with some horses belonging to Lone Wolf's band. Five more days of heavy going, with no Indians seen, brought him into Miles's camp on the Sweetwater.

There Davidson rested a day and then moved on to the North Fork of Red River. He scouted along that stream and toward the headwaters of McClellan Creek, flushed and captured a lone Cheyenne warrior, and then turned southward along the edge of the Staked Plain. He reached the breaks of Red River on September 29 through "some of the most broken country I ever saw in all my long experience upon the plains." When Pratt and his scouts could find no sign of Mackenzie, Davidson decided to return to Fort Sill.

[15] *Annual Report of the Secretary of War for the Year 1875*, 79; Miles to the Asst. Adj. Gen., Department of the Missouri, Oct. 12, 1874, File No. 2815–1874.

His supplies were low, and the rough going had already cost him thirty-six horses and twenty-two mules.[16]

The first phase of operations by the columns of Miles, Price, and Davidson were thus concluded. They had killed few Indians but had succeeded in clearing a large area of hostiles and had driven the main body onto the Staked Plain, where it was expected that Mackenzie and Buell would strike them. Moreover, several bands had seen the handwriting on the wall and had turned eastward to surrender at their agencies.

On September 29 a few Kiowas and Cheyennes slipped into the friendly camps at the Cheyenne Agency. They were spotted by Colonel Thomas H. Neill's guards, however, and messengers were sent to the friendly Indians asking that these intruders be brought in. To Neill's surprise one of the Kiowas proved to be Big Tree. Under questioning the prisoner volunteered that Satanta, with twenty-four lodges, was encamped at Red Hills some thirty miles west of the agency and wished to surrender. Neill immediately telegraphed this intelligence to Pope, who ordered that everything possible be done to apprehend the famous chief.[17]

A friendly Kiowa-Apache and a Kiowa woman were now sent to Satanta's camp to urge him to come in. On October 3, Satanta, Woman's Heart, and Poor Buffalo, with thirty-five warriors, forty women, sixty-six children, and two old men, reached the agency and surrendered. Both Satanta and Big Tree told Neill that they had paid an unauthorized but friendly visit to the Wichita Agency, had become frightened when the fighting broke out, and had fled to the Plains. They had harmed no whites and committed no depredations since leaving Fort Sill; they had merely stayed clear of the troops.[18]

---

[16] Davidson to the Asst. Adj. Gen., Department of Texas, Oct. 10, 1874, File No. 2815–1874; Woodward to Grierson, Aug. 12, 1874, Grierson Letters; Post Returns, Fort Sill, Sept., 1874.

[17] Neill to the Asst. Adj. Gen., Department of the Missouri, Oct. 1, 1874, File No. 2815–1874.

The report of Satanta's surrender made necessary an immediate formulation of some specific policy of disposing of Indian prisoners of war. General Sherman recommended that all who in the last two years had committed murder or had stolen cattle should be tried by a military commission; that the captured horses be sold at auction and the proceeds invested in cattle for the tribes, and that the ringleaders be imprisoned. Satanta, he felt, should be sent back to Texas.[19]

Secretary of War Belknap approved these recommendations and forwarded them to President Grant. The Interior Department, while in agreement with such a policy in general, urged that leniency be shown Satanta. Commissioner of Indian Affairs E. P. Smith and Superintendent Enoch Hoag both believed the chief guilty only of a momentary panic and felt that he did not deserve a return to the penitentiary. Grant, however, ordered Sherman's suggestions carried out in full. He also authorized a separation of the ringleaders from their people and their confinement in a seacoast prison.[20]

The Kiowas who had surrendered at the Cheyenne Agency were, therefore, taken to Fort Sill, where they arrived on October 19. Satanta was then returned to Huntsville prison while the other chiefs and warriors awaited trials to determine their fate. Before the month was out, over one hundred Kiowa and Comanche warriors had reached Sill and given up the struggle.[21]

---

18 Neill to the Asst. Adj. Gen., Department of the Missouri, Oct. 4, 1874, File No. 2815–1874; *Annual Report of the Commissioner of Indian Affairs for the Year 1874*, 236.

19 Secretary of War Belknap to President Grant, Oct. 6, 1874, File No. 3490–1874.

20 *Ibid.; Annual Report of the Commissioner of Indian Affairs for the Year 1874*, 215; Belknap to Sheridan, Oct. 5, 1874, File No. 2815–1874; Smith to the Secretary of Interior, Oct. 6, 1874, in *ibid.*

21 Neill to Pope, Oct. 3, 1874, in *ibid.;* Galveston *Daily News* (Oct. 20, 1874); *Annual Report of the Commissioner of Indian Affairs for the Year 1874*, 272; Post Returns, Fort Sill, Oct., 1874. Satanta's health declined rapidly following this second incarceration. On August 15, 1878, Superintendent Goree of the penitentiary wrote the Kiowa Agent at Fort Sill as follows: "Satanta is here in declining health, and very feeble. If he remains here can not live long. Will heartily second any effort made for his release." Two months later the chief threw himself from an upper-story window of the prison and died in-

Meanwhile the operations of Mackenzie and Buell were offering an even greater stimulus to further surrenders. Mackenzie received orders from General Augur on July 23, 1874, to search the headwaters of Red River and the adjacent region for hostile Indians. Acting with his usual promptness and energy, Mackenzie concentrated eight troops of the Fourth Cavalry and five companies of the Tenth Infantry at Fort Concho. He formed the cavalry into two battalions under Captains Napoleon B. McLaughlen and E. B. Beaumont, while Major T. M. Anderson commanded the infantry. A force of about thirty scouts, mostly Seminole and Tonkawa Indians, was assigned to Lieutenant William A. Thompson.[22]

The command left Fort Concho on August 23 and a week later reached the old supply camp on Catfish Creek. There additional supplies were hauled from Fort Griffin, final preparations were made, and scouting parties were thrown out. Then on the morning of September 20 the long column moved northward, marched past the head of the Big Wichita, through the valley of the Quitaque, and up the steep bluffs to the Staked Plain. Lashed by a cold wind and rain, the command turned westward and on September 25 encamped near the head of Tule Canyon.[23]

Early in the evening some of Thompson's scouts came in to report that a large Indian camp had been discovered in Palo Duro Canyon about thirty miles to the northwest. Shortly after 10:00 P.M., a strong force of warriors made a sudden dash at the camp, yelling and waving blankets in an effort to stampede the horses, but this time Mackenzie was not caught napping. All the animals had been

---

stantly. See Supt. Goree to Agent P. B. Hunt, Aug. 15, 1878, Kiowa Files, Trial of Satanta and Big Tree; Mooney, "Calendar History," *loc. cit.*, 210.

[22] Augur to Mackenzie, July 23, 1874, File No. 2815–1874; Carter, *On the Border with Mackenzie*, 473–74; Post Returns, Fort McKavett, Aug., 1874; Col. Charles A. P. Hatfield, "The Comanche, Kiowa, and Cheyenne Campaign in Northwest Texas and Mackenzie's Fight in the Palo Duro Canyon," MS in Panhandle-Plains Museum, Canyon, Texas (hereinafter cited as Hatfield, MS).

[23] Hatfield, MS; Carter, *On the Border with Mackenzie*, 481–84; Bruce Gerdis, Tulia, Texas, to Frank Collinson, El Paso, Texas, Jan. 12, 1938, Bruce Gerdis Papers, Panhandle-Plains Museum, Canyon, Texas.

"staked, cross-side-lined, and hobbled" and the attempt failed. The Indians then retired to near-by ravines and ridges whence they fired ineffectually at intervals until morning.

At daybreak Mackenzie ordered Captain Peter Boehm with Troop E to drive off the hostiles while the rest of the command saddled and packed. Boehm, assisted by Thompson and his scouts, charged, put the warriors to flight, and launched a vigorous pursuit. He halted, however, after a three-mile gallop to return and report that the Indians had regrouped and moved off toward the east.

It was obvious from the direction which the retreating warriors had taken that they were attempting to mislead the command concerning the location of their camp. To give the appearance of falling for the strategem, Mackenzie followed them for a few miles at a leisurely pace and then went into camp as if for the night. When dark came the command mounted, turned off the trail, and marched rapidly northwest. Near 4:00 A.M. they reached the edge of Palo Duro Canyon and at daylight peered into its yawning depths. Far below where Ceta Creek emptied into the Prairie Dog Town Fork of Red River stood a literal forest of Cheyenne, Kiowa, and Comanche tipis.[24]

A quick search revealed a steep and tortuous path to the canyon floor. The command dismounted and in single file, with each trooper leading his horse, the descent began. Perhaps 150 yards had thus been covered when the noise of their approach alerted an Indian sentry, who fired his rifle, waved a red blanket, and disappeared among the rocks.[25]

The sound of the shot, echoing and re-echoing down the canyon, aroused the sleeping Indians. They poured from their lodges and sought safety either in wild flight up the canyon or among the rocks and crevices along its precipitous walls. Beaumont with Troop A

[24] Carter, *On the Border with Mackenzie*, 485–88; Hatfield, MS; Galveston *Daily News* (Oct. 22, 1874); Thompson, "Scouting with Mackenzie," *loc. cit.*, 431; Sherman to Townsend, Oct. 13, 1874, File No. 2815–1874.

[25] Hatfield, MS; Carter, *On the Border with Mackenzie*, 489. According to the Kiowas, the alarm was given by Red War Bonnet. See also Nye, *Bad Medicine & Good*, 200–201.

and Boehm with Troop E reached the bottom first, mounted and charged through the line of villages bordering the course of the Prairie Dog Town Fork. Troops H and L soon followed, with Mackenzie himself at their head.

The charge met little initial opposition and swept for two miles up the canyon before a hot fire by warriors concealed on its rugged sides forced a halt and then a slow retirement. Beaumont, meanwhile, in a rapid sweep, had rounded up over fourteen hundred horses and mules—nearly the entire herd—and had driven them back down the canyon. While lively skirmishing continued, all the lodges and winter supplies, including much sugar, flour, and dried buffalo meat, were destroyed.[26]

This had been accomplished by midafternoon, and when Mackenzie detected a movement designed to seal off the trail by which he had entered he ordered his troops out of the canyon. Skirmishers kept the Indians engaged while the rest of the command, driving the captured herd, regained the rim. There the troops, formed in a "living corral" around the herd, moved back to the camp at Tule Canyon. Next morning, after allowing the Tonkawas to select some of the best ponies, the rest were shot.[27]

Mackenzie's loss was placed at one man and fourteen horses wounded. Four Indians were known to have been killed and a number wounded. Despite the light casualties, however, the Palo Duro battle was a catastrophe to the Indians for in it they had lost their ponies and a winter's supply of food. With mobility gone and hunger eroding their will to resist, many of them turned to the agencies and surrendered.

[26] Hatfield, MS; Carter, *On the Border with Mackenzie,* 489–90, 492; Hatfield to Bruce Gerdis, Feb. 12, 1923, Gerdis Papers.

[27] Carter, *On the Border with Mackenzie,* 493; Carter to Floyd Studer, May 27, 1934, Gerdis Papers. The number of animals killed was approximately 1,050. The Galveston *Daily News* (Oct. 22, 1874) gave the number as 1,046; *Army and Navy Journal,* Vol. XII (Oct. 17, 1874), 148, placed the total at 1,048. Mackenzie in his official report merely said "over 1,000." The bones of these animals were a prominent landmark in the area for many years. See Sherman to Townsend, Oct. 13, 1874, File No. 2815-1874.

During the first week of October, Mackenzie made an intensive scout north and west of the Palo Duro. He found no Indians but intercepted a party of *comancheros* with ammunition and other supplies for the Kwahadis. The command then moved northeastward toward McClellan Creek, but as accumulating evidence showed that a large party of hostiles had gone south toward Red River, he turned and followed them. However, both his men and his horses were now badly in need of rest, and he pursued only as far as Mulberry Creek and the breaks of Red River. He then marched for his supply camp on Catfish Creek, arriving on October 23.

After a week's rest Mackenzie put his troopers to work on a simple but effective plan of operations. Since it was the winter custom of the Kwahadis to break into small parties and camp at various water holes, he proposed to march from one such hole to another in order to strike at them. For the next five weeks, under miserable weather conditions, he doggedly pushed this campaign. On November 3, while operating around the headwaters of the Double Mountain Fork of the Brazos, he struck the camp of a hunting party, killed 2 warriors, captured 19 women and children, and rounded up 144 of their ponies. Two days later, in the same area, a few of his scouts killed 2 Indians and were able to capture 26 horses and mules.[28]

Rain, sleet, snow, and mud hampered the command's movements, and made the problem of supply difficult in the extreme. Nevertheless, scouting columns searched north toward McClellan Creek, west around Tahoka and Twin lakes, in the rugged canyons of Red River, and along the Quitaque. At length, on December 3, with his command worn to the point of exhaustion, Mackenzie decided to break up the expedition and move in to Fort Griffin. Because few Indians had been found in the later phases of his

[28] Thompson, "Scouting with Mackenzie," *loc. cit.*, 432; Carter, *On the Border with Mackenzie,* 503–506; Mackenzie to Augur, Nov. 8, 1874, File No. 2815–1874.

operations Mackenzie was convinced that they were in full flight toward the reservations.[29]

Buell too had been keeping the hostiles constantly on the move. On October 9 he had struck a small camp on the headwaters of the Salt Fork of Red River near the Staked Plain, killed one warrior and destroyed the lodges. He continued the pursuit upriver, driving an ever-increasing number of Indians before him. In rapid succession he burned Kiowa and Cheyenne villages of fifteen, seventy-five, and finally of four hundred lodges. Their erstwhile occupants, with Buell close on their heels, fled to the edge of the Staked Plain and northward across the headwaters of McClellan Creek, the North Fork of Red River, and on to the Canadian.[30]

There most of the Cheyennes turned westward. The Kiowas gave up the unequal struggle and moved toward their agency. Buell, now three hundred miles from his base, communicated with Miles on October 18, informed him of his movements, and then sent his worn-out force directly into Fort Sill. He retained, however, a picked detachment of sixty men with whom he proposed to scout eastward along the Washita and the North Fork before coming in.[31]

The campaigns of Mackenzie and Buell had the effect of driving the Indians back on Davidson and Miles, who, after a brief respite, had resumed full-scale operations. Davidson left Fort Sill on October 21 and advanced northwestward as far as Fort Cobb, and thence due west, with scouting detachments thrown far out.[32] Three days later on Elk Creek Major G. W. Schofield, with three troops of

[29] Mackenzie to Augur, Nov. 27 and Dec. 2, 1874, File No. 3490–1874; Thompson, "Scouting with Mackenzie," *loc. cit.*, 432; Carter, *On the Border with Mackenzie*, 506; Mackenzie's reports are the despair of the historian for they are short, to the point, and contain little if any detail.

[30] Sheridan to Sherman, Oct. 24, 1874, File No. 2815–1874; Organizational Returns, Tenth Cavalry, Nov., 1874.

[31] Buell to Miles, Oct. 18, 1874, File No. 2815–1874; Buell to the Asst. Adj. Gen., Department of Texas, Nov. 8, 1874, File No. 2815–1874.

[32] Sheridan to Sherman, Oct. 24, 1874, File No. 2815–1874; Davidson to the Asst. Adj. Gen., Department of Texas, Dec. 22, 1874, File No. 3490–1874.

the Tenth Cavalry, surprised a large camp of Comanches under Tabananica, White Wolf, Little Crow, Big Red Food, and Black Duck. These chiefs raised a white flag and surrendered along with 64 of their warriors and 250 women and children. Included in Schofield's net were about 2,000 horses.[33]

In the Pond Creek area another detachment of the Tenth under Captain L. H. Carpenter crossed the trail of some of the Kiowas fleeing from Buell and followed them into Fort Sill, where their chiefs were arrested.[34]

Davidson continued his westward march and on November 8 struck a Cheyenne camp on the North Fork of Red River. He destroyed seventy-five lodges and pursued the fleeing hostiles for more than ninety miles. The chase finally ended on the Canadian, where the command's horses gave out. There cold rain, sleet, and snow struck the column, froze one hundred of the animals to death, and caused Davidson to turn back to Fort Sill.[35]

On December 7, Davidson ordered Major Schofield into the field for a final strike. He marched to the Washita above Fort Cobb and then searched upstream for Indian trails. No success attended his efforts until December 18, when an abandoned Cheyenne camp was found on Barry's Creek. Schofield detached Captain A. S. Keyes with Troop D to follow the trail, while the remainder of the command continued to search toward the Canadian.

Keyes pursued the Cheyennes eastward toward their agency, overtook them on Kingfisher Creek only 18 miles out, and captured 52 men, women, and children, along with 47 ponies and a mule. Schofield, after reaching the Canadian, turned southwest, scoured the area around Sergeant Major Creek, and finding no

---

[33] Davidson to the Asst. Adj. Gen., Department of Texas, Oct. 30, 1874, File No. 2815–1874; *Annual Report of the Commissioner of Indian Affairs for the Year 1875*, 272; *Army and Navy Journal*, Vol. XII (Nov. 14, 1874), 213; *Record of Engagements*, 42.

[34] Lt. R. H. Pratt to the Asst. Adj. Gen., Fort Sill Column, Nov. 29, 1874, File No. 3490–1874.

[35] Davidson to Augur, Nov. 23, 1874, File No. 2815–1874.

Indians, returned to Fort Sill where he arrived on December 31, having scouted over 350 miles.[36]

This concluded Davidson's campaign, and even though few casualties had been inflicted, his operations, combined with those of the other columns, took the heart out of the hostile Kiowas and Comanches. Small bands, in a steady stream, were coming in to surrender. In each instance their animals were confiscated, their warriors were confined, and their chiefs were put in irons. As the new year dawned Davidson prepared to attempt persuasion rather than force in getting the bands still out to come in and surrender.[37]

Miles proved to be the nemesis of the proud Cheyennes. By mid-October he was operating with five far-flung columns, whose principal purpose was to push the Indians ever eastward toward their agency, while at the same time steadily contracting their area of maneuver. After a four month's campaign marked by a number of sharp engagements, the main body of Cheyennes gave up their arms and accepted defeat.[38]

On October 13, Captain A. R. Chaffee, commanding one of these regiments, discovered and charged a large camp between Gageby Creek and the Sweetwater in the Panhandle of Texas. Although the Indians escaped, Chaffee destroyed their lodges and most of their property, and then pursued them to the vicinity of their agency. It was not always this easy. On November 2, Lieutenant Farnsworth left Camp Supply with Troop H, Eighth Cavalry, for a scout along McClellan Creek. When only thirty miles out and at about 1:30 P.M. he ran headlong into a force of some one hundred well-armed and well-mounted Cheyennes. He was quickly driven into a hollow, where he managed to hold off the circling warriors

36 Post Returns, Fort Sill, Dec., 1874; Schofield to the Post Adj., Fort Sill, Dec. 31, 1874, File No. 3490–1874.

37 Davidson to Augur, Dec. 23, 1874, File No. 3490–1874; Augur to Sheridan, Feb. 1, 1875, File No. 3490–1874; *Annual Report of the Commissioner of Indian Affairs for the Year 1875*, 272.

38 Miles to Headquarters, Department of the Missouri, Oct. 14, 1874, File No. 2815–1874; Miles to Pope, Mar. 4, 1875, File No. 3490–1874.

until dark. Then, with his ammunition exhausted, he made a dash for Camp Supply. He succeeded in breaking through the encircling Indians but Private William Dencham was killed, the trumpeter Hermann Fehr suffered a chest wound, Corporal Thompson received a bullet through the intestines, and Private Robinson was shot through the hand.[39]

At this time Miles was encamped with the main command on Red River bordering the Staked Plain. On November 4 he organized a detachment under Lieutenant Baldwin consisting of the scouts, Troop D, Sixth Cavalry, and Company D, Fifth Infantry. They were ordered to escort a train of twenty-three empty wagons going to a camp on the Washita for supplies. Baldwin was also instructed to watch for Indian trails. If he found a likely one, he might pursue if he thought it advisable.[40]

The column left that same evening and made its way northeastward. On the night of November 7 they encamped in a cottonwood grove on the north branch of McClellan Creek. At daylight next morning Baldwin sent out scouts to examine the broken country just ahead. The rest of the command had just started out when Scout Schmalsle came back on the run to report a large hostile camp—he was sure it was Grey Beard's Cheyennes—hardly a mile to the front.

This was welcome news indeed for some captured Cheyennes had previously reported that four white girls were being held by Grey Beard's band, and Miles believed the captives to be Addie, Sophia, Catherine, and Julia German, survivors of a family of nine attacked by a Cheyenne war party on September 13 in western Kansas. All previous efforts to locate them had failed.[41]

After sending Schmalsle on to inform Miles, Baldwin ranged

[39] Price to Farnsworth, Nov. 2, 1874, File No. 2815–1874; Farnsworth to Price, Nov. 7, 1874, in *ibid.*; *Army and Navy Journal,* Vol. XII (Nov. 14, 1874), 212.

[40] Miles, *Personal Recollections,* 174; Alice B. Baldwin, *Memoirs of the Late Frank D. Baldwin,* 71; Miles to Pope, Nov. 8, 1874, File No. 2815–1874.

[41] Baldwin, *Memoirs,* 72. The story of the German family and the experiences of the four girls are told in detail by Grace E. Meredith in *Girl Captives of the Cheyennes.*

his command in a single line. He placed the wagons in a double column in the center and told the wagonmaster that he must keep up with the troops for there would be no guards for the train if it fell behind. The trumpeter then sounded the charge and troops, scouts, and wagons rushed for the village.

The Cheyennes, numbering four or five hundred, promptly stampeded, leaving their lodges and most of their property. Baldwin tore straight through the camp and pursued the Indians for twelve miles out on the Staked Plain. There they managed to outdistance him. Back in the village Addie and Julia German, ages five and seven respectively, were found under a large buffalo robe. There was no sign of the two remaining sisters.

Miles moved northward once more, fanning out over a broad front and sweeping the area along the North Fork, McClellan Creek, the Sweetwater, and Gageby Creek. If possible, no Indians in the region were to be permitted "a quiet night's sleep."[42] On the morning of December 2, First Sergeant Dennis Ryan, with twenty men of the Sixth Cavalry, surprised a band of Cheyennes on Gageby Creek. He put them to flight, captured and killed seventy ponies, and destroyed most of their property, including some ammunition.

Continuing the program of harassment, Miles marched on to the Canadian and then west along that stream to a point near Adobe Walls. Reports from the Cheyenne Agency indicated that the Indians, with much of their property in ashes, were dispirited, hungry, and utterly miserable. Surrenders were increasing daily. The main body was still out, however. Those under Grey Beard were said to be encamped on the headwaters of Red River, and those under Stone Calf farther east and much closer to their agency. According to Indian informants, Sophia and Catherine German were in Stone Calf's camp.[43]

[42] Baldwin, MeMoirs, 73–74; Miles, *Personal Recollections,* 174–75; Miles to the Asst. Adj. Gen., Department of the Missouri, Mar. 4, 1875, File No. 3490–1874.

[43] Miles to the Asst. Adj. Gen., Department of the Missouri, Dec. 5, 1874, File No. 2815–1874; Miles to the Asst. Adj. Gen., Department of the Missouri, Mar. 4, 1875, File No.

Miles gave his troops a brief rest, gathered supplies, and on January 2, 1875, embarked upon a final circuitous swing to the south and west. The column marched down the eastern edge of the Staked Plain, crossed Red River, turned west to the head of the Tule, and then moved back eastward along the stream to its junction with Red River. From there Baldwin and the scouts went northwest to reconnoiter along the Salt Fork while the rest of the command continued almost due east.

The two columns converged at the Elm Fork. There were struck many trails leading toward Fort Sill. More than four hundred Indians, men, women, and children, just ahead of the command, had arrived to surrender. From Fort Sill, Miles marched to a supply camp on the North Fork of Red River, where he arrived on February 3. With intelligence indicating an early capitulation by both Grey Beard and Stone Calf, Miles moved on to Camp Supply and thence back to Fort Dodge. There he broke up the expedition and so ended almost six months of constant field operations.[44]

As early as the latter part of January, Colonel Neill at the Cheyenne Agency had learned from Indian prisoners that Stone Calf and probably Grey Beard wished to come in and surrender.[45] James Morrison, an interpreter with an Arapaho hunting party, supplied more definite information on February 18, when he told Neill that he had talked with Stone Calf four days before at the site of Custer's battle on the Washita. The chief had said that the Cheyennes were coming in as rapidly as the cold, wet weather would permit.[46]

On March 6 the main body of Cheyennes, some sixteen hundred

3490–1874; Sheridan to Headquarters, Military Division of the Missouri, Dec. 26, 1874, File No. 2815–1874; Miles to Agent Haworth, Jan. 21, 1875, File No. 3490–1874; *Army and Navy Journal,* Vol. XII (Feb. 13, 1875), 421.

[44] Miles to the Asst. Adj. Gen., Department of the Missouri, Mar. 4, 1875, File No. 3490–1874; *Army and Navy Journal,* Vol. XII (Feb. 27, 1875), 453; Post Returns, Fort Dodge, Feb., 1875.

[45] Five Cheyennes of Stone Calf's band surrendered at their agency on January 28. They told Neill that their chief wished to come in but that Grey Beard was still reluctant. See Neill to the Asst. Adj. Gen., Department of the Missouri, Feb. 7, 1875, File No. 3490–1874.

[46] Neill to Pope, Feb. 18, 1874, in *ibid.*

in number, under Stone Calf, Grey Beard, Heap of Birds, and Bull Bear, surrendered to Neill a short distance from the agency. With them were Catherine and Sophia German. In his report of the event the officer wrote:

> The surrender was a beautiful sight. Stone Calf in front with a white flag was followed by a line of three divisions of Indians on foot, a center and two wings; they halted, threw down their arms in line on the ground and then sat down on the ground. The behavior on this occasion was orderly and decorous.[47]

To agent John B. Miles, however, they did not make such a "beautiful sight":

> A more wretched and poverty-stricken community than these it would be difficult to imagine. Bereft of lodges, and the most ordinary of cooking apparatus; with no ponies, or other means of transportation for wood or water; half starved . . . scarcely anything that could be called clothing, they were truly objects of pity. . . . for the first time the Cheyennes seemed to realize the power of the Government, and their own inability to cope successfully therewith.[48]

Stripped of their guns and animals, the Cheyennes were held under close guard until the ringleaders of the outbreak could be singled out for punishment.

At Fort Sill, Davidson's policy of persuasion was crowned with success. With the invaluable assistance of the faithful Kicking Bird, the noted raider Big Bow was prevailed upon to come in and was promised immunity from punishment if he would persuade other hostile Kiowas to surrender. It proved an excellent bargain, for Big Bow returned on February 26 with Lone Wolf, Red Otter, Swan, Dohasan, Poor Buffalo, 252 of their followers, and 400 head of stock.[49]

---

[47] Neill to the Asst. Adj. Gen., Department of the Missouri, Mar. 7, 1875, in *ibid.*

[48] *Annual Report of the Commissioner of Indian Affairs for the Year 1875,* 269.

[49] *Ibid.,* 272; Augur to Sheridan, Feb. 1, 1875, File No. 3490–1874; *Record of Engagements,* 47. Tabananica, Big Red Food, and Cheevers also rendered assistance. See Davidson to Augur, Dec. 23, 1874, File No. 3490–1874.

Davidson did not remain at Fort Sill long enough to witness the culmination of his policy, for in March he was transferred to Texas along with the Tenth Cavalry and was succeeded by Colonel Mackenzie and his veteran Fourth Cavalry. Mackenzie continued Davidson's program and on April 18 received the surrender of Mow-way and nearly 200 other Comanches. Next day that master of the hit-and-run, the redoubtable White Horse, also came in.[50]

Only the Kwahadis remained in their old hide-outs on the Staked Plain, but a peace mission sent out by Mackenzie late in April located these last holdouts and in a three-day powwow persuaded them to surrender. It was June 2, however, before this large band, numbering 407 people, reached Fort Sill. They gave up their arms and more than 1,500 head of stock. Mackenzie confined the warriors for a short time and then released them. He returned as well 500 of their horses.[51]

The process of separating from their people the Kiowa and Comanche ringleaders for their transfer to a seacoast prison went forward rapidly and smoothly at Fort Sill. The Kiowas adjudged guilty were Lone Wolf, Woman's Heart, White Horse, Double Vision, Bird Chief, and Buffalo Bull's Entrails, all chiefs, and nineteen warriors. Although a far greater proportion of the Comanches as a tribe had participated in the outbreak than the Kiowas, only nine were found guilty and of these only one, Black Horse, was a chief.

The same process at the Cheyenne Agency was anything but smooth. Colonel Neill lined up the erstwhile hostiles and with the assistance of Catherine and Sophia German first selected two warriors and one woman whom the sisters identified as having participated in the attack on their family. Determination of the guilt of the remaining leaders then proceeded. In all, thirty-four Cheyennes and two Arapahoes were found guilty. Among the Cheyennes

[50] Post Returns, Fort Sill, Mar., 1875; Mackenzie to Pope, Apr. 19, 1875, File No. 3490–1874.

[51] Carter, *On the Border with Mackenzie*, 527–28; *Annual Report of the Commissioner of Indian Affairs for the Year 1875*, 272; Post Returns, Fort Sill, June, 1875.

were Grey Beard, Heap of Birds, Medicine Water, Minimic, and Bear Shield. Left Hand was the most prominent Arapaho. Stone Calf escaped punishment when Sophia and Catherine German testified that he had treated them kindly and had deplored the war.

So far all had gone well but trouble was near at hand. On the afternoon of April 6 a detachment of camp guards under Captain Andrew Bennett, Fifth Infantry, brought some of the prisoners to the agency blacksmith to have their shackles fitted. A group of women sitting near by taunted the warriors as they were placed in irons. Shame and anger overcame young Black Horse. Near 2:00 P.M., as his leg irons were being adjusted, he suddenly kicked the blacksmith, broke free, and made a mad dash for the Cheyenne camp a short distance away.

The guards shouted at him to halt, and when he continued his flight, they fired and killed him instantly. Some of the shots penetrated the Cheyenne camp and brought a return volley of arrows which seriously wounded one of the sentinels. Neill ordered some cavalry to Bennett's support, and their appearance brought on a stampede which virtually cleared the camp.

Between 100 and 150 warriors and a few women and children went to a sand hill on the south side of the North Fork of the Canadian, retrieved some guns and ammunition buried there prior to the surrender and entrenched themselves. Captain William A. Rafferty, Sixth Cavalry, with Troop M, first approached the Indian positions, dismounted his troop, and, withholding his fire, slowly advanced. When a short distance away, the Indians poured a volley into the troop, driving it back.

Troops M and D, Tenth Cavalry, under Captains S. T. Norvell and A. S. Keyes, now came up, and as Rafferty tried to work in close from the east, they moved in from the southwest. The Cheyennes stood their ground, however, and held them off. Colonel Neill reached the scene about 2:30 P.M. and ordered a mounted assault, but Norvell and Keyes reported the terrain on their front made this impossible. Neill then brought up a Gatling gun and at four hundred yards sprayed the Indian positions. This done, he ordered the troops to advance on foot.

Rafferty moved forward, but as Norvell and Keyes failed to support him, he was forced to retire. Again the Gatling gun was used and again Neill ordered a charge. This time the troops advanced but the Cheyennes beat them off. With dusk approaching, Neill suspended operations. Nineteen of his men had been wounded, four seriously, while three horses had been killed and six wounded.[52]

Every available man was called up, and preparations were made for a charge at dawn. However, the Indians fled during the night and when the troops reached the sand hill next morning they found only dead bodies: six warriors and one woman. Neill sent two troops in pursuit and telegraphed General Pope that the Cheyennes were moving north. The latter alerted Major H. A. Hambright, Nineteenth Infantry, commanding at Fort Wallace. Lieutenant Austin Henely, Sixth Cavalry, with forty troopers, two wagons, and fifteen days' rations, left the post in an effort to intercept the fugitives.

Henely struck the trail on April 20 south of the Smoky Hill River and followed it across the stream to the Kansas Pacific Railroad. There, near Monument Station, the Indians had scattered and the trail was lost. The detachment then marched for the headwaters of the Solomon River, arriving on the night of April 21. No trails were found and next day Henely moved northeast for the Beaver. During the morning the column encountered three white hunters, who told Henely that the Indians he was looking for had robbed their camp the day before and were encamped on the North Fork of Sappa Creek. With the hunters acting as guides, they found the camp on the night of April 22.

Henely attacked next morning at daybreak, effecting a complete surprise, but marshy ground slowed his charge and allowed many

[52] Neill to Lt. Col. R. Williams, Asst. Adj. Gen., Department of the Missouri, Apr. 7, 1875, Adjutant General's Office, Letters Received, 1875; *Annual Report of the Commissioner of Indian Affairs for the Year 1875*, 269; *Organizational Returns*, Tenth Cavalry, April, 1875. Private Clark Young, Troop M, died of his wounds.

of the Indians to escape. Nineteen warriors, however, entrenched themselves and fought to the last. All were killed, with the eight women and children who had remained with them. Henely then burned the abandoned property, rounded up 134 horses, and returned to Fort Wallace, where he arrived on April 25. His loss had been two men killed.[53]

On this tragic and bloody note the campaigns of 1874–75 came to an end. Most of the Cheyennes who had stampeded on April 6 soon came in to the peaceful Whirlwind's camp, while thirty-two of the thirty-four chiefs and warriors selected for confinement had failed to get away.

Lieutenant R. H. Pratt, Tenth Cavalry, was detailed to take charge of all the Indian prisoners of war, Kiowas, Comanches, Cheyennes, and Arapahoes, and escort them to Fort Marion, Florida. The transfer was accomplished in May, 1875, and only one incident marred the journey. The brooding Grey Beard tried to escape near Houston, Florida, and was shot and killed.

The close of the war marked the end of a way of life for the wild tribes of the Southern Plains. That they must henceforth adapt themselves to the ways of their white conquerors was recognized, however reluctantly, by even their most warlike chiefs. Shortly before their departure for Florida, Grey Beard and Minimic had Lieutenant Pratt write a letter for them to Agent Miles. It contained this message to their people:

> Your Grey Beard and Minimic want me to write you to tell their people to settle down at their Agency, and do all that the Gov't. requires of them. They say tell them to plant corn, and send their children to school, and be careful not to get in any trouble. . . . that we want them to travel in the white man's road. The white men are as many as the leaves on the trees and we are only a few people, and we should do as the white man wants us to, and live at peace with him.[54]

[53] *Annual Report of the Commissioner of Indian Affairs for the Year 1875,* 269; *Annual Report of the Secretary of War for the Year 1875,* 88; Lt. Henely to Maj. Hambright, Apr. 25, 1875, File No. 3490–1874.

[54] Pratt to Miles, May 9, 1875, Cheyenne-Arapaho Files, Prisoners and Warfare.

The columns of Miles, Mackenzie, Davidson, and Buell in what Sheridan described as "not only very comprehensive but the most successful of any Indian campaign in this country" had cleared the way for impatient whites to settle the Southern Plains. The transformation was now amazingly rapid. Towns and cities arose upon many a formerly favored Indian haunt. Even in wild and rugged Palo Duro Canyon, within a mile of Mackenzie's battle-field, stands a symbol of the white man's civilization: a modern tourist cabin.

Bibliography

I. Manuscript Materials

A. National Archives, Washington, D. C.
  1. Records of the Office of Indian Affairs.
    a. Letters Received, Kiowa Agency, 1864–80.
    b. Letters Sent, Vol. LXXXVI, February 26 to June 9, 1868; Vol. LXXXVII, June 10 to September 24, 1868.
  2. Records of the War Department, Adjutant General's Office.
    a. Consolidated File Number 1653 (1875), Affairs on the Rio Grande and Texas Frontier, 1875.
    b. Copies of Records Relating to the Mackenzie Trail, File No. 2236858.
    c. The History of the Fifth United States Cavalry from March 3, 1855, to December 31, 1905, File No. 1102491.
    d. Letters Received, Annual Reports of the Department of Texas for the Year 1869 and 1873.
    e. Letters Received, Annual Report of the Military Division of the Missouri for the Year 1871.

236

f. Letters Received, Selected Documents, 1866–72, 1872–76.

g. Letters Received, Map of the Frontier Posts in Texas for the Year 1869, File No. 1538–M–1869.

h. Letters Received, Files No. 726–M–1869, 1161–M–1869, 1166–M–1869, 1305–1871, 4447–1873, 2815–1874, 3144–1874, 3300–1874, and 3490–1874.

i. Organizational Returns, Ninth Cavalry.

j. Organizational Returns, Tenth Cavalry.

k. Post Returns: Fort Concho, Fort Dodge, Fort Griffin, Fort Harker, Fort Hays, Fort Larned, Fort McKavett, Fort Richardson, Fort Sill, Fort Stockton, Camp Supply, and Fort Wallace.

l. Tabular Statement of Murders, Outrages, Robberies and Depredations Committed by Indians in the Department of Missouri and Northern Texas in 1868 and '69 (exclusive of military engagements) and Officially Reported to Headquarters, Department of the Missouri.

m. Tabular Statement of Expeditions and Scouts against Indians and Etc., Made in the Department of Texas during the Year Ending September 30, 1873.

B. Illinois Historical Society, Springfield, Illinois.

  1. The Papers of Benjamin H. Grierson.

    a. Military, 1868–72.

    b. Miscellaneous Letters, 1867–75.

C. Oklahoma Historical Society, Oklahoma City, Oklahoma.

  1. Indian Archives Division.

    a. Cheyenne-Arapaho Files: Agents and Agency, Arms and Ammunition, Battles, Ben Clark, Captives, Depredations, Federal Relations, Foreign Relations, Hunting and Fishing, Indian Wars, Lawlessness, Military Relations, Murders, and Prisoners and Warfare.

    b. Kiowa Files: Agents and Agency, Agents' Reports, Arms and Ammunition, Arrest, Captives, Chiefs, Deaths, Depredations, Federal Relations, Foreign Relations, Medicine Lodge Treaty, Military Relations, Thefts, and Trial of Satanta and Big Tree.

      1) Record of Indian Depredations, 1869–76, Kiowa Agency Journal.

D. University of Oklahoma, Norman, Oklahoma.
  1. The Phillips Collection.
    a. Forsyth, George A., to Brevet Brigadier General C. M. Mc-Keever, Assistant Adjutant General, Department of the Missouri, March 31, 1869. "Report of the Organization and Operations of a Body of Scouts Enrolled and Equipped at Forts Harker and Hays, Kansas, August 24, 1868." MS.
    b. Extracts from Inspector General R. B. Marcy's Journal of an Inspection Tour while Accompanying the General in Chief during the Months of April, May, and June, 1871. University of Oklahoma copy.
    c. The Sherman-Sheridan Papers. University of Oklahoma Transcript.
E. Panhandle-Plains Historical Society, Canyon, Texas.
  1. The Library.
    a. The Bruce Gerdis Papers.
    b. Hatfield, Colonel Charles A. P., "The Comanche, Kiowa, and Cheyenne Campaign in Northwest Texas and Mackenzie's Fight in the Palo Duro Canyon, September 26, 1874." MS.
    c. The Papers of Lieutenant J. W. Myers.

II. Government Publications

A. Federal
Annual Report of the Board of Indian Commissioners for the Years 1869–75.
Annual Reports of the Commissioner of Indian Affairs for the Years 1850–75.
Annual Report of the Secretary of Interior for the Years 1865–75.
Annual Report of the Secretary of War for the Years 1865–75.
Bureau of American Ethnology, *Fourteenth Annual Report.* Washington, Government Printing Office, 1896.
Congressional Globe, 40 Cong., 2 sess., Washington, Office of the Congressional Globe, 1868.
Heitman, Francis B. *Historical Register and Dictionary of the United States Army.* 2 vols. Washington, Government Printing Office, 1896.

Hodge, Frederick Webb. *Handbook of American Indians North of Mexico, Bulletin No. 30,* Bureau of American Ethnology. Washington, Government Printing Office, 1912.

Hornaday, William T. "The Extermination of the American Bison," *Annual Report of the United States National Museum.* Washington, Smithsonian Institution, 1889.

Johnson, Willard D. "The High Plains and Their Utilization," *Twenty-first Annual Report of the United States Geological Survey,* Part IV. Washington, Government Printing Office, 1889.

Kappler, Charles J. *Indian Affairs: Laws and Treaties.* 3 vols. Washington, Government Printing Office, 1903.

Mooney, James. "Calendar History of the Kiowa," *Seventeenth Annual Report of the Bureau of American Ethnology, 1895–1896.* Washington, Government Printing Office, 1898.

Report of the Joint Special Committee on the Condition of the Indian Tribes. Washington, Government Printing Office, 1867.

Royce, Charles C. "Indian Land Cessions in the United States," *Eighteenth Annual Report of the Bureau of American Ethnology. 1896–1897.* Washington, Government Printing Office, 1899.

United States Army, Military Division of the Missouri. *Record of Engagements with Hostile Indians within the Military Division of the Missouri from 1868–1882.* Washington, Government Printing Office, 1882.

United States Congress, House. *H.R. Exec. Doc. No. 4,* 29 Cong., 2 sess.

———. *H.R. Exec. Doc. No. 2,* 35 Cong., 1 sess.

———. *H.R. Exec. Doc. No. 97,* 40 Cong., 2 sess.

———. *H.R. Exec. Doc. No. 239,* 40 Cong., 2 sess.

———. *H.R. Exec. Doc. No. 1,* 41 Cong., 2 sess.

———. *H.R. Exec. Doc. No. 240,* 41 Cong., 2 sess.

———. *H.R. Misc. Doc. No. 139,* 41 Cong., 2 sess.

———. *H.R. Misc. Doc. No. 142,* 41 Cong., 2 sess.

———. *H.R. Exec. Doc. No. 1,* 42 Cong., 2 sess.

———. *H.R. Exec. Doc. No. 39,* 42 Cong., 3 sess.

———. *H.R. Exec. Doc. No. 43,* 42 Cong., 3 sess.

———. *H.R. Exec. Doc. No. 277,* 42 Cong., 2 sess.

——. *H.R. Report No. 98,* 42 Cong., 3 sess.

——. *H.R. Exec. Doc. No. 1,* 42 Cong., 3 sess.

——. *H.R. Report No. 26,* 42 Cong., 3 sess.

——. *H.R. Exec. Doc. No. 282,* 43 Cong., 1 sess.

——. *H.R. Misc. Doc. No. 289,* 43 Cong., 1 sess.

——. *H.R. Exec. Doc. No. 1,* 43 Cong., 2 sess.

——. *H.R. Exec. Doc. No. 65,* 43 Cong., 2 sess.

——. *H.R. Misc. Doc.* No. 37, 44 Cong., 1 sess.

——. *H.R. Report No. 343,* 44 Cong., 1 sess.

——. *H.R. Exec. Doc. No. 1,* 44 Cong., 2 sess.

——. *H.R. Exec. Doc. No. 10,* 45 Cong., 1 sess.

——. *H.R. Exec. Doc. No. 13,* 45 Cong., 1 sess.

——. *H.R. Exec. Doc. No. 18,* 45 Cong., 1 sess.

——. *H.R. Exec. Doc. No. 14,* 45 Cong., 2 sess.

——. *H.R. Misc. Doc. No. 64,* 45 Cong., 2 sess.

United States Congress, Senate. *Sen. Exec. Doc. No. 171,* 30 Cong., 1 sess.

——. *Sen. Exec. Doc. No. 91,* 33 Cong., 2 sess.

——. *Sen. Exec. Doc. No. 2,* 36 Cong., 1 sess.

——. *Sen. Report No. 156,* 39 Cong., 2 sess.

——._*Sen. Exec. Doc. No. 7,* 40 Cong., 1 sess.

——. *Sen. Exec. Doc. No. 13,* 40 Cong., 1 sess.

——. *Sen. Exec. Doc. No. 113,* 40 Cong., 1 sess.

——. *Sen. Exec. Doc. No. 59,* 40 Cong., 2 sess.

——. *Sen. Exec. Doc. No. 60,* 40 Cong., 2 sess.

——. *Sen. Exec. Doc. No. 74,* 40 Cong., 2 sess.

——. *Sen. Exec. Doc. No. 7,* 40 Cong., 3 sess.

——. *Sen. Exec. Doc. No. 13,* 40 Cong., 3 sess.

——. *Sen. Exec. Doc. No. 18,* 40 Cong., 3 sess.

——. *Sen. Exec. Doc. No. 36,* 40 Cong., 3 sess.

——._*Sen. Exec. Doc. No. 40,* 40 Cong., 3 sess.

——. *Sen. Misc. Doc. No. 59,* 41 Cong., 2 sess.

——. *Sen. Misc. Doc. No. 60,* 41 Cong., 2 sess.

——. *Sen. Misc. Doc. No. 61,* 41 Cong., 2 sess.

——. *Sen. Misc. Doc. No. 37,* 42 Cong., 1 sess.

——. *Sen. Misc. Doc. No. 16,* 45 Cong., 2 sess.

United States Statutes at Large. Vols. IV, X, XIII, XV.

The War of the Rebellion: A Compilation of the Official Records of the Union and Confederate Armies. 130 vols. Washington, Government Printing Office, 1880–1901.

B. State

Gammel, H. P. N., comp. *The Laws of Texas, 1822–1897.* 10 vols. Austin, Gammel Book Co., 1898.

Lamar, Mirabeau Buonaparte. *The Papers of Mirabeau Buonaparte Lamar.* Ed. by Charles Gulick, Jr., and Katherine Elliott. 6 vols. Austin, Texas State Library, 1921–.

Winfrey, Dorman H., ed., *Texas Indian Papers, 1825–1916,* 4 vols. Austin, Texas State Library, 1959–61.

III. Publications of Learned Societies

Allgood, Samuel Y. "Historic Spots and Actions in the Washita Valley up to 1870," *Chronicles of Oklahoma,* Vol. V (June, 1927).

Barrett, Arvie. "Western Frontier Forts of Texas, 1845–1861," *West Texas Historical Association Yearbook,* Vol. VII (June, 1931).

Barrett, Lenora. "Transportation, Supplies, and Quarters for the West Texas Frontier under the Federal Military System, 1848–1861," *West Texas Historical Association Yearbook,* Vol. V (June, 1929).

Beach, James H. "Old Fort Hays," *Transactions of the Kansas State Historical Society,* Vol. XI (1910).

Bender, A. B. "The Texas Frontier, 1848–1861," *Southwestern Historical Quarterly,* Vol. XXXVIII (October, 1934).

Bieber, Ralph P. "Some Aspects of the Santa Fe Trail, 1848–1880," *Chronicles of Oklahoma,* Vol. II (March, 1924).

Brininstool, E. A. "The Rescue of Forsyth's Scouts," *Collections of the Kansas State Historical Society,* Vol. XVII (1928).

Bryan, Frank. "The Llano Estacado: The Geographical Background of the Coronado Expedition," *Panhandle-Plains Historical Review,* Vol. XIII (1940).

Buntin, Martha. "The Quaker Indian Agents of the Kiowa, Comanche, and Wichita Indian Reservations," *Chronicles of Oklahoma,* Vol. X (March, 1932).

———. "The Removal of the Wichitas, Kiowas, Comanches, and

Apaches to the Present Agency." *Panhandle-Plains Historical Review,* Vol. IV (1931).

Butler, Joseph. "Pioneer School Teaching at the Comanche-Kiowa Agency School, 1870–1873," *Chronicles of Oklahoma,* Vol. VI (December, 1928).

Campbell, C. E. "Down among the Red Men," *Collections of the Kansas State Historical Society.* Vol. XVII (1928).

Campbell, Walter S. "The Cheyenne Dog Soldiers," *Chronicles of Oklahoma,* Vol. I (January, 1923).

Clark, Mrs. Olive A. "Early Days along the Solomon Valley," *Collections of the Kansas State Historical Society,* Vol. XVII (1928).

Connelley, William E. "John McBee's Account of the Expedition of the Nineteenth Kansas," *Collections of the Kansas State Historical Society,* Vol. XVII (1928).

——. "The Treaty Held at Medicine Lodge," *Collections of the Kansas State Historical Society,* Vol. XVII (1928).

Crane, R. C. "Old Man Keeler," *West Texas Historical Association Yearbook,* Vol. IV (June, 1928).

——. "Settlement of Indian Troubles in West Texas, 1874–1875," *West Texas Historical Association Yearbook,* Vol. I (June, 1925).

——. "Some Aspects of the History of West and Northwest Texas since 1845," *Southwestern Historical Quarterly,* Vol. XXVI (July, 1922).

——. "Some Early History of the Panhandle-Plains Region," *Panhandle-Plains Historical Review,* Vol. VIII (1935).

——. "General Mackenzie and Fort Concho," *West Texas Historical Association Yearbook,* Vol. X (July, 1934).

Crimmins, Colonel M. L. "The First Line; Or, Army Posts Established in West Texas in 1849," *West Texas Historical Association Yearbook,* Vol. XIX (June, 1943).

——. "Fort McKavett, Texas," *Southwestern Historical Quarterly,* Vol. XXXVIII (July, 1934).

——. "W. G. Freeman's Report on the Eighth Military Department," *Southwestern Historical Quarterly,* Vol. LII (July, 1949).

Debo, Angie. "History and Customs of the Kiowas," *Panhandle-Plains Historical Review,* Vol. VII (1934).

——. "The Social and Economic Life of the Comanches," *Panhandle-Plains Historical Review,* Vol. III (1930).

Doran, Thomas F. "Kansas Sixty Years Ago," *Collections of the Kansas State Historical Society,* Vol. XV (1923).

Foreman, Carolyn T. "Colonel Jesse Leavenworth," *Chronicles of Oklahoma,* Vol. XIII (March, 1935).

——. "General Benjamin Grierson," *Chronicles of Oklahoma,* Vol. XXIV (Summer, 1946).

——. "General William Babcock Hazen," *Chronicles of Oklahoma,* Vol. XX (December, 1942).

Foreman, Grant. "Historical Background of the Kiowa-Comanche Reservation," *Chronicles of Oklahoma,* Vol. XIX (June, 1941).

Freeman, Winfield. "The Battle of the Arickaree," *Transactions of the Kansas State Historical Society,* Vol. VI (1900).

Garfield, Marvin. "Defense of the Kansas Frontier, 1864–1865," *Kansas Historical Quarterly,* Vol. I (February, 1932).

——. "Defense of the Kansas Frontier, 1866–1867," *Kansas Historical Quarterly,* Vol. I (August, 1932).

——. "Defense of the Kansas Frontier, 1868–1869," *Kansas Historical Quarterly,* Vol. I (November, 1932).

——. "The Military Post as a Factor in the Frontier Defense of Kansas," *Kansas Historical Quarterly,* Vol. I (November, 1931).

Grinnell, George B. "Bent's Old Fort and Its Builders," *Collections of the Kansas State Historical Society,* Vol. XV (1923).

Hadley, James A. "The Kansas Cavalry and the Conquest of the Plains Indians," *Collections of the Kansas State Historical Society,* Vol. X (1908).

Haley, J. Evetts, "The Comanchero Trade," *Southwestern Historical Quarterly,* Vol. XXXVIII (January, 1935).

Harmon, George D. "The United States Indian Policy in Texas, 1845–1860," *Mississippi Valley Historical Review,* Vol. XVII (December, 1930).

Harrison, Mrs. Emily Haines. "Reminiscences of Early Days in Ottawa County in Kansas," *Collections of the Kansas State Historical Society,* Vol. X (1908).

Hazen, William B. "Some Corrections of *Life on the Plains,*" *Chronicles of Oklahoma,* Vol. III (December, 1925).

Hobart, Mrs. T. D. "Pioneer Days in the Panhandle-Plains," *Panhandle-Plains Historical Review,* Vol. VIII (1935).

Holden, William C. "The Buffalo of the Plains Area," *West Texas Historical Association Yearbook,* Vol. II (June, 1926).

———. "Frontier Defense, 1846–1860," *West Texas Historical Association Yearbook,* Vol. VI (June, 1930).

———. "Frontier Defense, 1865–1889," *Panhandle-Plains Historical Review,* Vol. II (1929).

———. "Frontier Defense in Texas during the Civil War," *West Texas Historical Association Yearbook,* Vol. IV (June, 1928).

———. "Immigration and Settlement in West Texas," *West Texas Historical Association Yearbook,* Vol. VII (June, 1931).

Howard, Jacob. "Letter From an Ex-Soldier," *West Texas Historical Association Yearbook,* Vol. II (June, 1926).

Hull, Myra E. (ed.). "Soldiering on the High Plains: The Diary of Byram Hull, 1864–1866," *Kansas Historical Quarterly,* Vol. VII (February, 1938).

Hurst, John, and Sigmund Shlesinger. "Battle of the Arickaree," *Collections of the Kansas State Historical Society,* Vol. XV (1923).

Jacob, Captain Richard T. "Military Reminiscences of Captain Richard T. Jacob," *Chronicles of Oklahoma,* Vol. II (March, 1924).

Jenness, George B. "The Battle on Beaver Creek," *Transactions of the Kansas State Historical Society,* Vol. IX (1906).

Koch, Lena Clara. "Federal Indian Policy in Texas," *Southwestern Historical Quarterly,* Vol. XXVIII (January, 1925); Vol. XXIX (July, 1926).

Lockard, F. M. "A Version of a Famous Battle," *Chronicles of Oklahoma,* Vol. V (September, 1927).

Mead, James R. "The Little Arkansas," *Transactions of the Kansas State Historical Society,* Vol. X (1908).

Mellor, William J. "Military Investigation of Colonel John M. Chivington Following the Sand Creek Massacre," *Chronicles of Oklahoma,* Vol. XVI (December, 1938).

Montgomery, Mrs. Frank C. "Fort Wallace and Its Relation to the Frontier," *Collections of the Kansas State Historical Society,* Vol. XVII (1928).

———. "United States Surveyors Massacred by Indians (Lone Tree, Meade County, 1874), *Kansas Historical Quarterly,* Vol. I (May, 1932).

Mooar, J. Wright. "The First Buffalo Hunting in the Panhandle," *West Texas Historical Association Yearbook,* Vol. V (June, 1930).

Moore, Horace L. "The Nineteenth Kansas Cavalry," *Transactions of the Kansas State Historical Society,* Vol. VI (1900).

Muckleroy, Anna. "The Indian Policy of the Republic of Texas," *Southwestern Historical Quarterly* Vol. XXVI (October, 1922).

Murphy, John. "Reminiscences of the Washita Campaign, and of the Darlington Indian Agency," *Chronicles of Oklahoma,* Vol. I (June, 1923).

Nesbitt, Paul. "Battle of the Washita," *Chronicles of Oklahoma,* Vol. III (April, 1925).

Nye, Captain W. S. "An Indian Raid into Texas," *Chronicles of Oklahoma,* Vol. XV (March, 1937).

———. "Excitement on the Sweetwater," *Chronicles of Oklahoma,* Vol. XVI (June, 1938).

Peery, Dan W. "The Kiowa's Defiance," *Chronicles of Oklahoma,* Vol. XIII (March, 1935).

Porter, Kenneth W. "Negroes and Indians on the Texas Frontier," *Southwestern Historical Quarterly,* Vol. LIII (October, 1949).

———. "The Seminole Negro-Indian Scouts, 1870–1881," *Southwestern Historical Quarterly,* Vol. LV (January, 1952).

Richardson, Rupert N. "The Comanche Indians and the Adobe Walls Fight," *Panhandle-Plains Historical Review,* Vol. IV (1931).

———. "The Comanche Reservation in Texas," *West Texas Historical Association Yearbook,* Vol. V (June, 1929).

——— (ed.). "Documents Relating to West Texas and Her Indian Tribes," *West Texas Historical Association Yearbook,* Vol. I (June, 1925).

Rister, Carl Coke. "Colonel A. W. Evans' Christmas Day Indian Fight," *Chronicles of Oklahoma,* Vol. XVI (September, 1938).

——— (ed.). "Early Accounts of Indian Depredations," *West Texas Historical Association Yearbook,* Vol. II (June, 1926).

———. "Fort Griffin," *West Texas Historical Association Yearbook,* Vol. I (June, 1925).

———. "Harmful Practices of Indian Traders of the Southwest, 1865–1876," *New Mexico Historical Review,* Vol. VI (July, 1931).

———. "Satanta, Orator of the Plains," *Southwest Review,* Vol. XVII (1931).

———. "The Significance of the Destruction of the Buffalo in the Southwest," *Southwestern Historical Quarterly,* Vol. XXXIII (July, 1929).

———. "Significance of the Jacksboro Indian Affair of 1871," *Southwestern Historical Quarterly,* Vol. XXIX (January, 1926).

Schmitt, Karl. "Wichita-Kiowa Relations and the 1874 Outbreak," *Chronicles of Oklahoma, Vol.* XXVIII (Summer, 1950).

Sheffy, L. F. (ed.). "Letters and Reminiscences of General Theodore A Baldwin: Scouting after Indians on the Plains of West Texas," *Panhandle-Plains Historical Review,* Vol. XI (1938).

Steele, Aubrey L. "Lawrie Tatum's Indian Policy," *Chronicles of Oklahoma,* Vol. XXII (Spring, 1944).

Tahan, "The Battle of the Washita," *Chronicles of Oklahoma,* Vol. VIII (September, 1930).

Taylor, Alfred A. "Medicine Lodge Peace Council," *Chronicles of Oklahoma,* Vol. II (March, 1924).

Thoburn, Joseph B. "Horace P. Jones, Scout and Interpreter," *Chronicles of Oklahoma,* Vol. II (December, 1924).

Wallace, Edward S. "General Ranald Slidell Mackenzie, Indian Fighting Cavalryman," *Southwestern Historical Quarterly,* Vol. LVI (January, 1953).

Wellman, Paul. "Some Famous Kansas Frontier Scouts," *Kansas Historical Quarterly,* Vol. I (August, 1932).

Whiting, Albe B. "Some Western Border Conditions in the 50's and 60's," *Collections of the Kansas State Historical Society,* Vol. XII (1912).

Whitney, Chauncey B. "Dairy of Chauncey B. Whitney," *Collections of the Kansas State Historical Society,* Vol. XII (1912).

Wilson, Hill P. "Black Kettle's Last Raid—1868," *Transactions of the Kansas State Historical Society,* Vol. VIII (1904).

Winsor, M., and J. A. Scarbrough. "Jewell County," *Collections of the Kansas State Historical Society,* Vol. XVII (1928).

Wissler, Clark, "Costumes of the Plains Indians," *Anthropological Papers of the American Museum of Natural History,* Vol. XVII (1915).

Wright, R. M. "Personal Reminiscences of Frontier Life in Southwest Kansas," *Transactions of the Kansas State Historical Society,* Vol. VII (1902).

IV. PERIODICALS

A. Special Articles

Carnal, Ed. "Reminiscences of a Texas Ranger," *Frontier Times,* Vol. I (December, 1924).

Davis, Theodore R. "The Buffalo Range," *Harper's Monthly Magazine,* Vol. XXXVIII (January, 1869).

———. "A Summer on the Plains," *Harper's Monthly Magazine,* Vol. XXXVI (February, 1868).

———. "A Winter on the Plains," *Harper's Monthly Magazine,* Vol. XXXIX (June, 1869).

Dorst, Captain Joseph H. "Ranald Slidell Mackenzie," *Cavalry Journal,* Vol. X (December, 1897).

Forsyth, George A. "A Frontier Fight," *Harper's Monthly Magazine,* Vol. XCI (June, 1895).

Godfrey, Brigadier General E. S. "Some Reminiscences, Including an Account of General Sully's Expedition against the Southern Plains Indians, 1868," *Cavalry Journal,* Vol. XXXVI (July, 1927).

———. "Some Reminiscences, Including the Washita Battle," *Cavalry Journal,* Vol. XXXVII (October, 1928).

Hoyt, A. W. "Over the Plains to Colorado," *Harper's Monthly Magazine,* Vol. XXXV (June, 1867).

Hunt, F. A. "Adobe Walls Argument: An Indian Attack on a Party of Buffalo Hunters," *Overland Monthly,* Vol. LIV (May, 1909).

———. "Plain Pursuit," *Overland Monthly,* Vol. LIV (September, 1909).

———. "Subjugation of Black Kettle," *Overland Monthly,* Vol. LIV (July, 1909).

Hunter, J. Marvin (ed.). "The Battle of Palo Duro Canyon," *Frontier Times,* Vol. XXI (January, 1944).

King, Edward. "Glimpses of Texas," *Scribner's Monthly,* Vol. VII (February, 1874).

Leeper, Paul S. "Satanta and His Trial," *Frontier Times,* Vol. VII (April, 1930).

"List of Actions, Etc., with Indians and Other Marauders, Participated in by the Tenth United States Cavalry, Chronologically Arranged—1867 to 1897," *Cavalry Journal,* Vol. X (December, 1897).

Nichols, Colonel G. W. "The Indian: What We Should Do with Him," *Harper's Monthly Magazine,* Vol. XL (April, 1870).

Pratt, Richard H. "Some Indian Experiences," *Cavalry Journal,* Vol. XVI (December, 1906).

Robertson, Walter, "Reminiscences of Walter Robertson, the Loss [*sic*] Valley Fight," *Frontier Times,* Vol. VII (December, 1929).

Shlesinger, Sigmund. "The Beecher Island Battlefield—Diary of Sigmund Shlesinger," *Colorado Magazine,* Vol. XXIX (July, 1952).

Smith, Colonel C. C. "Old Military Posts in the Southwest," *Frontier Times,* Vol. VII (June, 1930).

Thompson, Major W. A. "Scouting with Mackenzie," *Cavalry Journal,* Vol. X (December, 1897).

B. Newspapers and Magazines

Army and Navy Journal.

Daily Express (San Antonio, Texas).

Daily Herald (Dallas, Texas).

Daily Herald (San Antonio, Texas).

Daily Journal (Austin, Texas).

Daily State Journal (Austin, Texas).

Flake's Daily Bulletin (Galveston, Texas).

Harper's Weekly Magazine.

Nation, The.

Tribune (New York, New York).

Weekly Democratic Statesman (Austin, Texas).

V. BOOKS

Abel, Annie Heloise. *The Indian as a Participant in the Civil War.* Cleveland, Arthur H. Clark Co., 1919.

Bibliography

Adams, James T. (ed). *Atlas of American History*. New York, Charles Scribner's Sons, 1943.

Allen, J. A. *History of the American Bison*. Washington, Government Printing Office, 1877.

Armes, Colonel George A. *Ups and Downs of an Army Officer*. Washington, D. C., 1900.

Atkinson, Mary J. *The Texas Indians*. San Antonio, Naylor Co., 1935.

Babb, Theodore Adolphus. *In the Bosom of the Comanches*. Dallas, John F. Worley Printing Co., 1912.

Baldwin, Alice B. *Memoirs of the Late Frank D. Baldwin, Maj. General, United States Army*. Los Angeles, Wetzel Publishing Co., 1929.

Bancroft, Hubert Howe. *History of Nevada, Colorado, and Wyoming, 1540–1888*. San Francisco, History Company, 1890.

———. *North Mexican States*. 2 vols. San Francisco, A. L. Bancroft & Co., 1883–89.

Barde, Frederick S. *Life and Adventures of "Billy" Dixon of Adobe Walls, Panhandle, Texas*. Guthrie, Oklahoma, 1914.

Barker, Eugene C. (ed.). *History of Texas*. Dallas, Southwest Press, 1929.

Bates, Charles Francis. *Custer's Indian Battles*. Bronxville, New York, 1936.

Bates, Ed. F. *History and Reminiscences of Denton County*. Denton, Texas, McNitzky Printing Co., 1918.

Battey, Thomas C. *The Life and Adventures of a Quaker among the Indians*. Boston, Lee and Shephard, 1875.

Bedford, Hilary G. *Texas Indian Troubles*. Dallas, Hargreaves Printing Co., Inc., 1905.

Bernhardt, Christian. *Indian Raids in Lincoln County, Kansas, 1864 and 1869*. Lincoln, Kansas, Lincoln Sentinel, 1910.

Beyer, W. F. and J. Keydel (eds.). *Deeds of Valor*. 2 vols. Detroit, Perrien-Keydel Co., 1906.

Blackmar, Frank W. *Kansas*. 2 vols. Chicago, Standard Publishing Co., 1912.

Boyd, Mrs. Orsemus Bronson. *Cavalry Life in Tent and Field*. New York, J. S. Tait and Sons, 1894.

Brady, Cyrus T. *Indian Fights and Fighters.* New York, McClure, Phillips and Co., 1904.

Brill, Charles J. *Conquest of the Southern Plains.* Oklahoma City, Golden Saga Publishers, 1938.

Brininstool, E. A. *Troopers with Custer.* Harrisburg, Pa., Stackpole Co., 1952.

Brown, John Henry. *Indian Wars and Pioneers of Texas.* Austin, Texas, L. E. Daniell, n.d.

Brown, Ralph H. *Historical Geography of the United States.* New York, Harcourt, Brace and Co., 1948.

Bruce, Robert. *The Fighting Norths and Pawnee Scouts.* New York, 1922.

Buell, J. W. *Heroes of the Plains.* Philadelphia, Historical Publishing Co., 1891.

Burton, Harley T. *A History of the JA Ranch.* Austin, Texas, Von Boechmann-Jones Co., 1928.

Carrington, Frances C. *Army Life on the Plains.* Philadelphia, J. B. Lippincott Co., 1910.

Carter, Robert G. *The Old Sergeant's Story.* New York, Frederick H. Hitchcock, 1926.

———. *On the Border with Mackenzie.* Washington, D. C., Eynon Printing Co., 1935.

Carter, Major General William Harding. *The Life of Lieutenant General Chaffee.* Chicago, University of Chicago Press, 1917.

Catlin, George. *North American Indians.* 2 vols. Edinburgh, John Grant, 1926.

Cody, William F. *Adventures of Buffalo Bill.* New York, Harper and Brothers, 1904.

Conover, G. W. *Sixty Years in Southwest Oklahoma.* Anadarko, Oklahoma, N. T. Plummer, Book and Job Printer, 1927.

Cook, John R. *The Border and the Buffalo.* Topeka, Kansas, Crane and Co., 1907.

Crawford, Samuel J. *Kansas in the Sixties.* Chicago, A. C. McClurg and Co., 1911.

Cullum, George W. *Biographical Register of Officers and Graduates of the United States Military Academy at West Point, New York, 1802–1867.* 2 vols. New York, D. Van Nostrand, 1868.

Custer, Mrs. Elizabeth. *Following the Guidon.* New York, Harper and Bros., 1890.

———. *Tenting on the Plains; Or, General Custer in Kansas and Texas.* New York, C. L. Webster and Co., 1887.

Custer, George A. *Wild Life on the Plains.* St. Louis, Royal Publishing Co., c.1891.

Dale, Edward Everett. *The Indians of the Southwest.* Norman, University of Oklahoma Press, 1949.

Deaton, E. L. *Indian Fights on Texas Frontier.* Hamilton, Texas, C. M. Boynton, 1894.

DeShields, James T. *Border Wars of Texas.* Tioga, Texas, Herald Co., 1912.

Dixon, Olive K. *Life of "Billy" Dixon.* Dallas, P. L. Turner Co., 1914.

Dodge, Richard I. *The Hunting Grounds of the Great West.* London, Chatto & Windus, 1877.

———. *Our Wild Indians.* Hartford, A. D. Worthington and Co., 1890.

Douglas, C. L. *The Gentlemen in the White Hats.* Dallas, Southwest Press, 1934.

Downey, Fairfax. *Indian-fighting Army.* New York, Charles Scribner's Sons, 1943.

Eastman, Charles A. *Indian Heroes and Great Chieftains.* Boston, Little, Brown and Co., 1924.

Eastman, Elaine Goodale. *Pratt: The Red Man's Moses.* Norman, University of Oklahoma Press, 1935.

Evans, Harold C. *Kansas, A Guide to the Sunflower State.* New York, Viking Press, 1939.

Forsyth, George A. *The Story of the Soldier.* New York, D. Appleton and Co., 1900.

———. *Thrilling Days in Army Life.* New York, Harper and Bros., 1902.

Franks, J. M. *Seventy Years in Texas.* Gatesville, Texas, 1924.

Freeman, G. D. *Midnight and Noonday; Or, The Incidental History of Southern Kansas and the Indian Territory.* Caldwell, Kansas, 1892.

Fritz, Percy S. *Colorado, the Centennial State.* New York, Prentice-Hall, Inc., 1941.

Fry, James B. *Army Sacrifices.* New York, D. Van Nostrand and Co., 1879.

Ganoe, William Addleman. *The History of the United States Army.* New York, D. Appleton and Co., 1924.

Garretson, M. D. *The American Bison.* New York, 1938.

Gittinger, Roy. *The Formation of the State of Oklahoma (1803–1906).* Berkeley, University of California Press, 1917.

Glass, Major E. N. *History of the Tenth Cavalry.* Tucson, Acme Printing Co., 1921.

Grant, Blanche C. *Kit Carson's Own Story of His Life.* Taos, New Mexico, Santa Fe New Mexican Publishing Corp., 1926.

Grinnell, George B. *The Cheyenne Indians.* 2 vols. New Haven, Yale University Press, 1928.

———. *The Fighting Cheyennes.* New York, Charles Scribner's Sons, 1915.

———. *Two Great Scouts and Their Pawnee Battalion.* Cleveland, Arthur H. Clark Co., 1928.

Haley, J. Evetts. *Fort Concho and the Texas Frontier.* Kansas City, H. C. Revercomb-Americana, 1953.

———. *The XIT Ranch of Texas and the Early Days of the Llano Estacado.* Chicago, Lakeside Press, 1929.

Hancock, Almira R. *Reminiscences of Winfield Scott Hancock.* New York, C. L. Webster & Co., 1887.

Hill, Luther B. *A History of the State of Oklahoma.* New York, Lewis Publishing Co., 1908.

Holden, W. C. *Alkali Trails.* Dallas, Southwest Press, 1930.

Hough, Emerson. *The Passing of the Frontier: A Chronicle of the Old West.* New Haven, Yale University Press, 1918.

Howbert, Irving. *The Indians of the Pike's Peak Region, Including an Account of the Battle of Sand Creek, and of El Paso County, Colorado, during the War with the Cheyennes and Arapahoes in 1864 and 1868.* New York, Knickerbocker Press, 1914.

Humfreville, J. Lee. *Twenty Years among Our Hostile Indians.* New York, Hunter and Company, Publishers, 1899.

Hunt, Elvid. *History of Ft. Leavenworth, 1827–1927.* Ft. Leavenworth, Kansas, General Service Schools Press, 1926.

Hunt, Frazier. *Custer, the Last of the Cavaliers.* New York, Cosmopolitan Book Corp., 1928.

Hunter, John Marvin. *The Bloody Trail in Texas: Sketches and Narratives of Indian Raids and Atrocities on Our Frontier.* Bandera, Texas, J. M. Hunter, 1931.

————. *The Boy Captives.* Bandera, Texas, Frontier Times, 1927.

Hyde, George E. *Indians of the High Plains.* Norman, University of Oklahoma Press, 1959.

————. *Red Cloud's Folk.* Norman, University of Oklahoma Press, 1937.

Jackson, A. P., and E. C. Cole. *Oklahoma, Politically and Topographically.* Kansas City, 1885.

Jackson, Helen Hunt. *A Century of Dishonor.* New York, Harper and Bros., 1881.

Junkin, D. X., and Frank H. Norton. *The Life of Winfield Scott Hancock.* New York, D. Appleton and Co., 1880.

Keim, De Benneville R. *Sheridan's Troopers on the Borders: A Winter Campaign on the Plains.* Philadelphia, D. McKay, 1885.

Kelsey, D. M. *Our Pioneer Heroes and Their Daring Deeds.* Philadelphia and St. Louis, Scammell and Co., 1883.

Kelsey, Rayner W. *Friends and the Indians, 1655–1917.* Philadelphia, Associated Executive Committee of Friends on Indian Affairs, 1917.

Kroeber, A. L. *Cultural and Natural Areas of Native North America.* Berkeley, University of California Press, 1939.

Lehmann, Herman. *Nine Years among the Indians, 1870–1879.* Austin, Texas, J. Marvin Hunter, 1927.

Leupp, Francis E. *Indians of the Southwest.* Philadelphia, David McKay, 1897.

McConnell, H. *Five Years a Cavalryman.* Jacksboro, Texas, J. N. Rogers and Co., 1889.

McConnell, Joseph C. *The West Texas Frontier.* N.p., 1933.

McCreight, Major Israel. *Buffalo Bone Days.* Sykesville, Pa., Nupp Printing Co., 1939.

Macleod, William C. *The American Indian Frontier.* New York, Alfred A. Knopf, 1928.

Manypenny, George W. *Our Indian Wards.* Cincinnati, Robert Clarke & Co., 1880.

Marcy, Randolph B. *Thirty Years of Army Life on the Border.* New York, Harper and Bros., 1866.

Meredith, Grace E. *Girl Captives of the Cheyennes.* Los Angeles, Gem Publishing Co., 1927.

Methvin, Reverend J. J. *Andele; Or, The Mexican-Kiowa Captive.* Anadarko, Oklahoma, Plummer Printing Co., 1927.

———. *In the Limelight; Or, History of Anadarko.* Anadarko, Oklahoma, n.d.

Miles, Nelson A. *Personal Recollections of General Nelson A. Miles.* Chicago and New York, Werner Co., 1896.

Milner, Joe E., and Earl R. Forrest. *California Joe.* Caldwell, Idaho, 1935.

Mishkin, Bernard. *Rank and Warfare among the Plains Indians.* New York, J. J. Augustin, 1940.

Moffett, Thomas C. *The American Indian on the New Trail.* New York, Macmillan Co., 1914.

Morrison, William B. *Military Posts and Camps in Oklahoma.* Oklahoma City, Harlow Publishing Co., 1936.

Northrop, Henry D. *Indian Horrors; Or, Massacres by the Red Men.* Philadelphia, National Publishing Co., n.d.

Nye, Wilbur Sturtevant. *Bad Medicine & Good: Tales of the Kiowas.* Norman, University of Oklahoma Press, 1962.

———. *Carbine and Lance: The Story of Old Fort Sill.* Norman, University of Oklahoma Press, 1937.

Parker, James. *The Old Army: Memories, 1872–1918.* Philadelphia, Dorrance & Co., 1929.

Parrish, Randall. *The Great Plains.* Chicago, A. C. McClurg and Co., 1907.

Paxson, Frederic Logan. *The Last American Frontier.* New York, Macmillan Co., 1922.

Price, George F. *Across the Continent with the Fifth Cavalry.* New York, D. Van Nostrand Publishers, 1883.

Priest, Loring B. *Uncle Sam's Stepchildren: The Reformation of United States Indian Policy, 1865–1887.* New Brunswick, 1942.

Quinn, Vernon. *War-Paint and Powderhorn.* New York, 1929.

Ramsdell, Charles W. *Reconstruction in Texas.* New York, Longmans, Green and Co., 1910.

Richardson, Rupert N. *The Comanche Barrier to South Plains Settlement.* Glendale, Arthur H. Clark Co., 1933.

Rister, Carl Coke. *Border Captives: The Traffic in Prisoners by Southern Plains Indians, 1835–1875.* Norman, University of Oklahoma Press, 1940.

———. *Border Command: General Phil Sheridan in the West.* Norman, University of Oklahoma Press, 1944.

———. *The Southwestern Frontier, 1865–1881.* Cleveland, Arthur H. Clark Co., 1928.

———, and Rupert Norval Richardson. *The Greater Southwest.* Glendale, Arthur H. Clark Co., 1934.

Rodenbough, General Theo. F. *Sabre and Bayonet.* New York, G. W. Dillingham Co., 1897.

Roe, Mrs. Francis M. A. *Army Letters from an Officer's Wife, 1871–1888.* N.p., n.d.

Roenick, Adolph. *Pioneer History of Kansas.* N.p., 1933.

Sabin, Edwin L. *Building the Pacific Railway.* Philadelphia, J. B. Lippincott Co., 1919.

———. *Kit Carson Days, 1809–1868.* 2 vols. New York, Press of the Pioneers, 1935.

———. *Wild Men of the West.* New York, Thomas Y. Crowell Co., 1929.

Saunders, J. Marvin (ed.). *The Trail Drivers of Texas.* Nashville, Tennessee, Cokesbury Press, 1925.

Schmeckebier, Laurence F. *The Office of Indian Affairs: Its History, Activities, and Organization.* Baltimore, Johns Hopkins Press, 1927.

Schmitt, Martin F., and Dee Brown. *Fighting Indians of the West.* New York, Charles Scribner's Sons, 1948.

Seger, John Homer. *Early Days among the Cheyenne and Arapaho Indians.* Edited by Stanley Vestal. Norman, University of Oklahoma Press, 1934.

Seymour, Flora W. *Indian Agents of the Old Frontier.* New York, D. Appleton-Century Co., 1941.

———. *The Story of the Red Man.* New York, Longman's, Green and Co., 1929.

Shaw, Luella. *True History of Some of the Pioneers of Colorado.* Hotchkiss, Colorado, Coburn, Patterson and Shaw, 1909.

Sheridan, Philip H. *Personal Memoirs.* 2 vols. New York, Chester L. Webster and Co., 1888.

Sherman, General W. T. *Memoirs of General W. T. Sherman.* 2 vols. New York, Charles L. Webster and Co., 1892.

Shipman, Mrs. D. L. *Taming the Big Bend,* N.p., 1926.

Smith, Clinton L. and Jeff D. *The Boy Captives.* Hackberry, 1927.

Smith, J. Russell, and M. Ogden Phillips. *North America.* New York, Harcourt, Brace and Co., 1925.

Smith, Mrs. White Mountain. *Indian Tribes of the Southwest.* Palo Alto, California, Stanford University Press, 1933.

Smithwick, Noah. *The Evolution of a State; Or, Recollections of Old Texas Days.* Austin, Texas, 1900.

Smythe, H. *Historical Sketch of Parker County and Weatherford, Texas.* St. Louis, Louis C. Lavat, Printer, 1877.

Sowell, A. J. *Early Settlers and Indian Fighters of the Southwest, 1815–1875.* Austin, Texas, 1900.

Spaulding, Oliver Lyman. *The United States Army in War and Peace.* New York, G. P. Putnam's Sons, 1937.

Spotts, David L. *Campaigning with Custer and the Nineteenth Kansas Volunteer Cavalry on the Washita Campaign, 1868–69.* Los Angeles, Wetzel Publishing Co., 1928.

Stanley, Dorothy (ed.). *The Autobiography of Sir Henry Morton Stanley.* Boston, Houghton Mifflin Co., 1909.

Stanley, Henry M. *Early Travels and Adventures in America and Asia.* 2 vols. New York, Charles Scribner's Sons, 1905.

Stratton, Ella R. *Wild Indians and Their Daring Deeds.* Washington, 1902.

Strong, Captain Henry W. *My Frontier Days and Indian Fights on the Plains of Texas.* N.p., n.d.

Swett, Morris. *Fort Sill, a History.* Fort Sill, Oklahoma, 1921.

Tatum, Lawrie. *Our Red Brothers and the Peace Policy of President Ulysses S. Grant.* Philadelphia, J. C. Winston and Co., 1899.

Taylor, Drew K. *Taylor's Thrilling Tales of Texas.* N.p., 1926.

Thoburn, Joseph B., and Muriel H. Wright. *Oklahoma, A History of the State and Its People.* 4 vols. New York, Lewis Historical Publishing Co., 1929.

Thorndike, Rachel S. (ed.). *The Sherman Letters, Correspondence between General and Senator Sherman from 1837 to 1891.* New York, Charles Scribner's Sons, 1894.

Tilghman, Zoe A. *Quanah, the Eagle of the Comanches.* Oklahoma City, 1938.

Toulouse, Joseph H. and James R. *Pioneer Posts of Texas.* San Antonio, Naylor Co., 1936.

Trimble, W. J. *The Mining Advance into the Inland Empire.* Madison, University of Wisconsin, 1914.

Tuttle, Charles R. *History of the Border Wars of Two Centuries.* Chicago, C. A. Wall and Co., 1874.

Van De Water, Frederic F. *Glory-Hunter, a Life of General Custer.* New York, Bobbs-Merrill Co., 1934.

Vestal, Stanley. *Kit Carson.* Boston. Houghton Mifflin Co., 1928.

———. *Warpath and Council Fire.* New York, Random House, 1948.

Walker, Francis A. *The Indian Question.* Boston, James R. Osgood and Co., 1874.

Wallace, Ernest, and E. Adamson Hoebel. *The Comanches: Lords of the South Plains.* Norman, University of Oklahoma Press, 1952.

Ward, Robert D. *The Climates of the United States.* Boston, Ginn and Co., 1925.

Webb, George W. *Chronological List of Engagements between Regular Army of the United States and Various Tribes of Hostile Indians Which Occurred during the Years 1790–1898, Inclusive.* St. Joseph, Missouri, Wing Printing and Publishing Co., 1939.

Webb, W. E. *Buffalo Land.* Cincinnati, E. Hannaford & Co., 1872.

Webb, Walter Prescott. *The Great Plains.* Boston, Ginn and Co., 1931.

———. *The Texas Rangers; A Century of Frontier Defense.* New York, Houghton Mifflin Co., 1935.

Wellman, Paul I. *Death on the Prairie.* New York, Macmillan Co., 1944.

Wharton, Clarence R. *History of Texas.* Dallas, Turner Co., 1935.

———. *Satanta, the Great Chief of the Kiowas and His People.* Dallas, B. Upshaw and Co., 1935.

Wheeler, Homer W. *Buffalo Days.* New York, Bobbs-Merrill Co., 1925.

———. *The Frontier Trail; Or, From Cowboy to Colonel.* Los Angeles, Times-Mirror Press, 1923.

Wilbarger, J. W. *Indian Depredations in Texas.* Austin, Texas, Hutchings Printing House, 1889.

Wilder, Daniel W. *The Annals of Kansas*. Topeka, George W. Martin, Kansas Publishing House, 1875.

Wissler, Clark. *Indians of the United States*. New York, Doubleday and Co., 1946.

———. *North American Indians of the Plains*. New York, 1912.

Wooten, D. G. *Comprehensive History of Texas*. N.p., n.d.

Wortham, Louis J. *A History of Texas*. 5 vols. Fort Worth: Wortham-Molyneaux Co., 1924.

VI. Unpublished Materials

Buntin, Martha L. "History of the Kiowa, Comanche, and Wichita Indian Agency." Unpublished Master's thesis, Department of History, University of Oklahoma, 1931.

Carmichael, Jeanne. "The Kiowa Indians as Government Wards, 1867–1875." Unpublished Master's thesis, Department of History, University of Oklahoma, 1941.

Ensey, Joseph W. "Indian Hostilities of the Southwest, 1865 to 1875." Unpublished Master's thesis, Department of History, University of Oklahoma, 1931.

Holden, William C. "Frontier Problems and Movements in West Texas, 1846–1900." Unpublished Ph.D. dissertation, Department of History, University of Texas, 1928.

Jenks, Edward L. "The Federal Military Policy in Western Oklahoma." Unpublished Master's thesis, Department of History, University of Oklahoma, 1935.

Nunn, William C. "Texas during the Administration of E. J. Davis." Unpublished Ph.D. dissertation, Department of History, University of Texas, 1938.

Parker, Bruce L. "Indian Affairs and the Frontier of Texas, 1865–1880." Unpublished Master's thesis, Department of History, University of Texas, 1925.

Parrish, Cora H. "The Peace Commission of 1867 and the Western Indians." Unpublished Master's thesis, Department of History, University of Oklahoma, 1948.

Ruckman, Caroline S. "The Frontier of Texas during the Civil War."

Unpublished Master's thesis, Department of History, University of Texas, 1932.

Skinner, Francis. "The Trial and Release of Satanta and Big Tree: State-Federal Relations during the Reconstruction Era." Unpublished Master's thesis, Department of History, University of Texas, 1937.

Index

The text of *The Military Conquest of the Southern Plains* has been set in twelve-point Linotype Granjon, with two points of leading between lines. Granjon is a modern machine adaptation of the sixteenth-century Garamond face, which has been used on the title page and as the handset display initial letter of the chapter openings.

University of Oklahoma Press

Norman

Leckie, William H
    The military conquest of the southern plains. [1st ed.]
Norman, University of Oklahoma Press [1963]

269 p. illus. 24 cm.

Includes bibliography.

1. Indians of North America—Wars—1866–1895. 2. Frontier and
pioneer life—Great Plains. 3. Indians of North America—Great
Plains.   I. Title.

E83.866.L4   970.5   63–17160 ‡

Library of Congress   [5]